SECOND EDITION

Youth
IN CONFLICT
WITH THE LAW

Paul S. Maxim
The University of Western Ontario

Paul C. Whitehead
The University of Western Ontario

THOMSON
NELSON

Australia   Canada   Mexico   Singapore   Spain   United Kingdom   United States

THOMSON

NELSON

Youth in Conflict with the Law
Second Edition

Paul Maxim and Paul Whitehead

Editorial Director and Publisher:
Evelyn Veitch

Executive Editor:
Joanna Cotton

Marketing Manager:
Lenore Taylor

Senior Developmental Editor:
Edward Ikeda

Production Editor:
Carrie Withers

Senior Production Coordinator:
Hedy Sellers

Copy Editor/Proofreader:
Rohini Herbert

Creative Director
Angela Cluer

Cover Design:
Katherine Strain

Interior Design:
Sarah Battersby

Interior Design Modifications:
Katherine Strain

Compositor:
Brenda Prangley

Indexer:
Belle Wong

Printer:
Webcom Limited

National Library of Canada Cataloguing in Publication

Maxim, Paul S., 1950–

Youth in conflict with the law / Paul Maxim, Paul Whitehead. —2nd ed.

Includes bibliographical references and index.
ISBN 0-17-622478-5

1. Canada. Young Offenders Act.
2. Juvenile justice, Administration of — Canada.
3. Youth — Legal status, laws, etc. — Canada.
4. Juvenile delinquency — Canada.
I. Whitehead, Paul C., 1942–
II. Title.

KE9445.M39 2003   345.71'03
C2003-901291-3

KF9780.ZA2M9 2003

For Nancy and Doreen

Contents

CHAPTER 5: ARRESTING AND QUESTIONING YOUNG PERSONS 85

CHAPTER 6: EXTRAJUDICIAL MEASURES 107

CHAPTER 7: DETAINING AND PROCESSING YOUNG PERSONS 119

Preface

The primary difference between this edition and the first edition of *Youth in Conflict with the Law* is the focus on the new *Youth Criminal Justice Act (YCJA)*. There are several marked and important distinctions between the *YCJA* and the *Young Offenders Act*, which it replaces, and a number of these changes are of particular relevance to the discharge of policing responsibilities.

Other key changes to be found in the Second Edition include the following: (1) updated statistics on youthful offending; (2) a new chapter on extrajudicial measures and the preference for their use; (3) expanded discussion of custodial sentences, the conditions under which they are presumed not to apply, and the facilities in Ontario that are available, in cases where such sentences are received; (4) a glossary of terms; and (5) an updated *Instructors' Manual/Test Bank*.

Many police officers do not view dealing with young offenders as a very glamorous aspect of policing. From a social point of view, however, dealing with young people who come into conflict with the law is one of the most important parts of policing. Young persons, particularly those who are 16–17 years old, proportionally commit more crimes that any other age group. Criminologists have determined that most serious adult offenders start their criminal careers as young offenders. On the other hand, criminologists know that most young offenders do not go on to become adult criminals.

Despite all of the resources we put into providing school counsellors, social workers, and child care workers, it is the police who most often meet young people at a time of crisis. It is the police who are called to intervene in domestic disputes between parents, and between parents and their children. The police may be called to intervene when a minor ruckus breaks out in the school yard or when some "punks" are being an annoyance in the neighbourhood or at a local shopping mall. They are certainly called when a young person commits an infraction of criminal law.

Handling this range of problems is one of the greatest challenges the police officer can face. Successful intervention with an angry or misguided young person, or one who comes from a highly dysfunctional family, can be a rewarding experience for the police officer and a benefit for the society. Such interventions do not generate newspaper headlines the way a solved murder or significant fraud case does, but then again, most police officers rarely get to crack a really "big case."

Most police officers do have families, though, and most officers appreciate how difficult it is to raise children. Most are also aware of how difficult growing up can be. These experiences contribute to the good judgment that needs to be exercised in dealing with young people in a wide array of circumstances, including on the job.

There are many ways of writing about young people and the law, even for a targeted audience. In this instance, we have chosen not to deal with legislation in its entirety. Instead, we have chosen to focus on how the *YCJA* requires the police to handle young persons in ways different from handling adults. The *YCJA* is the fundamental document on which our summaries and interpretations are based.

As a final point, both the *YCJA* and the *Criminal Code of Canada* make reference to law enforcement personnel as "peace officers." The term "peace officer," as defined by the *Criminal Code of Canada*, covers a range of individuals from mayors, to justices of the peace, to police officers, to (in some circumstances) aircraft pilots. Given our audience, we have chosen to use the term "police officer," instead of, the more general term "peace officer" in most situations.

INSTRUCTORS' MANUAL/TEST BANK [0-17-641646-3]

The *Instructors' Manual/Test Bank* includes the following features that have been requested by professors who used the previous edition: (1) answers to the True or False and Multiple Choice questions that appear in the exercises in the text; (2) additional True or False and Multiple Choice items that can be used for the purpose of setting examinations; and (3) a copy of the Glossary that contains detailed responses to each of the definition questions on the text. In addition, all of the items mentioned in 1 and 2 are available in digital format, to facilitate the creation of examinations, with the items that appear in the text clearly distinguished from the ones that only appear in the *Instructors' Manual/Test Bank*. Contact your local sales representative for a copy of the digital files.

ACKNOWLEDGMENTS

In preparing this book, the authors have benefited considerably from the information, advice, and wisdom provided by many people. In particular, we wish to acknowledge the assistance of the following persons: Chief Brian Collins and Inspector Ian Peer, London Police Service; Lee Tustin of the Child Welfare and Young Offenders Branch of the Ministry of Community, Family, and Children's Services; and Glen Semple of the Ministry of Public Safety and Security. Very special thanks go to Miriam Bloomenfeld, Counsel, *YCJA* Implementation, Criminal Law Policy Branch, Ministry of the Attorney General, who repeatedly fielded our inquiries and assisted us with information and interpretations that were not otherwise available to us.

The advice provided by Gino Arcaro, Coordinator and Professor for the Police Foundations Program, Niagara College, and John Grime, Coordinator and Professor, Law and Security Administration, Mohawk College, with the first edition continued to be helpful as we crafted this one. Other reviewers included Dana Lennox (Algonquin College), Paul Macisaac (Georgian College), and Larry White (Mohawk College).

P.S.M.
P.C.W.
London, Ontario
6 January, 2003

Offending by Young People in Historical Perspective

Learning Outcomes

Students who have mastered this chapter will have the ability to do the following:

- Identify *what* mens rea *and culpability have to do with the notion of offences by young people, rather than adult crime.*
- Know *the legal roots of Canadian criminal law and the Canadian correctional system.*
- Explain *the view of young people in British common law.*
- Describe *the impact of the Industrial Revolution on the legal rights of young people.*
- Explain *why juvenile criminality became linked to concerns for the social welfare of children.*
- Distinguish *between "prisons" and "houses of refuge."*
- Explain *the doctrine of* parens patriae *and its relation to the "child-saving" movement.*
- Understand *the North American roots of the juvenile court.*
- Distinguish *between reformatories and how young people were previously jailed.*
- Explain *how the manner in which children were viewed affected how they were treated and punished.*

THE MEANING OF DELINQUENCY

The questions of which behaviours should be considered delinquent and how society should deal with young offenders are not recent ones. These concerns have kept legal scholars busy for centuries. Traditionally, the main issues have revolved around the problems of *mens rea* and **culpability**. That is, can young people form criminal intent, and if they can, should we hold them accountable for their actions?

All societies recognize that very young children—infants and those in their formative years—are different from adults. Only recently, however, have we accepted the notion of the pre-teen years and adolescence being different from adulthood. Often, society saw youths or juveniles as miniature adults—with all the capabilities of adults—except that they appeared in smaller packages. Thus, the law often treated children beyond their formative years no differently from how it treated adults.

Much of the debate over the meaning of delinquency has its roots in unique historical conditions. Consequently, it is only through an examination of history that we can make sense out of the many conflicting views on the law-violating behaviour of young people. The notion of delinquency did not evolve in a vacuum. Rather, it grew out of particular historical circumstances and the prevailing social and moral spirit of the times. Societies put in place social policies that they consider to be solutions to the problem of young people committing offences. Often, those "solutions" are not seen as totally adequate, even at the time that they are suggested. The longer the social policies stay in place, the more likely it is that they become accepted as the normal way of doing things. Thus, we are still living with the consequences of many earlier "solutions."

This chapter reviews some elements of the historical background of delinquency. This will provide a framework for understanding many present-day issues and practices. It is important to remember that Canada is a country held together by a constitution that makes many arbitrary distinctions in governmental responsibility. Often, those distinctions are based on political compromise, rather than logic. Furthermore, Canadian law and Canadian legal institutions are not unique. Most Canadian legal institutions do not have their origins in responses to Canadian problems. Our nation draws its common and civil law traditions from its ancestral roots in Britain and France. On the other hand, its welfare and correctional systems have been modelled largely on American experience and experimentation.

Delinquency as a Social Problem

Historically, within the Anglo-American culture, the lot of a youth has not been an easy one. The law rarely made any distinction between the legal responsibilities of young persons and those of adults. On the other hand, children (and women, for that matter) have usually been denied many legal rights granted to adult males. Women and children were often viewed as subservient to, and sometimes the property of, their fathers, guardians, or, in the case of women, their husbands.

The historical treatment of young persons under common law has been well documented. A 10th-century law of King Aethelstan, for example, called for the death penalty for persons over 12 years of age who were caught stealing amounts greater than 12 pence (Cavan and Ferdinand, 1975:4). Some (e.g., Sanders, 1945:42) have argued, however, that while the law allowed for the possibility of extreme penalties, the very severity of those penalties often made judges and juries reluctant to enforce the law to the fullest—especially when juveniles were involved. Judge Edward Waite has perhaps best illustrated the insecurity of the youth under English criminal law:

> It is recorded in the Year Books of Edward I that judgment for burglary
> was spared to a boy of twelve years....Yet in the seventeenth century, John

Dean, being of the age of eight years, was hanged at Abingdon for arson, and in 1833 the death sentence was pronounced upon a child who broke a pane of glass and stole two pennyworth of paint (taken from MacGill, 1925:5).

Under common law, young people were not held criminally responsible until they reached the age of seven years. Children under seven years of age were considered legal infants and were assumed not able to appreciate the moral aspects of the law fully. Consequently, they could not form criminal intent. It was expected, however, that when these children did break the law, their parents would deal with them. Usually, this took the form of serious beating. Between the ages of seven and 14 years, young people were held to limited legal responsibility. In theory, at least, the crown was obliged to make the case that the young offenders were legally mature and could appreciate the nature of the law and the consequences of their behaviour. All too often, little was required for the crown to convince a presiding magistrate.

Beyond the age of 14 years, and up to 21 years, young people were typically treated as adults. They could, however, argue that they suffered from diminished mental capacity. In such an instance, it would be maintained that the young person was "slow" and could not form the intent—the *mens rea*—expected of adults. While rarely leading to complete acquittal, this defence sometimes led to a far lighter sentence. At the age of 21 years, however, a person was considered a legal adult.

If the legal rights of young persons did not improve with the Industrial Revolution, their social conditions certainly deteriorated, since the age of mechanization drew heavily upon the labour of women and children. The excesses of industrialism spurred real reformers in the 19th century to reassess the social and legal statuses of children. The development of large cities with their high population densities displayed human misery much more intensely than was seen in the agrarian society. For example, the French scholar Villermé, who had studied the new industrial worker, wrote:

> One should see them moving into the town every morning and leaving it every evening. Among them are large numbers of women, pale, starving, wading barefoot through the mud...and young children, in greater numbers than women, just as dirty, just as haggard, covered in rags, which are thick with oil splashed over them as they toil by the looms (quoted in Kuckzynski, 1967:59).

Many others, however, saw the growth of industry not as a source of social disorder but as a social boon, since it allowed for the employment of formerly idle women and children. As Edith Abbott observed in America,

> the employment of children in the early factories was regarded from much the same point of view as the employment of women. Philanthropists who still cherished colonial traditions of the value of an industrious childhood, supported statesmen and economists in warmly praising the establishment of manufacture because of the new opportunities of employment for children. They point out the additional value that could be got from the six thousand girls in the country, between the ages of ten and sixteen, most of whom were "too young or too delicate for agriculture," and in contrast called attention to the "vice and immorality" to which children were "exposed by a career of idleness" (quoted in Kuckzynski, 1967:61).

While the new industrial state may have rescued many children from a "career of idleness," it also did much to foster crime and deviance among juveniles. The pressures placed on many children to engage in crime, simply for survival, were well documented in the popular literature of the time. Frances Trollope's 1840 novel *The Life and Adventures of Michael Armstrong* and Charles Dickens' *Oliver Twist* are two notable examples.

Some historians have argued that it was this combination of urban misery and social and moral upheaval that eventually led to juvenile criminality being combined with concerns for the social welfare of children. It was reasonable to link modern explanations of juvenile delinquency (e.g., deprived or broken homes and a lack of skills and resources to compete in the existing opportunity structure) to problems resulting from the growth of industrial society. Many reformers saw the cause of juvenile crime and immorality as lying in social welfare problems that followed from a society quickly losing its agrarian roots.

Many of the worst social conditions that existed in Europe or the large cities of the United States in the 19th century did not appear until much later in Canada. As an agriculturally based society, Canada's problem with youth crime paled beside that of its neighbour. As one Canadian historian writes,

> lawbreaking by young boys and girls developed in a distinct pattern from the earliest days of pioneer settlement. Much of it was minor in nature, consisting of violations of local ordinances, nuisance offences, vandalism, petty theft, and breaches of the moral laws. Males offended in larger numbers than females, while certain crimes such as prostitution, abortion, and infanticide were primarily committed by females (Carrigan, 1998:25).

Interestingly, many social problems that we experience with young people today appeared regularly in the past. Citizens in the growing colonial cities of Halifax, Montreal, and Toronto constantly complained about the problems posed by runaways, or "street kids" as we would now call them. One difference in the past was that most of those young people were either orphans or young servants who had run away from their masters. One area of similarity, however, is that many were living on the streets to escape abusive homes only to experience more and different forms of physical and sexual abuse on the streets.

Garrison and port towns, such as Halifax, faced particular problems as soldiers and sailors searched for female companionship. Many poor and unskilled adolescent girls were attracted into prostitution. Invariably, the trade was linked to heavy drinking and other forms of vice. Many prostitutes (and young servant girls, for that matter) became pregnant and solved their "problem" through abortion. Frequently, the young women in the sex trade were also involved in minor acts of theft. Either on their own initiative or at the urging of their pimp or brothel owner, they would steal from their often drunk clients. Prostitution was also a major problem in mining and lumber towns, where, again, there were large concentrations of single men, flush with money to spend on payday.[1]

This Canadian experience was quite different from what was typical of many parts of the United States. While it is true that America was primarily rural, there were also large cities where youth crime appeared rampant. Such cities as New York, Boston, and Philadelphia were home to juvenile gangs that often engaged in what we might best describe as ethnic warfare.

The overall pattern of youth crime changed little in Canada from colonial times until the 20th century. By that time, the population started to become more urbanized, and youth crime was starting to take a higher profile. However, as the historian Carrigan (1998:104) writes,

> the profile of the typical delinquent of the 1920s changed little from the previous century. Convicted offenders were still predominantly white, male, and Canadian-born. They were urban dwellers, usually from troubled

homes, who mixed with bad companions and had repeated run-ins with the law. One not untypical example was a Toronto boy who came from a family of seven. He grew up in poverty and an unkempt home with parents who quarrelled and drank heavily. While still young, his mother deserted the family and the boy started on a path of truancy and petty theft. By the time he was eleven, he had graduated to shop-breaking and stealing automobiles. He was in and out of detention until he eventually reached adulthood. He ended his career in Kingston Penitentiary on a fifteen-year sentence for armed robbery.

While many commentators of the time were quick to focus on youth crime, the situation in Canada seems more of an annoyance than a major social problem from our perspective. It is also worthwhile remembering that historically, young people made up a much larger segment of the population than they do now. Life expectancies were shorter, and birth rates were much higher. Consequently, there were fewer adults in relation to young people than we find today. When we consider that factor, the problem of youth crime appears to have been less of a challenge for Canadian society in the past than it is today.

It is also the case that the economy usually had more room for young people. Educational requirements for employment were different from those we have today. The dexterity and strength of young people were useful, both on the farm and in the factory, where machines were not the complete labour replacement items that they are now. Furthermore, many young people were accepted into personal service where they worked as servants.

Juvenile crime increased substantially in Canada through the 1920s and the 1930s. Again, most of it appears to consist of minor property offences. There were, however, increases in the rates of violent crime. Gang behaviour also started to become a more regular part of the urban scene, especially in the bigger cities, such as Montreal and Toronto. As in the United States, many of those gangs revolved around ethnic affiliations. Fortunately, in Canada, juvenile gangs never posed the serious problem that they did in the large American cities.

Exercise 1

DEFINITIONS

Please define the following terms:

1. *Mens rea:*

_____

_____

_____

_____

_____

_____

_____

_____

_____

_____

2. Culpability:

_____

_____

_____

_____

_____

_____

_____

_____

_____

TRUE OR FALSE

1.   T   F   The law has always treated children differently from adults.

2.   T   F   The correctional system of Canada is modelled, in part, on the American experience.

3.   T   F   *Mens rea* has to do with the formation of intent.

4.   T   F   Present ideas about juvenile delinquency are completely new.

5.   T   F   During the 1920s and 1930s, juvenile crime decreased considerably in Canada.

MULTIPLE CHOICE

1. Distinctions made in the constitution of Canada are best described as

    a) logical
    b) based on compromise
    c) rooted in the law of God
    d) neither logical nor arbitrary

2. Canada draws its common and civil law traditions from

   a) United States and Britain
   b) United States and France
   c) United States, Britain, and Australia
   d) Britain and France

3. The historical treatment of children in English common law

   a) has included harsh punishments for relatively minor offences
   b) has consistently protected children from exploitation
   c) has always held that children are not criminally accountable until they reach the age of 12 years
   d) none of the above

4. Runaways and "street kids"

   a) are an entirely modern condition
   b) were a problem in Europe for a long time but which have only recently come to North America
   c) were a problem in the colonial cities of Halifax, Montreal, and Toronto
   d) were never involved in prostitution

SHORT ESSAY

1. Identify some effects of the industrial revolution on women and children.

_____

_____

_____

_____

_____

_____

_____

_____

_____

_____

_____

_____

_____

_____

_____

_____

_____

_____

_____

_____

_____

INSTITUTIONAL RESPONSES

Institutional responses to the problems of delinquent youth have their origins as far back as the 16th century. It is only in the past 150 years or so, however, that most developments have taken place. Traditionally, the punishment for a young offender was the same as that for an adult. Often, it consisted of a good whipping or lashing. Prison generally meant serving time with adults, and older youths were just as likely to be transported to the colonies as were adults. Occasionally, a young person could "avoid" civil punishment by being placed in military service. Of course, for many, life on board a ship or with "the regiment" was not any better than life in prison.

Prisons

Not all young criminals, however, were committed to institutions. England quite often dealt with child criminals in the same manner it did adults. Children were commonly flogged, pressed into naval service, transported to the colonies, or incarcerated in common jails along with adults. The following is a report on the English **prison hulks** (ships) of the early 19th century.[2] It reflects a typical mix of what conditions were like at the time.

> Among the criminals, lunatics, feeble-minded and outcasts of all kinds who were cooped up for periods generally varying between one and seven years…were young boys. An old table gives the number upon the hulks at that time, and we find the record of: one child of 2, two of 12, four boys of 14, four of 15 and altogether twenty persons less than sixteen years old. About 1824 they appear to have placed the boys on a special ship, the hulk 'Euryalus,' and there the youngest 'villain' was nine years old; some of the boys, the inspector reported, 'are so young that they can hardly put on their clothes.' Two thirds of them are described as being natural ["bastard"] or neglected children (Barnes, 1972:119).

There was usually no separation of prisoners in jails in either Europe or the United States until late in the 19th century. Men, women, and children were often kept together, whatever their crime—whether it was murder, bestiality, or the inability to pay their debts.

Houses of Refuge

One of the earliest answers to the problem of neglected and wayward youth was the establishment of Houses of Refuge (Barnes, 1972:201–203). The **Houses of Refuge** were an institutional response to the problem of juvenile crime. Their principal features were that they kept youth separate from adults and focused on hard work and discipline. They grew out of the juvenile sections of the English workhouses of the 16th and 17th centuries. They became common throughout most of western Europe. Holland had built a complete system of institutions by the 17th century. While most institutions of the time did not distinguish between "needy" and "criminal" youths, two notable exceptions existed. The Amsterdam House of Correction (Sellin, 1944) and the Hospice de St. Michel, opened by Pope Clement XI in 1704 (Sellin, 1930), focused mostly on wayward or criminal children and youths. Mennel (1973:3–4) notes that the growth of these Houses of Refuge marked a shift in the emphasis from family-centred discipline to the institutional control of young people by the state.

The idea of a House of Refuge was apparently brought to America from Europe by John Griscom, a Quaker, who travelled widely throughout Europe in the 1820s. The first House of Refuge opened in New York State in 1825, but the idea soon spread to neighbouring states. Eventually, however, most juvenile institutions came to take on the characteristics of adult prisons; the facilities were spartan, silence was usually enforced, and strict discipline maintained. As Sutherland and Cressey (1974:490) point out, "these institutions were, during the first half-century of their history, primarily prisons, and their principal contribution was the removal of juvenile prisoners from association with adult prisoners."

No matter how poorly these juvenile institutions achieved their goals, it is safe to state that the 19th century was the century of the institution. The apparent answer to the "youth crime problem" lay in the institutions. Reformers believed that given sufficient hard work, discipline, and moral training, a wayward youth could be moulded into a useful adult citizen. For the progressive reformer, the training or reform school promised to be a solution to the "juvenile crime problem."

Dissatisfaction with Institutions

Not everyone supported children's institutions, least of all many parents whose children were taken away from them. Gradually, reports of cruelty inside the institutions began to circulate in public. Even from the highly acclaimed cottage settings, there came disturbing reports of juveniles engaging in "unnatural" acts with the farm animals (Mennel, 1973:107–110). Many observers also began to notice that training schools were often schools for crime, rather than institutions where one learned skills for a legitimate career.

The intervention of the state into the family lives of the poor through these "child-saving" institutions became a serious problem. What we must remember is that only occasionally were clear distinctions made between young persons who had actually committed criminal acts and those who were unfortunate enough to have been born to impoverished parents. Despite the intentions of its founders, the New York House of Refuge, for example, was obliged to accept both youths who were committed for criminal acts and those who were committed for vagrancy. The core of the problem (and one that remains with us even today, to some degree) is that

> the nineteenth century viewed poverty almost as a crime and many of the terms were used synonymously. Thus vagrant, wayward, delinquent, depraved, dependent, vicious, neglected and perhaps other adjectives were used to describe basically the same children (Rendleman, 1971:81).

The nonpoor, for the most part, saw little wrong in separating pauper children from their families. The early Elizabethan Poor Laws supported this as a proper and benevolent act, if not a very functional one. Many poor parents, however, could not understand why the state had the right to take their children, especially in instances where the child had essentially committed no crime. The problem became acute in the latter half of the 19th century, in both Canada and the United States, with the mass influx of many Catholic immigrants. First-generation immigrants were especially prone to an impoverished lifestyle. Consequently, their children were prime targets for the Protestant institutions that saw the children as victims of both material and spiritual deprivation. The legal justification presented by reformers for their sometimes high-handed interference in family affairs was the old doctrine of *parens patriae*. Under this doctrine, the jurisdiction of the Chancery Court could be invoked to intercede on behalf of children when their parents or guardians were neglecting or mistreating them. More often, it was used when the property rights of the children of nobility were at risk (Rendleman, 1971:74–77).

Supporters of the child-saving movement relied heavily on this doctrine for legal support of their activities. Of course, the benevolence of the Chancery Court was highly romanticized to gain widespread popular support for their activities. By drawing on a long and continuous heritage of the state's right to be the ultimate father of the children within its jurisdiction, supporters of juvenile institutions could add a much needed legitimacy to their actions.

Toward the end of the century, however, the use of *parens patriae* to justify removing children from their families came under increased attack as capricious and unjust. At the same time, there was a the growing realization that they were simply not achieving their stated goals. As Mennel notes,

> by the late nineteenth Century, little remained of the enthusiasm and hope which had produced the asylum, the penitentiary, and the reform school. Internal as well as external attacks upon reform schools were indicative of a larger collapse of faith in the healing powers of...[these places]. By remembering the dimensions of this deterioration of confidence, we can more clearly comprehend the significance of the juvenile court (Mennel, 1973:124).

Exercise 2

DEFINITIONS

Please define each of the following terms:

1. Prison hulk:

_____

_____

_____

_____

_____

_____

_____

_____

_____

_____

2. House of Refuge:

_____

_____

_____

_____

_____

_____

_____

_____

_____

3. *Parens patriae:*

_____

_____

_____

_____

_____

_____

_____

_____

_____

_____

_____

TRUE OR FALSE

1. T   F   In pre-20th century England, it was not uncommon for children to be flogged.

2. T   F   A prison "hulk" refer to a ship.

3. T   F   It never bothered parents that their children could be taken away from them if the children behaved badly.

MULTIPLE CHOICE

1. Which of the following describes "Houses of Refuge"?

    a) Spartan facilities and enforced silence
    b) Enforced silence and visits from parents
    c) Strict discipline and time off for good behaviour
    d) Enforced silence and teaching of Latin

2. Traditionally, if young people were punished, the punishment they received was

    a) more harsh than that received by adults
    b) more lenient than that received by adults
    c) dependent on the education of their mothers
    d) similar to that received by adults

3. The separation of children and adults in prison settings

    a) occurred all through the 19th century, but not before
    b) was not done in Europe or America during most of the 19th century
    c) occurred for boys, but not for girls through most of the 1800s
    d) none of the above

SHORT ESSAYS

1. What does it mean to say that in the 19th century, the dominant response to juvenile crime was "institutional"?

    _____

    _____

    _____

    _____

    _____

    _____

    _____

    _____

    _____

_____

_____

_____

_____

_____

2. What is the relationship between the "child-saving movement" and the doctrine of *parens patriae?*

_____

_____

_____

_____

_____

_____

_____

_____

_____

_____

_____

_____

_____

THE JUVENILE COURT

The second half of the 19th century was a period of significant social reform. It saw the beginnings of the social welfare movement that gradually improved working conditions and the overall quality of life for most people in much of western Europe and North America. Many of those reforms and the social institutions that supported them were the result of private charity and philanthropy. Gradually, however, the state started to play an increasingly larger role. The state supported institutions and passed legislation to limit the punitiveness of criminal law, enhanced child welfare, reduced hours of work, and provided some support for the poor.

The view of children also changed, both about how they related to adults and about how they fitted into the social order. Children were seen less as adults in small packages and more as beings who were not only physically but also socially and intellectually less developed than adults. These views of children accelerated around the turn of the 20th century as the young social sciences started to broaden our understanding of human development.

Developmental psychologists, for example, provided empirical evidence to show that social and intellectual growth takes place not only in childhood but throughout adolescence. Psychologists Piaget (1951) and Kohlberg (1981) suggested that moral development in young people happens in a series of stages. Although there is significant interpersonal variability, the evolution of the individual into a socially, morally, and intellectually mature adult takes time. Other social scientists have made us aware that while many young people may be aware of certain social ideas and terms, such as justice, rights, fairness, and responsibility, their *understanding* of those terms develops only as they grow older.

The United States

The first formal **juvenile court** was opened in Chicago in 1899, after the presentation of the innovative *Juvenile Delinquents Act* to the Illinois state legislature the previous year. The juvenile court, it would appear, was an idea whose time had come. Although most jurisdictions were facing increasing difficulties with the manner in which they disposed of troublesome juveniles, Illinois was apparently in a particularly acute predicament. Several court cases in the late 1880s and 1890s began to erode the right of existing legislation to separate wayward youth from their parents in noncriminal situations. At the same time, however, the reformist or "child-saving" movement (see especially Platt, 1969) was still very strong and sought to intercede in the lives of deprived and delinquent juveniles. It was, states Mennel (1973:128), "under these circumstances [that] the legal fraternity in Illinois became concerned about the vacuum of state welfare power and sought a means to reassert the right of the state to assume parental power over delinquent children."

The juvenile court appeared to provide the ideal solution. It recognized the fact that childhood was a special status, qualitatively different from adulthood, and that children were simply not miniature adults. As such, children were protected from the harshness of the criminal sanction under adult courts. Furthermore, the courts could become informal affairs, with the judge acting in the capacity of a wise and judicious parent. The judge's role was not to accuse the child of a crime but to offer assistance and guidance. Because the court was not treating the matter strictly as a criminal issue, the hearing could be held in private, away from the prying eyes of the public and the press.

The new juvenile court also conformed to the rising ideology of the time, that the origins of criminal and antisocial behaviour existed in the mind and social environment of the individual (see Platt, 1969:Chapter 3). By focusing on the causes of criminal and deviant behaviours, the court allowed for a revitalization of the *parens patriae* doctrine and the right of the state to intercede for the juvenile. Attending to young delinquents and youths dwelling in environments that foster crime or exhibiting delinquent tendencies allowed the court to divert the juvenile from a potential life of adult criminality.

The problem with the classical framework, which had focused on culpability and legal rights, was that it could deal with a situation only after the fact. In contrast, the positivist school of criminology, which emerged at the turn of the 20th century, offered a greater opportunity to protect society from crime. The positivist's aim was to save a youngster from the ravishes of a life of crime by scientifically examining the causes of crime. By determining the causes of crime and by interceding at the appropriate instance, the juvenile court could become an active component of crime prevention instead of merely dealing with crime after the fact.

Canada

Institutional reforms were longer in coming to Canada than to many other parts of the world where common law prevails. Most major cities had jails and other facilities for adults. Few, however, had the type of institutional infrastructure of poor houses and houses of refuge found in Britain or the United States. For example, in 1815, the City of Halifax had a jail along with a regular courthouse. Carrigan (1998:37) reports that the courts usually imposed 39 lashes, rather than allowing young offenders to spend time in jail. As he states, "the sanction was preferable to putting them in detention because officials wanted to avoid the expense of providing board and lodging out of the taxpayers' money."

When they were housed in local jails, young offenders faced the same squalid conditions as adults did. The food was poor, sanitation was minimal, and the facilities were crude. When Upper Canada opened its first penitentiary at Kingston in 1835, the courts were ready to supply it with both young and old prisoners. Conditions in Kingston were never good. Young boys were kept with the general adult male population, and young girls were kept with adult women. All were subject to lashings for misbehaviour, including several youngsters under the age of 12 years.

In the late 1850s, new institutions, known as **reformatories,** started to appear. They were designed to hold young offenders only. The record of the first reformatories is mixed at best. They were often little more than adult jails designed for young people. Historians record much internal turmoil, high rates of escape, chronic mismanagement, and a general lack of progress. Some exceptions have been noted. After a rocky start, the Montreal Reformatory, run by the Brothers of Charity, was viewed as one of the more successful institutions. The Brothers placed great emphasis on trades training so that the young people in their care had a decent chance of getting a job upon release.

The latter part of the 19th century also saw the rise of the industrial school. **Industrial schools** were designed to fit between the ordinary public schools, which were coming into existence, and the reformatories. Wayward and neglected youths were targeted for the industrial schools as much as young offenders were. As with some reformatories, religious orders and charities as well as the state ran many industrial schools.

Exercise 3

DEFINITIONS

Please define each of the following terms:

1. Juvenile court:

_____

_____

_____

_____

_____

_____

_____

_____

_____

_____

_____

_____

2. Industrial revolution:

_____

_____

_____

_____

_____

_____

_____

_____

_____

_____

3. Reformatories:

_____

_____

_____

_____

_____

_____

_____

_____

_____

_____

4. Industrial schools:

_____

_____

_____

_____

_____

_____

_____

_____

_____

TRUE OR FALSE

1. T F The moral development of young people occurs in stages.

2. T F The first juvenile court was opened in Chicago in 1899.

3. T F In juvenile court, the judge's role is to accuse the child of a crime.

4. T F In juvenile court, the judge's role is to offer assistance and guidance.

MULTIPLE CHOICE

1. When it comes to the social welfare of children, the second half of the 19th century was a period of

   a) moving backward
   b) reform
   c) high expectations and low performance
   d) low expectations and low performance

2. Which of the following is not true about juvenile court? It recognized that

   a) childhood is a special status
   b) childhood is qualitatively different for adulthood
   c) children are simply miniature adults
   d) children should be protected from the kinds of longer sentences given in adult courts

3. In comparison to other common law countries, Canada

   a) led the way in institutional reforms

b) lagged behind in institutional reforms
c) modelled its reforms after those in Islamic countries
d) has displayed no interest in reform, even in this day

4. Which of the following groups helped advance our knowledge that social and moral growth takes place, not only in childhood, but throughout adolescence?

a) Police
b) Politicians
c) Social scientists
d) Social workers

SHORT ESSAYS

What do you consider were the principal problems with the way in which young offenders were treated in the latter part of the 19th century?

_____

_____

_____

_____

_____

_____

_____

_____

_____

_____

_____

_____

_____

_____

_____

_____

_____

_____

_____

_____

_____

_____

_____

ENDNOTES

1. To put this in context, Kiernan (1986:62) estimates that there were about 140 brothels in Toronto alone at the time of Confederation.

2. Because of a shortage of prisons in the London area, the British government used "hulks" to house prisoners. The hulks consisted of old warships anchored in the Thames river. The ships had their masts and most of the rigging removed. Usually, inmates were taken off the hulks during the day to join work parties repairing roads, docks, and other public facilities.

CHAPTER 2

Legislation Dealing with Young Canadians in Conflict with the Law: A Brief History

Learning Outcomes

Students who have mastered this chapter will have the ability to do the following:

- Distinguish *between "common law" and a "penal code."*

- Identify *what is meant by "legal infant."*

- Identify *the ways in which young people who committed crimes were treated in the 19th century.*

- Describe *why, in Canada, dealing with crime requires federal and provincial cooperation.*

- Distinguish *between the philosophical positions of "legal moralists" and "constitutionalists."*

- Explain *why the juvenile court was a type of social welfare agency.*

- Articulate *the range of behaviours that could lead a person to be found to be "in a state of delinquency."*

THE EARLY YEARS

Until the late 19th century, the laws of Great Britain applied almost directly to Canada. During colonial times, the Canadian legal system treated young people over the age of seven years the same way it treated adults. Canadian practice was similar to British practice, particularly as far as the courts were concerned. If, as Hobbes (1996) contended, life was nasty and brutish, then so was the legal system. Children were exposed to the same laws, the same court procedure, the same judges, and the same punishment, including prisons, as adults.

There were, however, some differences locally. In pre-Confederation Canada, one of the earliest signs of special concern for the treatment of young offenders was the passage in 1857 of *An Act for Establishing Prisons for Young Offenders* and *An Act for the More Speedy Trial and Punishment of Juvenile Offenders*. The *Prisons Act* also led to the construction of reformatory prisons in Canada, similar to those that were appearing in Britain and the United States at that time. The second act was concerned primarily with the pretrial conditions of youths who had not yet been convicted of a crime.

At the time of Confederation (1867), Canada inherited the British system of criminal law. A unique characteristic of British criminal law at that time was the total absence of a systematic criminal or penal code. In 1878, however, a Royal Commission was set up under the initiative of Sir James Fitzjames Stephen to systematize English common law concerning criminal matters and to produce a criminal code. Parliament drafted a Canadian criminal code in 1891, and it was adopted the following year (Mewett and Manning, 1978). Basically, this **Criminal Code of Canada** brought together and formalized what had been standard legal practice in criminal matters up to that time. Juveniles were, generally, subject to the same laws and rules of procedure as adults. One major distinction, however, was the common law rule that an individual's age was a key factor in defining culpability or criminal responsibility. Children under seven years of age were generally excluded from all criminal responsibility. Between the ages of seven and 21 years, individuals were held accountable in varying degrees.

British common law defined a person between the ages of seven and 14 years a **legal infant**, that is, a person with limited ability to form criminal intent. This assumption was open to challenge in specific cases, but the burden of proof was placed upon the Crown. To establish criminal liability, the prosecution had to show the court that children had adequate moral discretion and understanding to appreciate the wrongfulness of their actions. Common law saw persons between the ages of 14 and 21 years, both years inclusive, as being accountable for their actions. This assumption was open to rebuttal, however, with the burden of proof being placed upon the defence, rather than the prosecution.

In the middle of the 19th century, those children unfortunate enough to be convicted for indictable offences could look forward to the full brunt of Canadian justice. Perhaps the greatest outrages committed on children by the Canadian justice system were those found in the Kingston Penitentiary in the 1840s. From its opening, on June 1, 1835, the penitentiary experienced administrative strife, corruption, and overall mismanagement. Public criticism of the institution was such that in 1848, a commission was set up by the Governor General, Lord Elgin, to investigate the running of the prison. The commission's report provided a resounding condemnation of the institution's administration.

> The commissioners were especially severe in their condemnation of the treatment of child convicts. They point out the case of 10-year-old Peter Charbonneau, who was convicted on May 4, 1845, and given a seven-year sentence. They said, "…that Charbonneau's offences [in prison] were of

the most trifling description, such as were to be expected of a child of ten or eleven (like staring, winking, and laughing); and that for these he was stripped to the shirt, and publicly lashed 57 times in eight months." Then there was the case of convict Antoine Beauche, committed November 7, 1845, for three years: "…this eight-year-old child received the lash within a week of his arrival and that he had no fewer than 47 corporal punishments in nine months, and all for offences of the most childish character…" (Edmison, 1977).

As elsewhere, Canadian reformatories soon achieved a reputation of being harsh and severe institutions. In response to this, the Province of Ontario passed *An Act Respecting Industrial Schools* in 1874, providing an alternative source of residential treatment for "neglected, uncontrolled, and delinquent children" (Hagan and Leon, 1977:591).

The late 1880s were very eventful years in the field of child welfare legislation in Canada. After the American Humane Society held its annual convention in Toronto in 1888, the first provincial act dealing with neglected children was passed by the Ontario Legislature. Under this act, "children under 14 years of age could be committed to any society or institution willing to receive them." (MacGill, 1925:8). The legislation also provided for a special commissioner to try youthful offenders apart from adults.

In 1890, Ontario passed two statutes—*An Act Respecting the Custody of Juvenile Offenders* and *An Act Respecting the Commitment of Persons of Tender Years*—both of which further reduced the use of reformatories for children by diverting more juveniles to the industrial schools. Again, it is possible to see the growing disenchantment with institutions in Canada parallelling, though probably not equalling, the intensity of that in the United States and Britain. As previously noted, the first Canadian Criminal Code was adopted in 1892.

In 1893, Ontario passed the *Children's Protection Act* that "provided for the establishment of Children's Aid Societies and for the commitment of neglected and delinquent children to them by court order" (Scott, 1952:1). This act provided an essential element for the success of the juvenile court. The Ontario legislation, which served as a model for other provinces, provided operational facilities in the form of Children's Aid Societies, through which juvenile courts could dispose of many of their clients. Probation, which became an essential element of the juvenile court, since it provided a clear alternative to institutional supervision, was unknown as such in Canada at this time. The Children's Aid Societies, however, practised a type of probation by supervision of the children sent to them through court orders. The first real instance of juvenile probation in Canada seems to have been the appointment of two probation officers (one English-speaking, one French-speaking) by the Children's Aid Society of Ottawa.

Exercise 1

DEFINITION

Define the following terms:

1. *Criminal Code of Canada*:

_____

_____

_____

_____

_____

_____

_____

_____

_____

_____

2. Legal infant:

_____

_____

_____

_____

_____

_____

_____

_____

_____

_____

TRUE OR FALSE

1. T F   Until the late 19th Century, the laws of the United States applied almost directly to Canada.

2. T F   In colonial times, young people over the age of seven years and adults were treated similarly.

3. T F   In colonial times, there were separate prisons for adults and young people.

4. T F   Industrial schools in Ontario were in response to treatment in reformatories that was considered to be too lenient.

5. T F   Children's Aid Societies were established in Ontario before 1900.

MULTIPLE CHOICE

1. When Canada inherited the English system of criminal law if had the unique feature of

   a) a total absence of provisions for dealing with women who might violate the law
   b) a total absence of systematic penal code
   c) a highly structured and clearly defined criminal code
   d) allowing the penalty of capital punishment of young people for a very broad range of offences

2. English common law defined a person between the ages of 7 and 14 years as

   a) adults
   b) near adults
   c) legal infants
   d) having no ability to form criminal intent

3. In the 19th century, young persons under the age of 12 years in Canada

   a) were not imprisoned
   b) were sometimes lashed (or whipped)
   c) were never placed in the same institutions as adults
   d) were sometimes sent to a prison colony on Vancouver Island

4. Industrial schools were created in Ontario because treatment in reformatories was considered to be

   a) too harsh
   b) too lax
   c) inadequate to deal with girls
   d) too focused on the spiritual needs of young people

5. In Canada, Children's Aid Societies were first established in

   a) British Columbia
   b) Saskatchewan
   c) Ontario
   d) Nova Scotia

SHORT ESSAYS

1. Distinguish between a system based on "common law" and one that uses a criminal code.

   _____

   _____

   _____

   _____

   _____

_____

_____

_____

_____

_____

_____

_____

_____

_____

_____

_____

_____

2. What does it mean to refer to someone as a "legal infant"?

_____

_____

_____

_____

_____

_____

_____

_____

_____

_____

_____

_____

_____

_____

_____

_____

_____

_____

_____

_____

THE JUVENILE DELINQUENTS ACT

The Canadian *Juvenile Delinquents Act* was introduced to Parliament in 1907 and passed into legislation the next year. That act was based on legislation passed in the states of Illinois and Colorado. The architects of the act, however, found it very difficult to copy and adopt the American statutes in Canada.

The *Constitution Act of 1867* (which was originally known as the *British North America Act* or *B.N.A. Act*), is essentially the Canadian Constitution. It called for a clear jurisdictional split between federal and provincial responsibilities—a split aimed at the very heart of the philosophy of the juvenile court. Under the *Constitution Act*, the federal Parliament had sole jurisdiction over criminal law and procedure, but not over the composition of the criminal courts. The provincial legislatures, on the other hand, had jurisdiction over property and civil rights, local and private affairs and the administration of justice within the province, plus the criminal courts. Thus, it became an extremely complex matter for the authors of the *Juvenile Delinquent's Act* to include both the criminal concerns of the federal Parliament and the welfare concerns of the provincial legislatures without infringing upon provincial jurisdiction.

The attempt by Canadian reformers to copy the American experience and reduce the child's involvement with strictly criminal proceedings had unexpected consequences in Canada. They succeeded in broadening the scope of criminal law to include behaviour normally considered "criminal" plus "noncriminal" behaviour, by defining both as "acts of delinquency." Thus, the *Juvenile Delinquents Act* [sec. 1(1)] said that

> "juvenile delinquency" means any child who violates any provision of the Criminal Code or of any Dominion [federal] or provincial statute, or of any by-law or ordinance of any municipality, or who is guilty of sexual immorality or any similar form of vice, or who is liable for reason of any other act to be committed to an industrial school or reformatory under the provisions of any Dominion or provincial statute.

Having made virtually any form of juvenile misbehaviour a criminal act (thus allowing the federal government to intervene in welfare matters through the back door), something had to be done to express the nonpunitive philosophy of the juvenile court to soften the "criminal" orientation of the legislation. Thus, Section 38 of the *Juvenile Delinquents Act* states that

> this Act shall be liberally construed to the end that its purpose may be carried out, namely, that the care and custody and discipline of a juvenile delinquent shall approximate as nearly as may be that which should be given by its parents, and that as far as practicable, every juvenile delinquent shall be treated, not as a criminal, but as a *misdirected and misguided child*, and one *needing aid, encouragement, help, and assistance* [emphasis added].

This "liberal" construction of the *Juvenile Delinquents Act* required the cooperation and goodwill of the provincial governments. As we have noted, while Parliament was responsible for enacting the legislation, it depended on provincial resources for its effective application. Thus, despite the theoretical universality of the *Act* throughout the country, the practical application relied on the resources the provinces were willing to devote, or were capable of devoting, to juvenile justice. Throughout most of the history of the *Juvenile Delinquents Act*, there was a great variation in the facilities available across the country (Government of Canada, Department of Justice, 1965:31).

Scott summarized the major philosophical and ideological underpinnings of the 1908 legislation when he wrote that

> the rights of parents are sacred and ought not to be lightly interfered with, but they may be forfeited by abuse. Paramount to the rights of parents is the right of every child to a fair chance of growing up to be an honest, respectable citizen. What chance has the daughter of a prostitute, if left with her mother, to be other than a prostitute, or the son of a thief to be other than a thief?...[W]hy should this girl be condemned, through no fault of her own, to a life of prostitution, or that boy, unwittingly, to a career of crime? The State, too, has rights and ought not to stand idly by while children are trained, either by evil example or by neglect, to disobey her laws (quoted in Stewart, 1974:12).

From a humanitarian point of view, perhaps the greatest benefit gained from the establishment of the juvenile court was the simultaneous creation of a system of juvenile probation as an alternate disposition to incarceration. Yet, the creation of extensive probation services, combined with the fact that very often chance determined whether intervention into a juvenile's life was through welfare agents or the probation service, succeeded in bringing many children into contact with criminal law, children who perhaps ought not to have been there. This would not have been a problem if the needs of delinquent as well as neglected children were similar—as the early reformers believed. There was a growing belief, however, that juveniles who committed crimes (especially older juveniles) were different from cases of neglect and ought to be treated differently by social institutions designed specifically for that purpose. Although the juvenile court was under continuous question since its inception (e.g., Hurley, 1905; Waite, 1921), it was only in the 1960s that the underlying philosophy and structure came under broad critical attack. The major offensive against the philosophy and procedure of the court started in the United States, although it quickly spread to Canada.

"Legal moralists" argue that offenders ought to be punished. Punishment is functional to society because it expresses society's moral indignation regarding socially unacceptable behaviour. The constitutionalists argue for equal treatment under the law and due process.

It is the counterarguments to both positions that form the theoretical foundation of the juvenile court. First, the juvenile is qualitatively different from an adult and, as such, ought not to be held legally accountable to the same degree as an adult. Second, the aim of the juvenile court is not to adjudicate crime but to prevent crime by interceding in the life of a delinquent. Third, since the juvenile court is not a body whose aim it is to decide guilt or innocence, the issue of individual rights is not relevant. That is, the child does not *need* his or her rights "protected" because the court, in determining its disposition, is considering the best interests of the child. Thus, the court is guarding the child's civil rights, that is, the child's right not to be neglected, not to be exposed to a criminal environment, and to be provided the proper help, care, and guidance so as not to fall into a life of adult criminality.

The juvenile court was a "court" in name only—functionally it was supposed to be a social welfare agency. Unfortunately, the benevolence of the juvenile court was also dependent upon one's perspective. As Francis Allen (1964:18) indicates,

> whatever one's motivation, however elevated one's objectives, if the measures taken result in the compulsory loss of the child's liberty, the involuntary separation of a child from his family or even the supervision of a child's activities by a probation worker, the impact on the affected individual is essentially a punitive one. Good intentions and a flexible vocabulary do not alter this reality. This is particularly so when, as is often the case, the institution to which the child is committed is, in fact, a peno-custodial establishment...the business of the juvenile court...consists...[of] dispensing punishment. If this is true, we can no more avoid the problem of unjust punishment in the juvenile court than in the criminal court.

The response to this constitutional challenge, at least by some jurisdictions, was to delineate more clearly youths who have been engaged in criminal activities from those who are "noncriminal" delinquents. The New York *Family Court Act* of 1963, for example, created a separate category of youths appearing in front of the family court known as *persons in need of supervision* or **P.I.N.S.**. The P.I.N.S. classification was an attempt to deal with "obnoxious" or "undesirable" youthful behaviour not strictly of a criminal nature. Thus, the act stated that

> "juvenile delinquent" means any person over seven and less than 16 years of age who does any act which, if done by an adult, would constitute a crime.

> "Person in need of supervision" means a male less than 16 years of age and a female less than 18 years of age who is an habitual truant, or who is incorrigible, ungovernable, or habitually disobedient and beyond the lawful control of parent or other lawful authority (Presidential Commission on Law Enforcement, 1967).

The act also defined **neglected minors** as "any minor under 18 years of age...whose environment is injurious to his welfare or whose behaviour is injurious to his welfare or that of others."

Similar trends were occurring in Canada. As previously noted the constitutional relationship of the powers of the federal Parliament to the provincial legislatures led to the paradoxical situation of actually "criminalizing" previous social welfare problems when the *Juvenile Delinquents Act* was proclaimed, rather than "socializing" the treatment of criminal behaviour. To impose the *Act* uniformly throughout the country, the early supporters of the *Juvenile Delinquents Act* had the federal government define all "delinquencies" as criminal offences. As a result, the amorphous "state of delinquency" made no distinctions between serious antisocial behaviours, such as assault or robbery, and minor bylaw infractions, such as spitting in the street, or even occasionally, strictly welfare problems, such as being homeless.

It is this historical background of confusion and critical disagreement regarding juvenile delinquency that led the Federal government to attempt to change existing juvenile delinquency legislation. A concerted effort was made from the early 1960s onward to develop a juvenile policy around which a consensus could be achieved. That effort manifested itself primarily through the reports of several government committees created to study the issue. Foremost among those was the *Young Persons in Conflict with the Law* and the *Juvenile Delinquency in Canada* documents. Eventually, that reform effort resulted in the passage of the *Young Offenders Act* in 1985 and, more recently, the *Youth Criminal Justice Act* in 2001.

Exercise 2

DEFINITION

Define the following terms:

1. P.I.N.S.:

_____

_____

_____

_____

_____

_____

_____

_____

_____

2. Neglected minors:

_____

_____

_____

_____

_____

_____

_____

_____

_____

_____

TRUE OR FALSE

1. T F Welfare concerns are in the provincial jurisdiction.

2. T F The *Juvenile Delinquents Act* includes sexual immorality and vice in the definition of delinquency.

3. T F The implementation of the *Juvenile Delinquents Act* depended on the cooperation of the provinces.

4. T F In the *Juvenile Delinquents Act*, there was a clear distinction between criminal acts and other antisocial acts.

MULTIPLE CHOICE

1. Except which of the following do Canada's constitutional arrangements provide that provincial legislatures have jurisdiction over all?

   a) property and civil rights
   b) local and private affairs
   c) criminal courts
   d) criminal law

2. The crafting of the *Juvenile Delinquents Act* in the early 1900s

   a) was based on a straight application of statutes in Illinois and Colorado
   b) was based on the experience in Australia and New Zealand
   c) was complicated by the differences in political structures between Canada and the United States
   d) was based on a model where each province is responsible for writing its own criminal code

3. The *Juvenile Delinquents Act* defined acts of delinquency, including

   a) both criminal and noncriminal behaviour
   b) any criminal behaviour
   c) only noncriminal behaviour
   d) only those misbehaviours that are recognized as sins

4. The orientation of the *Juvenile Delinquents Act* was to care for young people in conflict with the law in a manner that

   a) was similar to what a parent would do
   b) was the same as an adult

c) reflected the child's need for corporal punishment

d) was 30 percent the severity of what an adult would receive

SHORT ESSAYS

1. Describe the role of the court relative to youthful offenders under the *Juvenile Delinquents Act.*

_____

_____

_____

_____

_____

_____

_____

_____

_____

_____

_____

_____

_____

_____

_____

2. Under the *Juvenile Delinquents Act,* what did it mean to be in a "state of delinquency"?

_____

_____

_____

_____

_____

_____

_____

_____

_____

_____

_____

_____

_____

_____

_____

_____

THE *YOUNG OFFENDERS ACT*

The federal government introduced the *Young Offenders Act* (*YOA*) in Parliament in 1982, and it became law on April 2, 1985. The former *Juvenile Delinquents Act* was designed more as social welfare legislation than criminal legislation. On the other hand, the *YOA* had at once far more limiting and yet far more complex objectives. Fundamentally, it attempted to do four things:

1. Hold young people more accountable for their behaviour
2. Provide greater protection to society from youthful offenders
3. Recognize the need to temper the impact of the criminal justice system on young people
4. Protect the legal rights of young people

Formerly, delinquency was a status offence. A **status offence** is an act that is considered to be an offence or crime that would not be an offence if committed by a person who was an adult. Because of their status as young people, juveniles could be considered criminal even if they did something that was not criminal if done by an adult. Young people could be in a "state of delinquency" or be "truant," and the *Juvenile Delinquents Act* defined this state as criminal. Under the *YOA*, there were no status offences, and the provinces had to use child welfare and child protection legislation to address other misbehaviour. By keeping behaviours defined as crimes separate from all other misbehaviour, the seriousness of those behaviours was highlighted.

Parliament meant the *YOA* to protect society from youthful criminals through several measures. First of all, the justice system was expected to divert as many young offenders as possible from the formal process. The assumptions here are twofold. First, the writers of the *YOA* expected more, and more varied, programs to be introduced than had existed under the old system. This would give the courts more options for intervention, and hopefully, those options would be more effective than what had been previously available. By providing flexibility in the legislation, the courts could encourage more use of community service orders and victim compensation. The belief is that offenders who are kept closer to the community will become more aware of the social harm they cause.

Second, the supporters of the *YOA* wanted to reserve the formal process for the most serious offenders. Throughout the 1960s and 1970s, a basic criticism of the *Juvenile Delinquents Act* was that it was too lenient on offenders. Many people hoped that the court's dispositions would be more punitive if the formal process were reserved for the most serious offenders.

The *YOA* recognized that young people are different from adults. While the prevailing philosophy of the *YOA* was to enhance accountability, it recognized that young people (even young offenders) needed special protections. This belief went beyond the traditional notion that young persons lacked the social and psychological maturity of adults. Those social scientists who considered themselves *labelling theorists* did an excellent job of influencing the drafters of the legislation. They successfully made the argument that defining young people as *delinquents* or *criminals* is detrimental to both their rehabilitation and their future development. Consequently, Parliament included a provision in the *YOA* prohibiting the publication of the young offenders' identities, restricting access to their records by adult courts, increasing the age of culpability from seven years of age to 12 years, and limiting the length of sentences.

Parliament also put procedures in place to respect further the young person's fundamental legal rights. For example, they included the right to legal representation in the *YOA*. The police were also expected to inform young suspects of their legal rights. Furthermore, police officers would not take confessions without a written waiver or the presence of the young person's lawyer or guardian. Other sections were written to introduce more "procedural fairness" into the process. Thus, the notion of "due process" had a broader application to the young offender than it did to adults.

Key Provisions of the *Young Offenders Act*

In addition to the provisions alluded to above, there are four provisions of the *YOA* that need to be understood: (1) age; (2) alternative measures; (3) rights; and (4) dispositions.

Age

The *YOA* defined young persons as individuals between the ages of 12 and 17 years, inclusive. Under 12 years of age, a person was considered a child and to be dealt with under provincial child welfare statutes. When people reach their 18th birthday, they were considered to be adults.

Alternative Measures

The *YOA* outlines a set of alternative measures. **Alternative measures** are ways of dealing with young persons who are in conflict with the law in a manner that reduces continued formal processing in the criminal justice system. They can be initiated by the police before a court appearance, by a judge before a finding of guilt, or by a judge after a finding of guilt. These measures may be used to deal with a young person alleged to have committed relatively minor offences (such as petty theft or minor acts of vandalism) under certain conditions, typically, a first offence. Several restrictions apply, but primarily, young persons must agree that they committed the act in question. The young person must "freely consent" to participate in the program; the young person must be advised of and be given the right to counsel; and, the disposition must take into consideration the best interests of society. The primary function of alternative measures is to divert young offenders from the formal court system.

Rights

Young persons have the same rights as adults as outlined in the *Canadian Charter of Rights and Freedoms*. Thus, arresting officers have an obligation to notify young offenders of their rights. Young offenders also have the right to legal counsel, the right to confer with their parents and the right to due care while in detention. The handling of young peoples' confessions is much more restricted under the *YOA* than for adults.

Dispositions

The *YOA* contained several sections that relate to the disposition of young offenders. Many dispositions are similar to those available in adult court. For example, the *YOA* allowed for both absolute and conditional discharges, fines, compensation or restitution orders, community service orders, prohibition orders, and probation. Youth court judges could also sentence young offenders to open or secure custody. **Open custody** consisted of removing the young person from his or her home and placing them in a group home for a fixed length of time. **Secure custody** generally implied that the young person is placed in a more restrictive, jail-type facility with bars and electronic surveillance.

Exercise 3

DEFINITION

Please define the following terms:

1. Status offence:

_____

_____

_____

_____

_____

_____

_____

_____

_____

2. Age of culpability:

_____

_____

_____

_____

_____

_____

_____

_____

_____

_____

3. Alternative measures:

_____

_____

_____

_____

_____

_____

_____

4. Open custody:

_____

_____

_____

_____

_____

_____

_____

5. Secure custody:

_____

_____

_____

_____

_____

_____

_____

_____

_____

TRUE OR FALSE

1. T F The *Young Offenders Act* was around for almost 100 years.

2. T F The *Young Offenders Act* was designed to keep young persons inside the criminal justice system for as long as possible.

3. T F The *Young Offenders Act* generally prohibited the publication of the identity of young persons.

4. T F Under the *Young Offenders Act*, young persons are treated differently from adults except for the length of the sentence.

5. T F Crimes are defined by the *Young Offenders Act*.

MULTIPLE CHOICE

1. Which of the following is not an objective of the *Young Offender Act*?

   a) hold young people accountable for their behaviour
   b) protection of society
   c) reward the good and punish the wicked
   d) protect the legal rights of young persons

2. Which of the following requires the use of alternative measures?

   a) that the young person has not really committed a crime
   b) that an appropriate program is not available
   c) that the young person admits guilt
   d) that a fine has already been paid

3. Alternative measures are for all of the following purposes, except

  a) dealing with minor offences
  b) punishing the guilty
  c) dealing with first-time offenders
  d) diverting some young offenders from the criminal justice system

4. The rights of young persons under the *Canadian Charter of Rights and Freedoms*

  a) are less than for adults
  b) are less than those of the police
  c) are the same as everyone else
  d) mostly disappear if they are suspected of having committed a crime

SHORT ESSAYS

1. Distinguish between "open custody" and "secure custody."

_____

_____

_____

_____

_____

_____

_____

_____

_____

_____

_____

_____

_____

_____

_____

_____

2. What do you suppose would make the difference as to whether a young person would get one of these dispositions rather than the other?

_____

_____

_____

_____

_____

_____

_____

_____

_____

_____

_____

_____

_____

_____

_____

_____

CRITICISMS OF THE *YOUNG OFFENDERS ACT*

As we have already seen and as we will continue to see, there are many and varied views about how best to deal with young people who come into conflict with the law. Different versions of the *YOA* were considered over more than two decades. Consultations with the provinces were conducted, expert panels were consulted, and a variety of professional and lay groups offered opinions.

From its inception, the *YOA* was criticized. It was criticized, on the one hand, for being too formal in its processing of young offenders, thereby making it more likely that they would see themselves as criminals. It was criticized, on the other hand, for being too soft on young offenders and thereby not "correcting" them and protecting society.

Most of the criticisms directed toward the *YOA* reflect differences in opinion over how we should treat young offenders. For example, many people argue that the *YOA* was "too soft" on young offenders. Some saw the minimum age of legal culpability of 12 years as literally allowing child criminals to get away with murder. Many in Ontario believed that the change in the age of adulthood from 16 to 18 years of age resulted in young adult criminals being "mollycoddled." These critics further suggested that the sentences available under the YOA were too light—that the maximum available limit for fines should have been higher and that institutional sentences should be longer. It was often heard that light sentences for youthful offenders who commit crimes only serve to encourage crime, not deter it.

Several areas of the YOA served as lightning rods for critics. Among the most often cited are the sections that encourage a wide range of noncustodial dispositions and the section dealing with transfer to adult court.

To be fair, the YOA's critics generally acknowledged that custodial sentences were not needed for first-time offenders who committed minor offences. Their attention was directed primarily toward "experienced" young offenders who continued to commit ever more serious offences. Even when they are incarcerated, the maximum sentence for a 16- or 17-year-old offender who committed the most serious offence was two years. Worse still, for these critics, once incarcerated, the young offender had the option of not participating in any treatment program.

The issue of transfer to adult court, on the other hand, was somewhat misdirected. The YOA did allow Crown prosecutors to petition the court to transfer young offenders age 14 years and over, who commit particularly serious offences (such as murder and aggravated sexual assault), to the jurisdiction of the adult courts. It was the youth court prosecutors, however, who were reluctant to use that option. Consequently, some critics argued for *mandatory* transfer to adult court for *all* serious crimes.

Other criticisms were directed at the privacy provisions of the YOA. The publication ban on names, for example, was the subject of some objections. Some argued that it placed the public at greater risk, since they were unaware of potentially dangerous young offenders who might be living in their neighbourhood. They also argued that the ban on publicizing names made it more difficult for the police to identify and find serious offenders, especially across police jurisdictions.

Hardline critics of the YOA also believed that there was excessive concern for the rights of offenders at the expense of the rights of victims. Such procedures as having to advise young suspects of their rights before questioning as well as requiring a written waiver or the presence of a lawyer or parent before the police can seek a confession were common examples of what they saw as "pandering" to civil libertarians. The primary concern of critics was that young people too easily learned how to manipulate the system. We were, they argued, sending the wrong message; that is, it was not important whether you had committed a wrong or not; what was important was that you were only guilty if the case could be proven in court. Criminal responsibility, therefore, became a cat-and-mouse game focused on legal nuances instead of issues relating to right and wrong, culpability, and social harm.

Other criticisms of the YOA were not directed at the legislation so much as the way in which it has (or has not) been carried out. Many critics from the social welfare perspective argued that the *Act* failed because there were insufficient resources for its implementation. These critics also argued that traditional sentences with an emphasis on punishment and incarceration did not work very well. They often mustered convincing support for the success of alternative dispositions. The problem, they argued, was in the lack of programs, personnel, and facilities to support the YOA's novel provisions.

Ironically, some social welfare critics also saw the growth of legalism, with it emphasis on procedure and due process, as a problem. Those who view delinquency as a mental health problem argued that mental health professionals should determine how young offenders are treated—not legal professionals. Lawyers do not treat physical illness, so why should they treat what is arguably a mental illness?

The perceived shortcomings of the *YOA* led to lengthy debate over issues that were not completely resolved with the passing of the *Youth Criminal Justice Act* in 2001.

Exercise 4

TRUE OR FALSE

1. T   F   The *Young Offenders Act* was well accepted and did not generate criticism.

2. T   F   Everyone agrees that the names of young offenders should not be published.

MULTIPLE CHOICE

1. Which of the following is not a criticism of the *Young Offenders Act?*

   a) the failure to provide custodial sentences for minor offences by first-time offenders
   b) the maximum sentence of 10 years
   c) the option of not participating in treatment
   d) the publication ban on names of offenders

2. Which of the following best expresses why there are criticisms of the *Youth Offenders Act?*

   a) The legislation is totally flawed.
   b) The legislation has no roots in our system of criminal justice.
   c) There are other well-proven ways of addressing the misbehaviour of young persons that we should be using.
   d) Reasonable people can reasonably disagree about how to address complex problems.

SHORT ESSAYS

1. Identify two disadvantages of not publishing the names of young offenders.

_____

_____

_____

_____

_____

_____

_____

_____

_____

_____

_____

_____

_____

_____

_____

_____

2. In your opinion, what was the most serious problem with the *Young Offenders Act*, and why do you think that this was so?

_____

_____

_____

_____

_____

_____

_____

_____

_____

_____

_____

_____

_____

_____

_____

_____

_____

Youth Crime in Canada

Learning Outcomes

Students who have mastered this chapter will have the ability to do the following:

- Explain *the value of official statistics on crime.*
- Explain *the value of different types of unofficial statistics on crime.*
- Distinguish *between "crimes known to the police" and "crimes cleared."*
- Indicate *what police discretion is and the extent to which it has an effect on the official rates of less serious and more serious crimes.*
- Explain *what "self-reports" of crime are and what they tell us about crime that is similar to and different from official statistics.*
- Explain *what "victimization surveys" of crime are and what they tell us about crime that is similar to and different from official statistics.*
- Distinguish *among ratios, proportions, and rates.*
- Manipulate *statistical information in order to calculate ratios, proportions, and rates.*
- Transform *ratios, proportions, and rates into one another.*
- Read *and understand tabular information.*
- Transform *tabular information into ratios, rates, and proportions.*

MEASURING CRIME

Besides the weather, one of the most common topics of conversation is the frequency of crime. Crime stories are the "bread and butter" of the news media and are the topic of much of our entertainment on television and at the movies. In fact, most people's knowledge of how much crime exists and where and when it takes place is moulded by the media. The constant diet of crime stories in the newspapers and on television tends to create the conventional wisdom that crime is ever on the increase. It is also part of the conventional wisdom that young people commit more crimes than they did in the past and that they are committing more serious crimes than ever before.

For people working in the criminal justice system, however, the question of how much crime there is in a community has far more practical consequences. Social scientists, such as criminologists and sociologists, use information on the distribution of crime to test explanations of crime. Politicians and planners use crime rates to decide whether there is a need for more police officers or if more courts or prisons should be built. Criminal justice administrators, on the other hand, use crime data to plan the allocation of resources. More police patrols, for example, are generally allocated to areas that have either more crimes or more serious crimes.

The amount of crimes that take place can be determined in different ways. Each way of counting crimes tells us something about crime. Depending upon our needs, some measures of crime are more useful than others. Criminologists generally identify four main sources of information on crime. The oldest and perhaps most commonly used source of information on crime is what is known as official statistics. **Official statistics** consist of information on crime collected by official agencies, such as the police, the courts, and the corrections system. Less frequently used sources of information on crime are self-report surveys and victimization surveys. As the names imply, **self-report surveys** ask people how much crime they commit. **Victimization surveys** ask people if they have been the victims of crimes. The fourth and least frequently used source of information on crime is a residual category of other techniques. Included here are such items as reports from private security firms, social scientists' field studies on gangs, direct surveillance techniques, and the results of social and psychological experiments.

We will examine each source of information separately with the aim of determining the strengths and weaknesses of those sources of information. We should note at the outset that no single source of data on crime is ideal. Each way of measuring crime has some strengths and some limitations. Each technique tends to give us a different estimate of the "true" amount of crime and each provides a different focus on the issue. Fortunately, criminologists have found that for most purposes, those different ways of measuring crime show similar patterns or distributions of crime even though the total counts do differ (for a detailed discussion, see Maxim and Whitehead, 1997).

Official Statistics

Most criminologists agree that the earliest consistent collection of crime statistics goes back to early 19th century France. In Canada, the Dominion Bureau of Statistics (now Statistics Canada) started systematically collecting national crime data in the early 1920s. Three basic sources of official statistics are reported: police statistics, court statistics, and prison statistics.

The most commonly reported official statistics are police statistics, particularly those referred to as **crimes known to police**. Crimes known to the police consist of just that—a count of all crimes that the police are aware of. Research shows that about

80 percent of the crimes known to the police results from calls for service from citizens. The remaining amount consists of crimes "discovered" by the police while on patrol or crimes uncovered through police initiated investigations. Official reports of crimes known to police consist of all offences known to the police minus those determined to be unfounded. **Unfounded crimes** are reported offences that did not take place or were determined to be not real crimes. For example, a report of stolen property may turn out to be simply misplaced property. A stolen car may have been borrowed, and a reported assault may be the result of a prank phone call.

A second count of crimes, one that is often reported in combination with crimes known to police, is a count of **crimes cleared**. A crime is most often cleared when an arrest takes place or the crime is otherwise "solved." For example, no arrest may take place in an episode of murder-suicide, but the determination of murder-suicide is enough to result in the case being closed. Either of these two sets of crime statistics is generally used as an official indicator of how much crime takes place in a community. They are also the figures most often quoted in the mass media.

Police statistics are not perfect indicators of the total amount of crimes that are committed in a community. Since most crimes known to police rely on detection by citizens, the onus is placed on the citizens to be aware that a crime has taken place and to take the initiative to make a complaint. Victims of crimes are among the most likely persons to report crimes, but witnesses do so as well. Sometimes, citizens are not aware that a crime has been committed against them. Two patrons in a bar who decide to "step outside" often do not define the situation as an assault. Stolen property may be forgotten or believed to have been mislaid. Occasionally, victims recognize that a crime has taken place but choose not to report it because they are afraid of retaliation, too embarrassed to report it, too indifferent, or are themselves engaged in an illegal activity. For example, few prostitutes report assaults on them committed by their clients, and almost no drug dealers report instances of theft, fraud, or assault.

Despite these limitations, police statistics are often our best indication of criminal activity. At the very least, they are reported on an annual basis and are assumed to have some level of consistency. Police statistics are also used as **workload data**. That is, they give us a general idea of how much crime the community thinks is important enough to report and the workload faced by the local police.

Even when a crime is reported by a citizen or detected by the police, there remains the difficulty of coming up with a good counting rule. Take the case of three young people who are armed and walk into a convenience store with the intention of committing a robbery. While in the store, they may assault a patron, rob the storekeeper, and do a significant amount of damage to the property. When generating an official report, what do we count? Should we count the number of offenders, the number of victims, or the number of offences? In this brief example, there are three offenders, two victims, and at least three possible offences that took place.

While Statistics Canada has produced a detailed handbook for generating counts, the general rule in Canada is to report *incidents* for statistics on crimes known to police. Our example consisted of one incident, and the type of incident (crime) will be defined by the most serious offence determined to have taken place. The other bits of information will eventually appear as official statistics somewhere in the system (for example, the number of offenders), but for all intents and purposes, the official report will remain as that of one crime—in this case, robbery.

We have mentioned other sources of official statistics on crime, specifically, court and prison statistics. These data are reported less often and clearly provide a count that is much smaller than the total amount of crimes that might exist in a community. When these statistics come to the attention of the public, however, it is usually in the context of how serious we are about punishing young offenders.

Self-Report Statistics

Another source of information on crime is self-report statistics. The first surveys that systematically asked a sample of people whether or not they had committed certain types of crimes took place in the 1940s. Since then, social scientists have conducted many studies based on self-reports. Most of those studies have been directed toward young people and inmates. It is likely that if you are aware of a self-report study, it is the one conducted by the Centre for Addictions and Mental Health, which, since 1968, has sought to measure substance abuse among young people.

As you might suspect, self-report studies indicate that much more crime takes place than is reported in official statistics. When they were first conducted, self-report studies shocked many people when they indicated that almost everyone commits some form of offence at some point in time. In particular, conventional notions that crime was the sole domain of certain social classes and ethnic and racial groups came under challenge. After half a century of self-report research, we can draw two firm conclusions. First, the reality is that everyone does commit some type of criminal act at some point in time. Second, it is also true that what distinguish those people who get caught from those who do not are the severity and the frequency of the offences they commit. That is, while *everyone* may commit an occasional offence, those persons most likely to show up in the official counts are those who self-report more frequent and more serious criminality.

Thus, for example, self-report studies suggest that as a group, young people from working class backgrounds and from broken homes pose more of a crime problem than do young people from a middle-class background and intact homes. Clearly, there are individual exceptions, since not all working class kids or kids from broken homes are young criminals, but there are significant differences at the group level.

From the researcher's point of view, self-report and victimization studies have the advantage of being able to provide "richer" information about criminality. Official statistics are often only broken down by age, gender, and type of offence. Self-report and victimization studies have the advantage of allowing us to look at other characteristics of young people, such as their social class, ethnicity, intelligence quotient (IQ), and school progress.

As with official statistics, however, self-report statistics have their limitations. Self-report studies require young people to perceive that their behaviour fits one of the definitions of crime as defined in the survey. Often, people forget their misbehaviours (particularly minor ones). Sometimes, respondents lie about or under-report infractions; at other times, they may exaggerate or report offences they have not committed. This is even the case when researchers promise anonymity on the survey. A common complaint by critics of self-report surveys is that they tend to be loaded with minor offences and with behaviours that may constitute sins, disobediences, and other wrongs, but not crimes. In the past, many researchers have not separated simple "bad acts" from crimes when they have reported the results. This led to the misperception that crime is universal.

Victimization Surveys

Victimization surveys are similar to self-report surveys, except that they ask people whether they have been the victims of offences, not if they have committed them. Victimization surveys are relatively recent developments. The first one of note was conducted in Washington, D.C. in 1967. Since then, annual national victimization surveys have been conducted in several countries, including the United States and the United Kingdom. There has been little enthusiasm, however, for conducting victimization surveys in Canada on a regular basis.

As with self-report studies, victimization surveys generally produce higher estimates of the total amount of crimes that are committed than we find in official statistics. As a consequence, many criminologists argue that victimization surveys get us closer to the "true" amount of crime that exists—the so-called "dark figure" of crime. Although there is a substantial difference between the estimates of the total amount of crime between official statistics and victimization surveys, there are similarities in both measures. Overall, both official statistics and victimization surveys rank crimes similarly in their order of prevalence.

By their nature, victimization surveys tell us little about the people who commit crimes, since most victims are either unfamiliar with their offenders or the crimes take place when the victims are absent from the crime scene. Most property offences, for example, take place when the victims are away. On the other hand, victimization surveys have provided some insight into the victim–offender relationship, in a situation where both are present at the time of the offence. Usually, these are incidents of crimes against individual persons. Thus, criminologists have learned a great deal more about the dynamics that take place in such crimes as domestic assaults and date rapes (Sacco and Kennedy, 1998).

Among the primary findings to come from victimization surveys is the one that young people are more at risk of criminal victimization than are older people. In general, we now know that victims share the same general profiles as offenders. Consequently, victims disproportionately tend to be young males from the working class—the same characteristics that commonly identify offenders. These profiles of victims are interesting, since surveys that tap into peoples' fear of crime suggest that those most likely to be victimized express the least fear of victimization. Usually, the elderly, women, and middle-class individuals express the greatest concern regarding the likelihood of victimization, even though they are, proportionally, less likely to be victimized.

We hold the view that it is the relative lack of fear of crime among those most likely to be victims that puts them at risk. Young males, for example, tend to engage in more reckless behaviour and to frequent locations (such as bars) which put them at greater risk of criminal victimization than in the case of other groups in society. It is the routine activities of one's lifestyle, some criminologists argue, that have the greatest impact on one's risk of victimization.

Victimization surveys also provide the police with other useful information beyond the amount of crime that exists. Most surveys ask people why they do not report crimes that take place—even the relatively serious ones. The most common reasons expressed for nonreporting are that the offences are too trivial to bother the police with and that for some offences, there is nothing the police can do. Less frequently, the reason is that the incident was "personal" or that "nothing was taken." The ability of young person to report victimization is even more restricted, since they normally do not have the same access to the police as do adults. Young person who are victimized usually report their concerns to parents, relatives, teachers, and other adults in supervisory roles who then decide whether or not to report the offences to the police.

Young persons face an additional reporting burden when their offender is a relative or an important adult in their lives. This is part of the reason that many incidents of sexual and physical abuse by parents and other adults in supervisory roles, such as coaches and priests, go unreported for so long.

While victimization surveys provide more systematic information about crime than do official statistics, they are not perfect. As with self-report surveys, the onus to recognize a criminal event is placed on the citizen. Many victims do not realize that they have been victimized. As we noted earlier, people often assume that stolen property has simply been mislaid or lost. Even when the victim is aware of the event, he or she must also be able to recognize it as a crime. While most people are able to distinguish crimes from other forms of unacceptable behaviour, there are many situations that are difficult to classify. As a consequence, victimization surveys will contain both false positives and false negatives: instances reported as crimes when they are not and crimes that are not acknowledged as such. Whether those errors cancel out or bias our results is not known with any degree of certainty.

Other Procedures

Criminologists have many other ways of measuring crime. For example, reports from private security firms are used to gain estimates of how much shoplifting takes place. Banks have estimates of how many credit-card and other frauds take place, even though much of that crime is not reported to the police. Other criminologists conduct field studies with gangs; they "hang out" with groups of young people or interview selected informants. Other sources of information include the use of surveillance cameras on the streets and the use of laboratory experiments. Most of these procedures do not give us better overall estimates of the total amount of crimes that are committed. Instead, they enhance our understanding of the who, why, and where of criminal behaviour.

One of the dangers of using some of these procedures is that they can colour our view of the overall problem of crime. For example, field workers who study juvenile gangs can easily be misled into believing that gang membership is more common than it really is. Police officers who work with young offenders often have to remind themselves that most young people are decent kids and not "punks" or "pukes."

Exercise 1

DEFINITIONS

Please define the following terms:

1. Official statistics on crime:

_____

_____

_____

_____

_____

_____

_____

_____

2. Self-report surveys:

_____

_____

_____

_____

_____

_____

_____

_____

3. Victimization surveys:

_____

_____

_____

_____

_____

_____

_____

_____

4. Crimes known to the police:

_____

_____

_____

_____

_____

_____

_____

_____

_____

_____

5. Unfounded crime:

_____

_____

_____

_____

_____

_____

_____

_____

6. Crimes cleared by arrest:

_____

_____

_____

_____

_____

_____

_____

_____

_____

_____

7. Workload data:

_____

_____

_____

_____

_____

_____

_____

_____

_____

_____

TRUE OR FALSE

1. T   F   Self-report surveys are an important source of official statistics on crime.

2. T   F   The oldest and most commonly used source of information on crime is in the form of surveys of victims.

3. T   F   Each technique (way) of measuring crime produces a *different* estimate of the amount of crime that actually exists.

4. T   F   Crimes known to police are only those violations of law that the police have witnessed with their own eyes.

5. T   F   The social categories of persons who least fear crime are those that have the greatest risk of being victims of crime.

MULTIPLE CHOICE

1. Which of the following sources of official statistics on crime would produce the highest estimates of the amount of crime

    a) crimes cleared by arrest
    b) number of persons incarcerated
    c) crimes known to police
    d) persons who are homeless

2. Surveys of victims are particularly helpful because they provide

    a) a good deal of information on those who commit crimes
    b) a good deal of information about those who commit property crimes, even if they provide much less about crimes against persons
    c) a good deal of information about those who commit property crimes *and* information about the relationships between the offenders and the victims
    d) none of the above

SHORT ESSAYS

1. For what three purposes can information on rates of crime can be used?

    1) _____

    _____

    2) _____

    _____

    3) _____

    _____

2. By what three agencies are official statistics on crime collected?

    1) _____

    2) _____

    3) _____

3. Identify two advantages of "crimes known to the police" as an indicator of the amount of crime in a city.

    1) _____

    _____

    2) _____

    _____

4. Identify two limitations of "crimes known to the police" as an indicator of the amount of crime in a city.

1) _____

_____

2) _____

_____

5. Discuss the truth or falsity of the following statement and give reasons for your position: "Police discretion is greatest in situations where the offence committed is a minor one."

_____

_____

_____

_____

_____

_____

_____

_____

6. Why are counts of crime expressed in different ways?

_____

_____

_____

_____

_____

_____

_____

7. What are the principal differences between official and unofficial counts of crime?

_____

_____

_____

_____

_____

_____

_____

_____

PROCESSING COUNTS OF CRIME

The total number of offences that take place in a community is useful to know for many reasons. It provides an estimate of the size of the crime problem plus an indication of the workload faced by criminal justice personnel. For most purposes, however, raw crime totals are not very useful. Common sense tells us that all else being equal, larger communities would record more offences in total than would smaller communities. Communities with greater proportions of their population in high-crime-prone categories, such as men and young people, will also have higher crime counts. Social scientists usually convert crime counts into different statistics to make them more useful. The most commonly used conversions are ratios, proportions, and rates.

Ratios consist of a comparison of one portion of a population count with another. For example, in a particular city of 350,000 people, 11,371 are arrested for theft involving under $5,000 in a given year. Of that total, 1,391 are women. The ratio of men to women arrested for theft involving under $5,000 is, therefore, 9,980:1,391 or about 7.2:1. In other words, approximately 7.2 men are arrested for one woman.

Proportions consist of the fraction of the population made up by a part of that population. Thus, the proportion of women arrested for theft is 1,391 of 11,371, or approximately 0.12. Multiplying a proportion by 100 give us a percentage; therefore, 0.12×100 or 12 percent of the people arrested in our example community are women.

Rates consist of the number of events in comparison with a standard-sized population or base. Usually, crime rates are based on the standard of 100,000 people, or sometimes, we use a base of 1,000 or 10,000 for more common events. Rates are calculated by the formula:

Events ÷ Population × 100,000 = Rate per 100,000

In this example, we calculate the rate for theft as:

$11,371 \div 350,000 \times 100,000 = 3,249$

We read this rate as 3,249 thefts per 100,000 population.

The primary advantage of ratios, proportions, and rates is that we can make comparisons across social and geographical units. Crime rates, for example, allow us to compare cities, nations, or other social groups of different sizes by assuming that the groups have similar population counts.

While they are useful, these statistics do have limitations. One major assumption we make when calculating a rate is that the population in the denominator is similar or homogeneous. When we make this assumption, we calculate what is known as a "crude rate." Different communities, however, may have different population compositions that make the comparison of crude rates a problem. For example, one community might have a higher proportion of young people (who are more prone to crime) than another community. Since the community with proportionately more young people will likely have a higher rate of crime, we find an estimate of the crude rate to be less useful. In those situations, we are inclined to break the population down into smaller groups based on the important crime-related factor. Thus, we might calculate age-specific rates where we estimate the number of crimes per 100,000 people in each age grouping (e.g., people under 15 years; 15–24 year of age; 24–35 years of age, and so on). It is common for social scientists to calculate separate age- or gender-specific crime rates for communities in order to allow for more precise comparisons.

The reluctance of social scientists simply to use crime totals when looking at a community stems from the fact that most things only have meaning when they are compared with something else. For example, the total amount of crime in a community makes much more sense when we look at it in comparison with the total population. The crime rate for Canada takes on more meaning when we compare it with that of another country that has characteristics similar to those of Canada.

Exercise 2

DEFINITIONS

Please define the following terms:

1. Ratio:

_____

_____

_____

_____

_____

_____

_____

_____

_____

2. Proportion:

_____

_____

_____

_____

_____

_____

_____

3. Rate:

_____

_____

_____

_____

_____

_____

_____

MULTIPLE CHOICE

1. Which of the following is a ratio?

    a) 10%
    b) 10:1
    c) 100 per 100,000
    d) 10

2. Which of the following is a proportion?

    a) 0.1
    b) 10:1
    c) 100 per 100,000
    d) 10

3. Which of the following is a rate?

    a) 10%
    b) 10:1
    c) 100 per 100,000
    d) 10

4. The calculation of crime rates is useful because

    a) all communities are basically the same size
    b) no community changes in size over time
    c) rates allow for the direct comparison of communities of different sizes
    d) the math is easy and it is fun to do

EXPRESSING COUNTS OF CRIME

1. Express the ratio that 80 percent of young persons charged with crime are males.

    The ratio is: _____:_____.

2. Express as a rate per 10,000 young persons that 400 younger persons appeared in youth court in a community that had 10,000 people between the ages of 12 and 17 years, inclusive.

    _____ per 10,000 young people.

3. Express as a proportion that females commit 20 of every 100 crimes.

    Females commit _____ of crimes.

4. Express as a ratio that young males commit 80 percent of property crimes and that young females commit the other 20 percent when such crimes are committed by young persons.

    _____

    _____

5. Express as a rate per 10,000 young persons that 800 young persons appeared in youth court in a community that had 20,000 people between the ages of 12 and 17 years, inclusive.

    _____

    _____

PROFILE OF OFFICIAL OFFENDERS

Demographics

Young persons between the ages of 12 and 17 years make up about 10 percent of the Canadian population. However, they represent about 20 percent of all the people charged with federal offences. In 2001, the charge rate for federal offences in Canada was 4,657 per 100,000—slightly over twice the charge rate for adults. In 2000–2001, approximately 2 percent of the youth population of Canada were convicted in court. Among those 16 and 17 years old, about 3 percent were convicted for offences. Given these statistics, it is clear that a large part of the workload facing the police is generated by young people.

The overall pattern of the relationship between age and criminality is illustrated in Figures 3.1 and 3.2. Figure 3.1 presents a graph of the percentage of people accused of property crimes in 1997 by the age of the accused. The data are taken from a non-random sample of police agencies that use the UCR reporting system.[1] Overall, those agencies handle almost half the total amount of crimes reported. These data show a pattern found in most Western countries. The peak for property offences appears among those in the 15-to-17-year age group.

Figure 3.2 displays a similar pattern, but for persons accused of violent crimes. The primary difference between these two figures is that unlike charges for property crimes, charges for violent crimes tend not to be clustered so exclusively among young people. There are some important similarities between the two figures, however. First, both show a steep increase in the amount of offending to a peak in mid-adolescence. Second, both indicate that while most official crimes occur among younger people, a clear and substantial drop does not take place until the 40-plus age category is reached.

Just as the young are over-represented among offenders, so are males. Of all those young offenders charged in 2001 for *Criminal Code of Canada* violations, only 21 percent were female. Among adults, the proportion of women charged was slightly lower at 17 percent. One of the more interesting patterns, however, is the difference between

Figure 3.1: Persons Accused of Property Crimes by Age, 1997

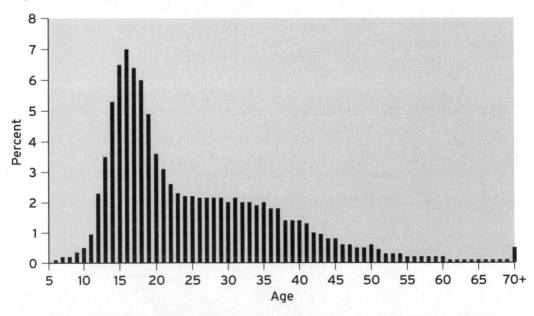

Source: Statistics Canada, "Canadian Crime Statistics, 1997." *Juristat Service Bulletin*, vol. 18, no. 11. Statistics Canada Cat. #85-002XPE, Figure 14a.

Figure 3.2: Persons Accused of Violent Crime by Age, 1997

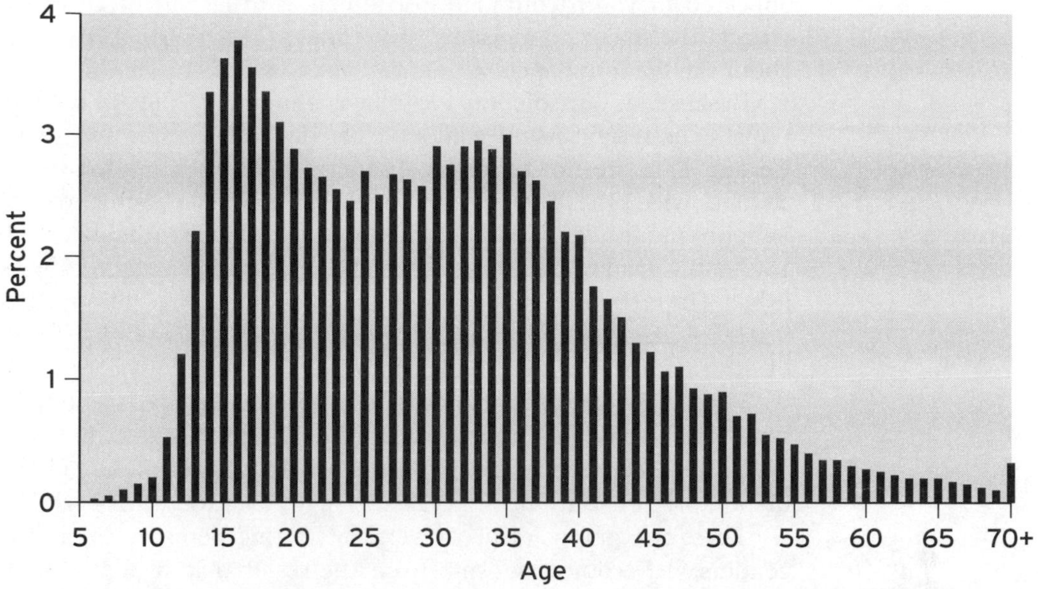

Source: Statistics Canada, "Canadian Crime Statistics, 1997." *Juristat Service Bulletin*, vol. 18, no. 11. Statistics Canada Cat. #85-002XPE, Figure 14b.

young and adult women in the matter of crimes of violence. Adult women account for about 22 percent of the adults charged for property offences and 15 percent of those charged for violent crimes. Young women, however, account for a similar 23 percent of young offenders charged for property offences, but of the young people charged for crimes of violence, it is higher at 26 percent.

Thus, while both male young offenders and male adult offenders make up the majority of offenders in all groups, proportionately, young women offenders are charged for more crimes of violence than their adult counterparts. The questions you might want to ask yourself are: To what degree is this difference due to the behaviour of young women? To what degree is it due to police officers' decisions to charge?

Offences

Table 3.1 presents selected rates of crime by major crime category based on the cases that appeared before the youth courts in 2001. The overall rate for all crimes was 466 per 10,000 young people. With a rate of 182.4 per 10,000, property crimes accounted for almost half the cases heard. Violent crimes had a rate of 94 per 10,000, which is about half the rate of property crimes but represents only slightly more than 20 percent of the total amount of crime.

Table 3.1 Rate per 10,000 Youths Charged, Canada, 2001

Offence Type	Rate per 10,000
Property crime	182.4
Violent crime	94.0
Other Criminal Code of Canada crime	137.6
Drug crime	33.9
Other federal statute crime	17.8
All incidents	465.7

Source: Statistics Canada, CANSIM II, Table 252-0014, last updated on 2002-06-11.

A more detailed breakdown is presented in Figure 3.3. Here, the offences that appeared in youth court are distributed as a percent of all cases heard. This graph reflects the major conclusions to be drawn from Table 3.1, where the point is made about the predominance of property offences.

Because of jurisdictional conflicts and financial restraints placed on Statistics Canada in recent years, national data on youth crime are reported inconsistently. Certain data are not reported annually, or the format in which they are presented changes with time. The primary source for national data on youth crime is the *Juristat* bulletin, published by the Canadian Centre for Justice Statistics, which is a division of Statistics Canada. The Canadian Centre for Justice Statistics (1999a) has recently published *The Juristat Reader*, which is a compendium of recent bulletins. It also releases the Statistics Canada publication *A Profile of Youth Justice in Canada*, which is a good source of information relating specifically to the youth justice system.

Figures 3.4 and 3.5 provide a temporal perspective on youth crime. Both figures show the absolute numbers of young people charged in Canada for the period 1989–2000. We have decided to display absolute numbers instead of rates, since the population base of youth has been relatively steady during this period.

These two graphs display several interesting elements. First, if we compare the two genders, it becomes evident (from the scale) that young women are charged with approximately one-quarter the number of offences as are their male counterparts. Second, with a few minor exceptions, the patterns for males and females track similarly.

Figure 3.3: Youth Court Cases, 2000/01

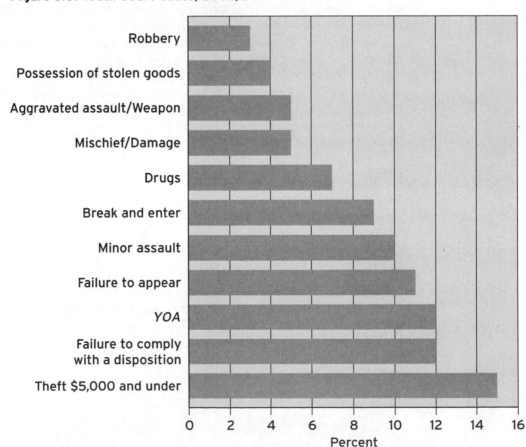

Source: Statistics Canada, "Youth Court Statistics, 2002/01." *Juristat*, vol. 22, no. 3.

Figure 3.4: Youths Charged (Males), Canada, 1989-2000

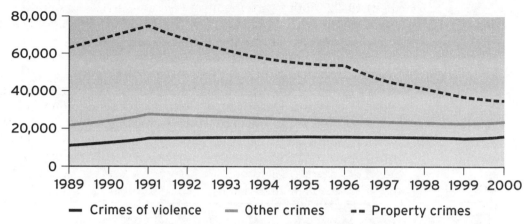

Source: Calculated from Statistics Canada, CANSIM II Table 109-5009, "Adults and Youths Charged, by Sex and Offence Category, Canada, Provinces and Territories Annual."

Figure 3.5: Youths Charged (Females), Canada, 1989-2000

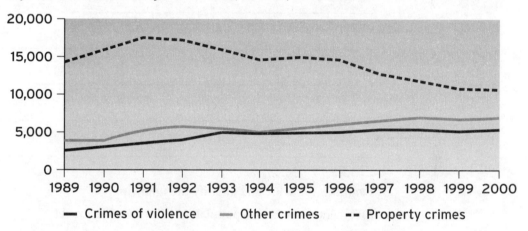

Source: Calculated from Statistics Canada, CANSIM II Table 109-5009, "Adults and Youths Charged, by Sex and Offence Category, Canada, Provinces and Territories Annual."

Third, after peaking in the early 1990s, charges for property crimes dropped considerably throughout the decade. However, there has been a slight increase in the number of charges for crimes of violence and other offences. The pattern is even more pronounced for young women. While it is not the purpose of this text to explore the underlying causes of criminal behaviour, the consensus among criminologists is that the changes are due to a combination of real behavioural changes on the part of young people. This has been combined with an increased willingness by police officers to deal with minor property offences in a nonjudicial manner.

Exercise 3

TABLE READING SKILLS

1. Examine Figure 3.1. Which of the following categories of age makes the greatest contribution to crime?

   a) 6–11

b) 12–18
c) 19–27
d) 30–55

2. Examine Figure 3.2. What does it mean?

_____

_____

_____

_____

_____

_____

_____

_____

_____

_____

3. Examine Table 3.1 and identify the following:

   a) The rate per 10,000 population of property crime is _____.

   b) The rate per 10,000 population of drug crime is _____.

4. Examine Figure 3.3. Which of the following is a more common category of case in youth court? Put an "X" on the line next to the correct answer.

   a) Drug offences _____

   b) Break and enter _____

5. Based on Table 3.2,

   a) the number of adults charged for all offences in 2000 is _____.

   b) the number of youths charged for all *Criminal Code of Canada* offences in 1990 is _____.

   c) the number of young males charged for violent crime in 2000 is _____.

6. Examine Table 3.3 and answer the following questions about cases heard in youth court with guilty findings.

   a) What year recorded the largest number of dispositions? _____

   b) The most "typical" disposition is _____.

Table 3.2 Youths and Adults Charged in Criminal Incidents by Gender

	1990	1995	2000
All offences			
Adults charged	490,280	454,465	433,902
Male	407,774	376,269	358,870
Female	82,506	78,196	75,032
Youths charged	131,155	128,809	111,104
Male	107,537	101,407	87,809
Female	23,618	27,402	23,295
All *Criminal Code of Canada*			
Adults charged	441,119	408,791	380,957
Male	364,928	337,061	313,777
Female	76,191	71,730	67,180
Youths charged	126,549	120,663	100,861
Male	103,771	94,649	77,566
Female	22,778	26,014	23,295
Violent crime			
Adults charged	319,738	327,637	327,412
Male	288,425	287,316	277,693
Female	31,313	40,321	49,719
Youths charged	41,261	58,657	60,010
Male	32,137	44,611	44,141
Female	9,124	14,076	15,869
Property crime			
Adults charged	188,591	159,128	124,366
Male	144,561	122,940	96,912
Female	44,030	36,188	27,454
Youths charged	83,741	68,105	46,248
Male	68,424	52,956	35,521
Female	15,317	15,149	10,727

Source: Statistics Canada, CANSIM II, Table 252-0002, last updated on 2002-06-11.

Table 3.3 Cases Heard by Youth Courts with Guilty Findings, by Most Significant Disposition (Canada)[1]

DISPOSITION	1994-1995	1996-1997	1998-1999	2000-2001
Secure custody	11,616	11,772	12,312	10,458
Open custody	13,596	13,506	12,857	10,351
Probation	35,627	37,960	35,451	29,053
Fine	4,472	3,574	4,081	3,502
Community service	4,866	4,594	4,988	3,906
Absolute discharge	2,413	1,464	1,130	1,044
Other[2]	1,379	1,927	2,142	1,727
Total guilty findings	73,969	74,797	71,961	60,041

[1] Includes other *Criminal Code of Canada* and federal statute crimes not listed above.

[2] Includes restitution, prohibition, compensations, pay purchaser, and other sentences, such as essays, apologies, counselling programs, and conditional discharges.

Source: Statistics Canada, Web site [http://www.statcan.ca/english/Pgdb/State/Justice/legal16.htm].

ENDNOTES

1. Some up-to-date information on crime and justice can be found on the Statistics Canada Web site, http://www.statcan.ca/english/Pgdb/State/justic.htm.

CHAPTER 4

Current Legislation Relating to Young People

Learning Outcomes

Students who have mastered this chapter will have the ability to do the following:

- Identify *federal and provincial responsibilities relative to the creation of criminal law and the prosecution of criminal cases.*
- Distinguish *between the criteria of defining a young person in conflict with the law under the* Juvenile Delinquents Act *and the* Young Offenders Act.
- Explain *the differences involved in being a "legal infant," a "young person," or an adult.*
- Specify *the ways in which the* Canadian Charter of Rights and Freedoms *has implications for young persons.*
- Understand *the basic objectives of the* Youth Criminal Justice Act.
- Articulate *the basis for the legal difference between young persons and adults.*
- Specify *ways in which young persons are treated differently from adults*
- Describe *what the* Child and Family Services Act *has to do with the behaviour of children.*
- Identify *some important features of the* Youth Criminal Justice Act.

THE YOUNG PERSON AND THE LAW

Because of the division of responsibilities outlined in Canada's constitution, no single level of government is responsible for handling young people who pose a social problem. The *Constitution Act, 1867* outlines the main divisions of responsibility among governments. Section 91(27) of the *Constitution Act* gives Parliament responsibility for defining criminal behaviour and for deciding what procedures should be followed in criminal cases. Thus, the *Criminal Code of Canada (CCC)* is federal legislation that outlines what makes up a crime, what criminal procedures to follow, and how to handle criminals. *The Youth Criminal Justice Act (YCJA)*, also federal, indicates how criminal law is to be applied to young persons. The federal government also has the responsibility for prosecuting criminal cases, but it has delegated much of that responsibility to the provinces.

The provinces, on the other hand, are primarily responsible for the implementation of justice. Thus, the provinces are responsible for local policing and for administering the criminal courts. Various parts of section 92 of the *Constitution Act* also state that the provinces are responsible for civil matters (which includes welfare issues) and for the enforcement of provincial laws. Thus, the provinces regulate matters of property and other civil concerns. The provinces are also responsible for stating what is appropriate procedure in civil cases.

Just as the federal government delegates some of its responsibilities to the provinces, so do the provinces delegate some of their responsibilities to municipal governments. Under this arrangement, the provinces give cities and municipalities the power to make and to enforce bylaws. Similarly, they allow many cities and municipalities to have their own police services whose duty it is to enforce criminal law, provincial statues, and municipal bylaws.

The federal and provincial governments share responsibilities for adults convicted of offences. Persons receiving a sentence of two years' incarceration or more are the responsibility of the federal corrections system. Persons receiving sentences of less than two years are the responsibility of the provincial correctional systems. Young persons in conflict with the law, however, are the sole responsibility of the provinces.

At times, this peculiar division of responsibility leads to political conflict. The provinces sometimes contend that it is unfair for the federal government to make the rules about young persons who violate the law when the provinces see themselves paying most of the bills. Different provinces have different views on how young offenders should be handled, and they sometimes argue that the federal government's rules do not fit local circumstances. Ontario has been one of the most vocal objectors on this score. In fact, Ontario sought and obtained an exemption that allowed it to delay the implementation of many sections of the *Young Offenders Act (YOA)* when it was first introduced. The federal government's response to the provinces is about equity. Ottawa argues that all Canadians should be treated the same whether they live in British Columbia, Ontario, or even (sometimes) Quebec.

The process of consultation over the *YCJA* was long and involved and revealed that there continue to be deep divisions among the provinces on how young violators of the law should be treated. After the *YCJA* was passed by Parliament, it was sent to the Senate for the "sober second thought" exercised in the "upper chamber." Ontario proposed more than 100 amendments for the Senate's consideration—most designed to toughen the language of the legislation. The Senate agreed to none of them.

In a constitutional sense, one of the most interesting features of the *YCJA* is that it allows the individual provinces to enact, or not, wide arrays of provisions that may—and most likely will—lead to quite different ways of dealing with young persons in different provinces. The principle that the law should apply uniformly appears to be violated. Whether this will lead to constitutional challenges remains to be seen.

It is interesting to note that the *YCJA* speaks of uniformity of application across "regions" [s. 38(2)(b)], which are undefined, but seems to allow differences, even within provinces.

The constitutional division of power also makes the provinces responsible for most "social" or common welfare issues. Consequently, the provinces are generally responsible for people who misbehave, but whose misbehaviour is not formally considered "criminal." This includes, for example, people who misbehave because of mental problems (they are handled under the *Mental Health Act*), children who are truant (they are handled under the *Education Act*), or children we see as too young to be handled by criminal law (they are handled under the *Child and Family Services Act*).

As we saw in Chapter 2, in 1908, the federal government tried to deal with some inconsistencies this division of responsibility created by defining most childhood misbehaviour as delinquency. Thus, the *Juvenile Delinquents Act* "criminalized" much behaviour that we might see as wrong, sinful, or immoral, but not necessarily criminal, if performed by an adult.

The introduction of the *YOA* resulted in a reduction of the federal government's control over young people, and this continues in the *YCJA*. A basic principle of the *YCJA* is that of fairness. The writers of both *Acts* believed that consistent definitions of criminality should apply to both young people and adults. Young persons generally should not be held criminally responsible for behaviours that would not be considered criminal if committed by an adult. Thus, the provinces again faced the problem of what to do with noncriminal, but socially unacceptable, youthful misbehaviour. With the *YCJA*, as with the *YOA* before it, Parliament set the minimum age of legal responsibility at the age of 12 years. At the upper end, it imposed a national maximum of 18 years of age for distinguishing young persons from adults.

THE CRIMINAL CODE OF CANADA

The *Criminal Code of Canada* indicates what behaviours are criminal. The *CCC* also specifies the procedures law enforcement officials must follow and the maximum penalties for committing a crime. The application of the *CCC*, however, is much more restricted when we are dealing with young persons instead of adults. The definition of what is criminal applies equally to young persons and adults with only **legal infants** (persons under the age of 12 years) being totally exempt. Many procedures, particularly those that relate to the notification of rights, the acceptance of confessions, and detention, apply only partially to young people. The *YCJA* alters and extends the basic principles that apply to adults cases. Furthermore, the sentences or dispositions outlined in the *CCC* have only partial bearing on the sentences that the youth justice courts might hand out. Again, the *YCJA* specifies the conditions that the youth justice courts can impose on young offenders. Police officers need to be familiar with the offences outlined in the *CCC*, since they form the basis of the substantive law as it applies to young persons.

THE CANADIAN CHARTER OF RIGHTS AND FREEDOMS

The *Canadian Charter of Rights and Freedoms*, which was introduced in 1982, has become an increasingly important document for criminal justice personnel—particularly police officers. The main purpose of the *Charter* is to protect all Canadians, including young people (and police officers), from arbitrary and excessive state intervention in their lives. The charter guarantees, among other things, equality before the law, whatever one's social characteristics (such as age, gender, religious affiliation, or ethnicity), and the right to due process. Sections 8 through 10 of the *Charter* indicate that everyone has the right

- to be secure against unreasonable search or seizure;
- not to be arbitrarily detained or imprisoned;
- to be promptly informed of the reason for being arrested or detained;
- to have and to instruct legal counsel without delay and to be informed of that right; and
- to be released if detention is unlawful or unwarranted.

Many citizens and criminal justice personnel think that minor violations of these charter rights automatically lead to a case being "thrown out" of court. This is not always the case. For example, subsection 24(2) of the *Charter* allows judges to admit physical evidence even in cases where a confession was improperly obtained. The key issue is whether "having regard to all the circumstances, the admission of it in the proceedings would bring the administration of justice into disrepute." To make this assessment, judges must examine the broader circumstances surrounding the violation of the *Charter*. Part of the misperception here is probably due to differences between Canadian and American jurisprudence. In the United States, constitutional provisions have been more narrowly interpreted. There, taking account of "all the circumstances" is not a consideration.

As we will see in the next chapter, the courts have also recognized that young persons are usually less aware of their rights than are adults. The courts believe young people are less able than adults to make prudent decisions. Consequently, they have interpreted many fundamental rights outlined in the *Charter* more broadly when applied to young people.

Exercise 1

DEFINITIONS

Define the following term:

Legal infant:

_____

_____

_____

_____

_____

_____

_____

_____

TRUE OR FALSE

1. T   F   Persons receiving sentences of two years or more are the responsibility of the provincial corrections system.

2. T   F   Provinces, not the federal government, are responsible for local policing.

3. T   F   All provinces have the same view of how young persons in conflict with the law should be handled.

4. T   F   Persons under the age of 12 years old are to be dealt with under the *Criminal Code of Canada,* rather than under the *Youth Criminal Justice Act.*

5. T   F   Procedures regarding the acceptance of confessions are different for young persons from what they are for adults.

MULTIPLE CHOICE

1. In Canada, the responsibility for defining criminal behaviour belongs to

   a) the police
   b) judges
   c) parliament
   d) the provinces

2. What piece of legislation identifies the procedures to be followed in handling young persons who have committed crimes?

   a) *Youth Criminal Justice Act*
   b) *Young Criminals Act*
   c) *Criminal Code of Canada*
   d) Canadian Constitution

3. Young persons in conflict with the law are the sole responsibility of

   a) the federal government
   b) the provinces
   c) their parents
   d) the Children's Aid Society

4. The *Youth Criminal Justice Act* applies to young people who are

   a) 10–16 years old
   b) 11–17 years old
   c) 12–19 years old
   d) at least 12 years, but not yet 18 years old

5. Whether a person is to be dealt with under the *Youth Criminal Justice Act* is determined by the person's age at the time

   a) the crime was committed
   b) of arrest
   c) of the court case
   d) most of the evidence was collected

ESSAY

1. Explain why there is sometimes conflict between the federal government and the provinces on how young persons in conflict with the law are to be dealt with.

_____

_____

_____

_____

_____

_____

_____

_____

_____

_____

_____

_____

_____

2. Why does Canada have the *Criminal Code of Canada* as well as the *Youth Criminal Justice Act*?

_____

_____

_____

_____

_____

_____

_____

_____

_____

_____

_____

_____

_____

_____

_____

3. When it comes to crime, what are the reasons for treating young persons differently from adults?

_____

_____

_____

_____

_____

_____

_____

_____

_____

_____

_____

_____

_____

_____

_____

_____

THE *CHILD AND FAMILY SERVICES ACT*

Description

Ontario deals with children under 12 years of age who commit criminal offences under the *Child and Family Services Act* (*CFSA*). Basically, the *CFSA* is child welfare legislation, and its provisions reflect that underlying philosophy. Consequently, child protection officers (including police officers) are directed to "return the child to the child's parents or other person having charge of the child" [*CFSA* 42(1)(a)], even when the child commits what would normally be a criminal offence. As Bala and Mahoney (1995) point out, "the only legal basis for intervention is if there is serious or repetitive offending behaviour combined with parental unwillingness or inability to provide an appropriate response." Theoretically, an 11-year-old who commits a serious assault would simply be placed in the custody of his or her parents.

Usually, however, children who kill or seriously injure someone or who commit more than one serious assault or act of property damage can be subjected to greater intervention. This is also the case where the child's parents either have clearly not provided adequate supervision or have actually encouraged the behaviour [*CFSA* 37(2) esp. (j-l)]. Under these circumstances, the police or a child welfare officer can ask the court to find the child to be "in need of protection."

What's Wrong with the *Child and Family Services Act*?

As indicated previously, the primary complaint directed toward the *CFSA* (from the perspective of criminal issues) is the difficulty of handling serious offenders who are under 12 years of age. Many commentators, including Bala and Mahoney (1995), have put forward good arguments to reconsider the minimum age of criminal responsibility. While few have argued for a return to the age of seven years, many suggest that 10 years of age might be reasonable. In 1992, the Centre for Justice Statistics issued the *Report on the Involvement of Children Under 12 in Criminal Behaviour*. While young people, under 12 years of age, are not a major problem, they suggested that 10 and 11-year-old children (primarily males) participated in many of the incidents of arson committed by persons under 18 years of age. A 1994 study, reported by Bala and Mahoney (1995), suggested that children under 12 years of age participated in about 10 percent of the sex offences committed by youths under 18 years of age.

Exercise 2

MULTIPLE CHOICE

1. Children under the age of 12 years who commit serious misbehaviour are dealt with under the

   a) *Criminal Code of Canada*
   b) *Youth Criminal Justice Act*
   c) *Child and Family Services Act*
   d) *Teenagers Reform Act*

2. Children under the age of 12 years

   a) almost never commit sex offences
   b) commit 75 percent of the sex offences committed by youths who are under 18 years of age
   c) commit 50 percent of the sex offences committed by youths who are under 18 years of age
   d) commit same-sex offences
   e) are involved in about 10 percent of these sex offences committed by young people under the age of 18 years

SHORT ESSAYS

1. What is the responsibility of a police officer who apprehends a 10-year old who has committed a serious violation?

   _____

   _____

   _____

   _____

   _____

   _____

   _____

   _____

_____

_____

_____

_____

_____

_____

_____

_____

2. Identify two advantages of lowering the minimum age of criminal responsibility to age 10 years.

1) _____

_____

2) _____

_____

3. Identify two disadvantages of lowering the minimum age of criminal responsibility to age 10 years.

1) _____

_____

2) _____

_____

THE YOUTH CRIMINAL JUSTICE ACT

The *Youth Criminal Justice Act* became law on February 2, 2002, replacing the *Young Offenders Act*. It came into force in Ontario on April 1, 2003.

Principles

The principles on which *YCJA* is based echo many of the principles of the *YOA*, for example, protection of society and protection of the rights of young people. However, it goes beyond the *YOA* with an emphasis on prevention and rehabilitation and on sensitivity to the needs of victims. Accordingly, the declaration of principles (s. 3) reads, in part, as follows:

> The Youth Criminal Justice System is intended to promote protection of the public by preventing crime by addressing the circumstances underlying the behaviour; rehabilitating and reintegrating young persons into society; and providing meaningful consequences for the offence to promote protection of the society.

The criminal justice system for young persons must be separate from that of adults and emphasize the following:

- Rehabilitation and re-integration
- Fair and proportionate accountability
- Timely intervention that reinforces the link between the offending behaviour and its consequences
- Promptness of enforcement

The measures taken against young people who commit offences should have the following features:

- Reinforce respect for societal values
- Encourage the repair of harm done to victims and the community
- Be meaningful to the young persons, given their needs and level of development, and, where appropriate, involve parents, extended family, the community and social or other agencies in the young person's rehabilitation and re-integration.

Special considerations that should apply to proceedings against young persons are the following:

- Protection of the rights and freedoms of young persons
- Courteous, compassionate, and respectful treatment of victims
- Victims should be provided with information about the proceedings and given the opportunity to participate
- Parents should be informed of measures and proceedings involving their children and encouraged to support them

Parliament meant the *YCJA* to protect society from youthful criminals through several measures. First of all, the justice system is expected to divert as many young offenders as possible from the formal process. The assumptions here are twofold. First, the writers of the *Act* expected more, and more varied, programs to be introduced than existed under the former system. This gives the police, crown prosecutors, and the courts more options for intervention and, hopefully, those options would be more effective than what had been previously available. By providing flexibility in the legislation, the courts can encourage more use of community service orders and victim compensation. The belief is that offenders who are kept closer to the community will become more aware of the social harm they cause and be more quickly re-integrated. Second, the *YCJA* reserves the formal process for the most serious offenders. It does this in three major ways. First, there is an emphasis on diverting many offenders out of the formal system through the use of extrajudicial measures that include warnings, cautions, and referral to programs, as well as Crown cautions. Second, for many types of offences and for many offenders, there is a presumption against the use of custody as an intervention. Third, serious offences by young persons who are at least 14 years of age can result in adult sentences, and in some cases, there is even the presumption that they will be handled in this manner. Each of these is discussed in more detail later in this book.

The *YCJA* recognizes that young people are different from adults. While the prevailing philosophy of the *YCJA* is to enhance accountability, it recognizes that young people (even offenders) need special protections. This belief goes beyond the traditional notion that young persons lacked the social and psychological maturity of adults. Provision of the *YCJA* prohibits the publication of the young offenders' identities, restricts access to their records, and limits the length of sentences. There is respect for the young person's fundamental legal rights, for example, the right to legal representation. The police are expected to inform young suspects of their legal rights. Furthermore, police officers cannot take confessions without a written waiver or the presence of the young person's lawyer or guardian. Due process, procedural fairness, and an emphasis on explaining the rights to young persons characterize the *YCJA*.

Key Provisions of the *Youth Criminal Justice Act*

The *YCJA* is a lengthy document that all police officers need to study. The next chapter addresses some specific details of the *YCJA* and its accompanying legislation as they relate to police work. For now, however, providing a broad overview of some key elements of the *Act* is sufficient.

A serious attempt is made to faithfully represent the elements of the legislation under discussion. Any variation that may exist between this rendition and the *Act* must be resolved in favour of the *Act*. The key *Act* in this case is the *YCJA*, and for that reason, a copy of it is provided along with this text. For most purposes, however, it will not be necessary for students to refer to the *Act*, but it is instructive to check sections of it if questions of interpretation do arise. In addition, it is useful to examine it in order to appreciate how legislation is structured and to be able to follow its requirements.

Young Persons

The *YCJA* defines "young persons" as individuals between the ages of 12 and 17 years, inclusive. Under 12 years of age, a person is considered a child and must be dealt with under provincial child welfare statutes. When people reach their 18th birthday, they are considered adults. It is important to note, however, that it is the age of the person *when the offence is committed* that is important—not the person's age at the time of arrest and charge. Thus, someone who commits a sexual assault when 17 years old but is not caught until age 19 years is still considered a young person and falls under the direction of the *YCJA*.

Crimes

The *YCJA* does not describe what makes up a criminal act. The *Criminal Code of Canada* defines what a criminal act is. Basically, the law holds young persons accountable for the same behaviours considered criminal if committed by an adult. Furthermore, the same rules of procedure and evidence outlined in the *CCC* and the *Canada Evidence Act* generally apply to young people as they apply to adults. Police officers must, therefore, be familiar with both documents.

Extrajudicial Measures

Immediately after the declaration of principles, the *YCJA* outlines a set of extrajudicial measures. **Extrajudicial measures** are ways of dealing with young persons who are in conflict with the law, in a manner that reduces continued formal processing in the criminal justice system. These measures can be initiated by the police, by the Crown prosecutor, or by a judge before or after a finding of guilt. Extrajudicial measures may be used to deal with a young person alleged to have committed relatively minor offences (such as petty theft or minor acts of vandalism) under certain conditions, typically, but not necessarily, when they are first offences. These measures range from no further action to referrals by the court. The primary function of nonjudicial measures is to divert young offenders from the formal court system through the use of less formal interventions that may be applied in a timely fashion to the ends of prevention, rehabilitation, and re-integration. The secondary function is to reserve courts and other more formal aspects of the justice system for severe offenders and those who cannot benefit from extrajudicial measures.

Youth Justice Courts

Under *YCJA*, any court that deals with a young person is a **youth justice court**. Youth justice courts are means of keeping young offenders separate from adults. In practice, while the courts hear cases involving young persons at different times from those of adult cases, youth justice court judges are Ontario Court (Provincial Division) judges. Thus, the same judges, court clerks, and Crown attorneys who handle adult cases often handle cases of young persons in the same courtrooms. Young persons are also to be kept in separate holding and detention facilities, although young persons and adults are sometimes kept in adjacent cells.

Notice to Parents

If the police arrest and detain a young person, the officer in charge has the responsibility to notify the young person's parents or relatives of the arrest as soon as possible. Parents are also to be notified of any summons or appearance notice that requires the young person to appear in court. In practice, courts often postpone proceedings until a responsible adult relative can be identified and notified.

Rights

Young persons have the same rights as adults as outlined in the *Canadian Charter of Rights and Freedoms*. Thus, arresting officers have an obligation to notify young offenders of their rights. Young offenders also have the right to legal counsel, the right to confer with their parents, and the right to due care while in detention. The handling of young peoples' confessions is much more restricted under the *YCJA* than it is for adults.

Procedures

Young persons who are detained have the same right to a bail hearing as adults. Unlike adults, however, young people are not released on their own recognizance. Once a young offender is found guilty, the court may ask for a pre-sentence report. This report generally contains more detailed information on the young person's character and life circumstances that the judge can use when detemining an appropriate sentence. When sentencing a young offender, we expect judges to fit the penalty to the crime. They are to do this while considering mitigating circumstances, the needs of the young person, and the protection of the community.

Sentences

The *YCJA* contains several sections that relate to the sentencing of young offenders. (The *YOA* referred to "dispositions.") Many sentences are similar to those available in adult court. For example, the *YCJA* allows for both absolute and conditional discharges, fines, compensation or restitution orders, community service orders, and prohibition orders. There are also provisions for "supervision orders," which are similar to parole for adults, but not the same. Youth justice court judges may also sentence young offenders to open or secure custody. **Open custody** consists of removing the young persons from their homes and placing them in a group home for a fixed length of time. **Secure custody** generally implies that a sentenced young person is placed in a more restrictive, jail-type facility with bars and electronic surveillance.

Privacy

We extend young offenders greater rights to privacy than in the case of adults. For example, the police, the press, and the courts are all forbidden to publicize a young offender's identity. Depending upon the sentence imposed, young offenders' records are sealed (but not necessarily destroyed) within one to five years after the young person reaches the age of 18 years. Once they become adults, the young offenders' fingerprints are transferred to a special repository and then destroyed after five years. The *YCJA* is more specific than was the *YOA* about the categories of persons with whom information about young persons in conflict with the law can be shared. It also makes provisions that allow the identification of young offenders to victims (on request, as well as in cases of investigation when the protection of the public is an issue.)

Exercise 3

DEFINITION

Please define the following terms:

1. Extrajudicial measures:

   _____

   _____

   _____

   _____

   _____

   _____

   _____

   _____

2. Youth justice court:

   _____

   _____

   _____

3. Open custody:

4. Secure custody:

_____

_____

_____

_____

TRUE OR FALSE

1. T   F   The *Youth Criminal Justice Act* has been around for so long that it is now almost 100 years old.

2. T   F   The *Youth Criminal Justice Act* is designed to keep young persons inside the criminal justice system for as long as possible.

3. T   F   The *Youth Criminal Justice Act* generally prohibits the publication of the identity of young persons.

4. T   F   Crimes are defined by the *Youth Criminal Justice Act*.

5. T   F   The *Youth Criminal Justice Act* is difficult to understand because it contains no statement of principles that would assist interpretation and application.

MULTIPLE CHOICE

1. Which of the following is not an objective of the *Youth Criminal Justice Act*?

   a) hold young people accountable for their behaviour
   b) protection of society
   c) reward the good and punish the wicked
   d) protect the legal rights of young persons

2. Parents of young persons have

   a) a right to be notified if a young person is arrested or detained
   b) no rights
   c) the same rights as the parents of adult criminals and no more
   d) to hire a lawyer before they can speak to the young person

3. The rights of young persons under the *Canadian Charter of Rights and Freedoms*

   a) are fewer than for adults
   b) are fewer than those of the police
   c) are the same as everyone else
   d) mostly disappear if they are suspected of having committed a crime

SHORT ESSAYS

1. A young person commits a serious crime three weeks before his 18th birthday. He is arrested nine months later and brought to court after his 19th birthday. Does the *Youth Criminal Justice Act* apply? If yes, why, and how? If no, why not?

_____

_____

_____

_____

_____

_____

_____

_____

_____

_____

_____

_____

_____

_____

_____

_____

_____

2. What three conditions must apply before a police officer can accept a confession from a young person:

1) _____

_____

2) _____

_____

3) _____

_____

3. Adults can be released "on their own recognizance." Why do you suppose that this does not apply to young persons?

_____

_____

_____

_____

_____

_____

_____

_____

_____

4. Distinguish between "open custody" and "secure custody."

_____

_____

_____

_____

_____

_____

_____

_____

_____

5. What do you suppose would make the difference as to whether a young person would get a particular sentence rather than another?

_____

_____

_____

_____

_____

_____

_____

_____

_____

ENDNOTES

1. Prior to the patriation of the Canadian Constitution by the Trudeau government, the *Constitution Act, 1867,* was known as the *BNA* or *British North America Act.*

CHAPTER 5

Arresting and Questioning Young Persons

Learning Outcomes

Students who have mastered this chapter will have the ability to do the following:

- Explain *what is meant by a "young person" under the* Youth Criminal Justice Act.
- Identify *the rights of the accused under the* Canadian Charter of Rights and Freedoms.
- Distinguish *between "indictable offences" and "summary offences."*
- Distinguish *between an "appearance notice" and a "summons."*
- Explain *the rules for taking statements from young persons.*
- Explain *the techniques that can be used to determine whether young persons understand the rights that have been stated to them.*
- Understand *the reasons why there are special protections for young persons.*
- Describe *the circumstances under which parents need to be notified.*
- Explain *the procedure to be used with persons under 12 years of age.*
- Explain *the responsibilities of a police officer who apprehends a person under 12 years of age.*

ARRESTING YOUNG PERSONS

The basic rules that govern the arrest and questioning of adults also apply to young offenders. Thus, for example, it remains good practice to touch the person you are arresting in order to indicate that you are "holding" them under arrest. The *Youth Criminal Justice Act* (*YCJA*) places additional requirements on the police to make sure that they protect the rights of the young person. Those requirements extend to include the admissibility of statements made by young offenders if they decide to enter a "not guilty" plea in court.

The relevant law that guides arrest and questioning is found in the *Criminal Code of Canada*, the *Canadian Charter of Rights and Freedoms,* and the *YCJA*. In many ways, the *YCJA* gives the police much more flexibility with respect to arrest than they have when dealing with adults. Both the statement of principles and many sections within the *YCJA* encourage the use of informal and extrajudicial measures. The *YCJA* requires police officers to consider *not* laying charges for the less serious cases, where a first-time offender is involved. In these instances, the law is satisfied if less formal measures are adequate. The *YCJA* recognizes that for many young people, simply being spoken to by the police may be a deterrent. This is particularly the case when the young person's parents are willing to take an active role in dealing with the young person's misbehaviour.

The latter part of this chapter will deal with some aspects of the province's *Child and Family Services Act (CFSA)*. Strictly speaking, children who are under 12 years of age cannot be *arrested*. They can, however, be *apprehended*. We will examine some sections of the *CFSA* since arrest and apprehension both result in the young person being placed in police custody, even if for only a short period.

Who Is a "Young Person"?

The *YCJA* defines a **young person** as someone "who is or, in the absence of evidence to the contrary, appears to be 12 years of age or more, but under 18 years of age" [*YCJA* 2 (1)]. The jurisdiction of the youth justice court extends to persons who are more than 18 years of age but who were under 18 years of age when they committed the offence.

Where there is some question about the offender's age, a parent's word is normally accepted. The *YCJA* also allows proof by standard documentary procedures, such as the submission of a birth certificate. Occasionally, young offenders lie about their age. Typically, this might be an attempt by someone over 17 years of age to avoid adult court. In these instances, the police must start treating the offender as a young person and not an adult. Practically, this involves segregating the young offender from other adults in custody and extending the rights provisions under the *YCJA*, including notifying the young person's parents. The opposite also occurs when some young offenders claim to be older than they are to avoid having the police notify their parents.

Because substantial differences exist in how we handle the cases of adult and young persons, the *YCJA* has provisions that avoid the loss of testimonial evidence when mistakes are made about the person's age. Under subsection 146(8), the youth justice court may accept statements or waivers given by young persons when it is believed that they are 18 years or older. The courts have also decided that when the police apprehend or charge adults for offences they committed as young persons, the police are not bound by all the restrictions imposed by the *YCJA*. Typically, this means that all the protections surrounding the questioning of young persons need not apply.

Basic Rights of the Accused

The sections on Legal Rights (sections 7 through 14) of the *Canadian Charter of Rights and Freedoms* outlines the general guidelines within which justice must be carried out.

The basic principle is outlined in section 7, which states that we should not deprive anyone of their life, liberty, and security, "except in accordance with the principles of fundamental justice." Among those principles of fundamental justice are the following rights:

- To be "secure against unreasonable search or seizure" [*CCRF* 8]
- To be "informed promptly" why they are being arrested or detained [*CCRF* 10(a)]
- To have access to legal counsel without delay [*CCRF* 10(b)]
- To be informed that they have the right to legal counsel, [*CCRF* 10(b)] to *habeas corpus*—the right to be brought before a justice within a reasonable time
- To determine whether their detention is lawful or necessary [*CCRF* 10(c)]
- To be informed of the specific charges against them [*CCRF* 11(a)]
- To be tried within a reasonable time [*CCRF* 11(b)]
- Not to be denied reasonable bail without just cause [*CCRF* 11(e)]
- Not to be subjected to any "cruel and unusual treatment or punishment" [*CCRF* 12]

These rights apply equally to young persons and adults.

Arrest

Sections 494 to 502 of the *Criminal Code of Canada* (*CCC*) outline the law that allows police officers to make arrests for criminal offences. The *CCC* distinguishes among three types of offences: (1) indictable offences, (2) summary offences, and (3) dual or "hybrid" offences. Indictable offences are usually the most serious offences. Specifically, **indictable offences** are those for which the potential penalty is either greater than six months in jail or a fine of more than $2,000. More often, indictable offences carry sentences of two or more years imprisonment (including life). Occasionally, the *CCC* does not indicate a maximum sentence for an indictable offence. For such offences, the maximum sentence is set at five years under section 730 of the *CCC*.

Summary offences are those for which the potential penalty is "to a fine of not more than two thousand dollars or to imprisonment for six months or to both" [*CCC* 787(1)]. **Hybrid offences**, such as some types of assault, can be treated as either summary or indictable offences. The distinguishing feature is usually how much harm or damage has been done. It is up to the Crown prosecutor to decide how to handle these cases.

From the law's point of view, "arrest" is a means of compelling a person to appear before a justice of the law. The law does not consider arresting an adult a form of punishment, although it may occasionally serve that function socially. The *YCJA*, however, recognizes that being arrested may have a significant impact upon many young persons. Consequently, the *YCJA* allows police officers the option of not compelling young persons to appear before the youth justice courts when they believe it is in the best interests of the young person and the community. These situations occur mostly when the young person has committed a minor offence and has little history of offending and appears to be genuinely sorry about the deed.

There are times, however, when compelling a young person to appear in court is the appropriate course of action. Arresting a young person is based on the rules for arresting an adult. Because different individuals and different circumstances require different levels of "compulsion," the law provides for different procedures for compelling an appearance. According to the *CCC*, a person may be compelled to appear before a justice by

- issuing an appearance notice [CCC 496],
- issuing a summons [CCC 509],
- arresting a person without a warrant [CCC 494(1) and 495(1)], or
- arresting a person with a warrant [CCC 513].

A police officer may issue an appearance notice to a person for an offence listed under section 553 of the *CCC*, for a hybrid offence, or for a summary conviction offence. In fact, subsection 495(2) of the *CCC* lists situations where officers are *not* to arrest a person who has committed one of those types of offences without a warrant. Officers should not make an arrest when no need exists to do any of the following: establish the identity of the person; secure or preserve evidence; prevent the continuation of or prevent an offence; or to make sure a person does not "fail to attend in court." Essentially, appearance notices are "issued by a police officer to a person not yet charged with an offence." Section 501 of the *CCC* indicates what should be included in the appearance notice. Form 9, which appears at the back of the *CCC*, provides a sample of what an appearance notice should contain.

Section 509 of the *CCC* sets out the requirements for summonses. Summonses are used for summary and hybrid offences. They cannot be used when an indictable offence has taken place. Unlike an appearance notice, a summons shows that the police have charged a person with committing an offence. Form 6, at the back of the *CCC*, provides an outline of a typical summons.

Sections 494 and 495 of the *CCC* present the conditions for arresting someone without a warrant. A police officer may arrest a person without a warrant if the person is found committing an indictable offence. Police officers may also arrest without a warrant when, on "reasonable grounds," they believe a person "has committed or is about to commit and indictable offence." Furthermore, an officer may arrest a person without a warrant if the officer believes a warrant of arrest or committal is outstanding for that person.

Arrest with a warrant is justified under section 513 of the *CCC*. Section 511 shows what needs to be included in the warrant. Form 7 of the *CCC* presents both the structure of a warrant and a listing of the reasons for which the court issues a warrant. Primarily, warrants are issued when a person fails to appear in court when asked to do so, when a person tries to avoid the serving of a summons, or when a person escapes or attempts to evade custody.

For adults, officers normally only execute warrants in the territorial jurisdiction of the court or justice that issues them. The primary exception is when they are involved in a fresh pursuit. Section 145 of the *YCJA*, however, allows youth court warrants to be executed anywhere in Canada.

Exercise 1

DEFINITIONS

Please define each of the following terms:

1. Young person:

    _____

    _____

    _____

    _____

    _____

    _____

_____

_____

_____

_____

_____

2. Indictable offence:

_____

_____

_____

_____

_____

_____

_____

_____

_____

3. Summary offence:

_____

_____

_____

_____

_____

_____

_____

_____

_____

_____

4. Hybrid offence:

_____

_____

_____

_____

_____

_____

_____

_____

_____

TRUE OR FALSE

1. T F All of the laws that are relevant to the questioning of young persons are found in the *Youth Criminal Justice Act*.

2. T F An 11-year-old person cannot be arrested.

3. T F Youth justice court warrants may be executed anywhere in Canada.

Indicate whether it is true or false that the items below are rights under the *Canadian Charter of Rights and Freedoms*.

4. T F to be secure against unreasonable search or seizure

5. T F to be informed of the right to marry

MULTIPLE CHOICE

1. Laws that guide arrest and questioning of young persons are found in

   a) the *Criminal Code of Canada*
   b) the *Youth Criminal Justice Act*
   c) the *Canadian Charter of Rights and Freedoms*
   d) all of the above

2. Which of the following should police officers consider when deciding to lay a charge?

   a) the gender of the young person
   b) the age of the young person
   c) the seriousness of the offence
   d) all of the above

3. When there is uncertainty about a person's age, it is best to

   a) treat the person as an adult
   b) afford the protections that would apply under the *Youth Criminal Justice Act*
   c) incarcerate the person until the matter of age is cleared up
   d) send the person to a mental hospital

4. Indictable offences carry potential sentences of

   a) two or more years imprisonment
   b) fines only
   c) no more than six months of imprisonment
   d) no more than six months of imprisonment and a $2,000 fine

5. Which of the following, according to the *Criminal Code of Canada*, is *not* a way to compel a person to appear before a justice?

   a) issuing a charge for a crime
   b) issuing a summons
   c) arresting a person without a warrant
   d) arresting a person with a warrant

SHORT ESSAYS

1. Under what circumstances, when a crime has been committed, should the police *not* make an arrest?

   _____

   _____

   _____

   _____

   _____

   _____

   _____

   _____

   _____

   _____

_____

_____

_____

_____

_____

_____

_____

_____

2. Under what conditions may a police officer arrest someone without a warrant?

1) _____

_____

_____

2) _____

_____

_____

3) _____

_____

_____

3. For what reasons are warrants issued?

1) _____

_____

_____

_____

2) _____

_____

_____

_____

3) _____

_____

_____

_____

QUESTIONING THE YOUNG PERSON

Asking questions is one of the primary investigative tools available to a police officer. Officers ask questions for many purposes, but ultimately, most officers question an accused in order to obtain a confession. For an adult suspect, a signed confession is one of the most helpful things an officer can provide to the Crown for its presentation of a case. When dealing with young offenders, however, statements tend not to be very useful in supporting the case. While this is a practical reality in many situations, it does not mean that one should not proceed to take statements when one can. While few statements might be used as evidence in the youth court, a statement might give the officer more insight into the incident—even to the point of deciding that the young person's involvement was not what it first seemed. Providing a statement might also be the first step in a process that allows young persons to come to grips with their culpability.

Since questions and confessions play such an important role in the criminal justice process, there are strict rules surrounding both. Questions, particularly those directed at young people, can only provide useful information if asked in the right manner, at the right time, and under the right circumstances. Similarly, confessions must be given "freely and voluntarily" in order to be acceptable as evidence. This is not a course dealing with either investigation or interrogation techniques. Consequently, we will not pursue the details of those issues. What we need to do, however, is to examine how those normal techniques of police procedure need to be modified to deal with young people.

One of the main differences between Anglo-American law, which forms the basis of Canada's legal system, and other legal systems is the right of the accused to remain silent. Traditional common law has long acknowledged that accused persons cannot be forced to testify in court and that both accused persons and witnesses cannot be forced to give self-incriminating evidence. So important is that concept to our view of justice that we have incorporated it into our *Charter of Rights and Freedoms* [sections 11(c) and 13].

The broader concept of the right of the accused to remain silent under other circumstances was recognized in the *Herbert* case, which was heard in the Supreme Court in 1990.[1] In that case, Madame Justice McLaughlin placed the right to silence within the context of one of the fundamental rights outlined in section 7 of the *Charter of Rights and Freedoms*. Essentially, the Supreme Court's stance is that accused persons should have the freedom to choose whether or not they wish to speak to the authorities or to refuse to make a statement.

The right of the accused not to make a statement does not prohibit the police from speaking to the accused. The police can encourage the accused to make a statement, particularly in light of available physical evidence. The key feature, however, is that the statement must be an informed one that is given freely and voluntarily. Statements taken under a threat (even an implied one) or statements made under a promise or inducement from the police or other officers of the court will likely not be admissible in court. And it must be remembered that the onus is not on the accused to prove that the statement was given voluntarily. If asked, the onus is on the Crown to show how the statement was given freely.

What constitutes a threat, inducement, or coercion (particularly an implied one) differs from one situation to another. Salhany (1997:197), however, provides some examples of statements that have been judged by the courts on various occasions to constitute a threat. These, for example, include the following statements:

- "It would be better for you if you told us what happened."
- "You will be arrested if you do not tell us where the stolen goods are."
- "You had better tell the truth."
- "It is necessary to give an explanation."

However, phrases such as the following have been seen as acceptable (Salhany, 1997:198):

- "Be sure to tell the truth."
- "Be a good girl/boy and tell the truth."

Salhany (1997:199–200) also indicates that it is easy for officers to unintentionally make promises or inducements that can invalidate the acceptance of a confession. Offering to speak to the judge about a lighter sentence if the accused person confesses or offering to arrange for therapy if a confession is forthcoming have been seen as inducements. This is even the case if the officer is making the offer in good faith and in what might be seen as in the best interests of the accused.

While police officers must exercise procedural care when questioning adults and taking their confessions, they must exercise extra care when dealing with young persons. The basic procedures in these areas apply to both adults and young people. The *YCJA* and the courts have imposed further rules on interactions between the police and young persons.

Although interpersonal dealings with young offenders may sometimes be more difficult than dealing with adult offenders, most young offender cases are easier to dispose of. Young persons have less experience and less well developed judgment than adults. Because of this, it is very important that police officers take young persons' statements correctly. Inadequate attention to the details of taking statements can easily result in a straightforward case becoming a series of problems.

The same basic rules that apply to adults for collecting evidence apply to young offenders. There are, however, two subsections of the *YCJA*—146(2) and 146(4)—that impose additional considerations on the taking of statements.

The rules for taking the statements of young persons apply to both peace officers and what the law defines as another "person in authority." Generally, a **person in authority** is someone who is considered to have a "direct role in the administration of justice or prosecution of offences" (Bala, 1997:123). This would normally include probation officers and anyone who is a peace officer. So far, the courts have not regarded parents, teachers, school principals, physicians, or psychiatrists as persons in authority (Bala, 1997:119–123). This distinction is important because the specific rules of caution outlined under subsection 146(2) of the *YCJA* apply only to police officers and persons in authority.

Statements made to other persons are subject to the normal rules of evidence. The court will usually accept them even if those "other persons" do not provide the normal cautions beforehand.

Subsection 146(2) of the *YCJA* states that no written or oral statement given by a young person to either a peace officer or a person in authority is admissible against the young person unless certain conditions apply. Specifically, those conditions are the following:

- The statement is voluntary.

- The young person is told before giving a statement, in language appropriate to the young person's age and understanding, that

  - the young person is under no obligation to give a statement,
  - any statement given may be used as evidence in court,
  - the young person has the right to consult legal counsel,
  - the young person has the right to consult a parent, relative, or another adult who might provide assistance, and
  - any statement they make must be made in front of their legal counsel or another appropriate adult, unless they desire otherwise.

- Before giving the statement, the young person must be given a reasonable *opportunity* to

  - consult with legal counsel,
  - consult with a parent, adult relative, or another appropriate adult chosen by the young person, and
  - make the statement in the presence of that parent, adult relative, or another adult.

Some police services give police officers a card outlining the main points that the officer needs to tell the young person. This is generally a good procedure. There are, however, some limitations to that approach. The main problem is that a standard explanation is not appropriate for all young persons. The *Act* requires the police to explain the young person's rights to them in a language that is appropriate to their age and ability to understand. Some police services use a detailed form to track the explanations provided to young persons as well as their responses. This is an important issue that we will cover in more detail in the next section.

It is good practice to advise the young person of their rights at several points in the arrest process. For example, the arresting officer should inform the young person of the charge and of his basic rights. The arresting officer should provide the same information again when turning the young person over to the officer in charge and, if the young person is temporarily detained, when he is released.

There are two exceptions to the need for an officer to give young persons a formal explanation of their rights. The first involves spontaneous oral statements made by the young person [*YCJA* 146(3)]. If the young person "blurts out" a confession or details of the case before the officer has a reasonable opportunity to comply with the subsection 146(2) requirements, that statement may still be admissible. In those circumstances, however, the officer must inform the young person of his rights as soon as is practical. Failure to do so will likely invalidate any further statements. The courts have often interpreted this section narrowly, usually favouring the young person. At the very least, the circumstances under which the statement was made must be consistent with being voluntary and spontaneous. Any element of duress will generally invalidate the statement (Bala, 1997:124–25).

Generally accepted examples would include situations where the officer is unaware that the young person was involved in an offence, but the young person makes an impulsive confession. Another example might be a candid admission when an officer first encounters the young person. An officer might ask the question, "What are you people doing here?" and the answer to it might be an admission of guilt.

The second exception occurs when the young persons *choose* to waive their rights. In such instances, the police have informed the young person of their rights, but they decide that they do not want to consult with counsel or parents before giving a statement. In this situation, subsection 146(4) requires that the waiver to be either videotaped or presented by the young person in writing. If they write down the waiver, the young persons must say that the police have informed them of their rights, and they must sign the document.

The special requirements outlined by subsection 146(2) of the *YCJA* only apply to young persons. Consequently, if the offender is over 18 year of age when a statement is made, the provisions of subsection 146(2) do not apply, even if the offender was under 18 years of age when the offence took place.

Explanations Appropriate to the Young Person's Age and Understanding

Social scientists have made us aware that while many young people may be aware of certain social ideas and terms, such as justice, rights, fairness, and responsibility, their *understanding* of those terms evolves only as they become older.

Abramovitch and associates (1993; 1995) conducted research into how well young offenders understand their right to legal counsel when the police advise them about it. Their conclusions are that most young persons claim to understand the advice given to them concerning their rights to silence and legal counsel, but the reality is that they have far less appreciation of the meaning attached to those warnings than do adults. Overall, young people have less understanding of the meanings of legal notions than do adults. They are also less likely to appreciate the consequences of giving up or waiving their rights.

Social scientists have also studied factors that go beyond the more limited ability of young people to understand legal concepts than in the case of adults. Disproportionately, being in conflict with the law is related to poor school performance and lower intelligence quotient (IQ) scores. There is still debate in the criminological literature over whether lower IQ or poor school performance *causes* delinquency; however, few dispute the fact that there is a relationship between these factors. Thus, despite the apparent worldliness, brashness, and knowledge of legal jargon exhibited by many young offenders, often they have little real appreciation of what is actually happening to them.

It is easy for police officers, regularly exposed to legal jargon, to assume that everyone else has the same level of understanding of those ideas as they have. This is particularly the case when confronted with a "smart Alec" young person who is spouting knowledge about his or her rights. The fact is that we have chosen to create a society based on law. Legal experts have created and defined many of the concepts included in our laws. Unfortunately, the emphasis is on precision, rather than on whether the language is understandable to the average adult citizen, let alone to immature young people.

Subsection 146(2)(b) of the *YCJA* is designed to address this problem of differing levels of understanding among young persons. It is also one area where the courts have paid a great deal of attention. The key phrase in that subsection is that the young person's rights must be "clearly explained...in a language appropriate to his age and understanding."

The courts have made it clear that police officers are to comply fully with the spirit of this section. Consequently, "rattling off" a statement of the young person's rights to silence and to counsel from a preprinted card is generally considered unacceptable. Young persons who seem particularly immature or who appear to have mental disabilities require special attention. While the judgment of what language is appropriate is obviously subjective, the courts are demanding increasingly that officers provide objective evidence that they have made the attempt. The statement outlined on the next page might be used as a good starting point. It covers the main points that we need to include in a caution. As indicated in the previous section, it is a good practice to restate the caution several times.

There are several ways in which the police officer can show that the explanation was at the appropriate level. For example, the officer might ask the young person a series of questions to "test" the young person's grasp of the explanation. We list a series of such questions below. The restatement of the young person's rights in different words is also helpful. Nicholas Bala (1997:115) suggests that an officer might ask the young person to state in their own words their rights as they understand them. A further suggestion is to ask the young person to write out the cautions in their own words. Some police services provide facilities for audio- and videotaping the cautioning segments of interviews with young persons.

The following are two examples of cautions that might be given to young offenders that outline their legal rights. The first version includes some wording used in the *YCJA*. According to the Flesch-Kincaid grade level index, it is written at a grade 10 level of understanding. We have rewritten the second version to simplify the vocabulary and the syntax. The rewritten version conforms to a grade 8 level of understanding as measured by the index.

Informing Young Offenders of their Right to Counsel

(Grade 10 Version)

It is my duty to tell you that you have the right to talk to a lawyer and to your parents or another adult relative. If they are not available, you may speak with some other adult you feel can assist you. If you speak to any of these people before giving a statement, they must be present while the statement is being taken, unless you do not want them to be present. You have the right to telephone any lawyer you wish. You also have the right to free advice from a Legal Aid lawyer. If you are charged with an offence, you may apply to the Ontario Legal Aid Plan for assistance. 1-800-265-0451 is a toll-free number that will put you in touch with a Legal Aid lawyer for free legal advice right now.

Informing Young Offenders of their Right to Counsel

(Grade 8 Version)

It is my duty to tell you that you have the right to talk to a lawyer. You can also talk to your parents or to another adult relative. If they are not available, you may speak with another adult you feel can help you. If you speak to any of these people before giving a statement, they must be with us when we are taking the statement. However, they do not need to be present if you do not want them to be here. You have the right to telephone any lawyer you wish. You also have the right to free advice from a Legal Aid lawyer. If we charge you with an offence, you may apply to the Ontario Legal Aid Plan for help. The toll-free number for a Legal Aid lawyer is 1-800-265-0451. That number will put you in touch with a Legal Aid lawyer for free legal advice right now.

Do you understand what I have just said? _____

Do you want to call a lawyer now? _____

Do you want to have a lawyer here with you? _____

Do you want to speak with one or both of your parents? _____

Do you want to have one or both of your parents here with you? _____

If a parent is not available, do you want to speak to an adult relative? _____

Do you want to have an adult relative here with you? _____

If an adult relative is not available, do you want to speak to another adult? _____

Do you want to have an adult here with you? _____

Exercise 2

DEFINITIONS

Please define each of the following terms:

1. Person in authority:

_____

_____

_____

_____

_____

_____

_____

_____

2. Age-appropriate explanation:

_____

_____

_____

_____

_____

_____

_____

_____

_____

_____

TRUE OR FALSE

Before giving a statement, a young person must be told that

1. T   F   there is no obligation to give a statement

2. T   F   the statement may be used in court

3. T   F   the young person has the right to legal counsel

4. T   F   the statement can be withdrawn after it is signed

5. T   F   the young person has the right to consult with other young persons who may have been accused of the same crime

MULTIPLE CHOICE

1. Which of the following is a "person in authority"?

    a) police officer
    b) school principal
    c) physician
    d) all of the above

2. Statements should be taken from young persons

    a) as quickly as possible
    b) before they speak to their parents
    c) only when certain conditions are met
    d) in private and without the distraction of other adults present

3. Young persons must have their rights explained to them in language that is

    a) French in Quebec and English in the rest of Canada
    b) the same as that used for adults
    c) appropriate to their age and ability to understand
    d) the same for every young person

4. In a situation where a young person waives rights to consult with counsel, a parent or another adult, what must the police do?

    a) videotape the waiver or have the young person present it in writing
    b) wait 12 hours

c) wait 24 hours

d) get a second police officer to be in the room

SHORT ESSAYS

1. A police officer approaches a young person who makes an immediate statement of admission to a crime. What is the next thing that the police officer should do? Explain why.

_____

_____

_____

_____

_____

_____

_____

_____

_____

_____

_____

_____

_____

_____

_____

_____

2. Why is there a concern that young people must have their rights explained to them clearly?

_____

_____

_____

_____

_____

_____

_____

_____

_____

_____

_____

_____

_____

_____

_____

3. Discuss the following statement: "If we make people aware of their rights, they will never tell us anything important."

_____

_____

_____

_____

_____

_____

_____

_____

_____

_____

_____

_____

_____

_____

_____

_____

_____

4. What kinds of things can a police officer do to ensure that young persons understand the rights that have been explained to them?

_____

_____

_____

_____

_____

_____

_____

_____

_____

_____

_____

_____

_____

_____

_____

_____

_____

_____

_____

_____

NOTIFICATION TO PARENTS

When a police officer arrests and keeps a young person in custody, section 26 of the *YCJA* obliges the officer to provide a **notification to the parent** of the young person as soon as possible. The parent must be contacted and told, either orally or in writing, where the young person is detained and the reason for the arrest. If the parents cannot be contacted, the officer in charge at the time of the detention should try to contact another adult relative who knows the young person and is likely to help him or her. If no other relative can be contacted, notice of the arrest may be given to another adult who knows the young person and is likely to assist him or her. Examples of other adults in this case include members of the clergy, scoutmasters, and big brothers or big sisters.

It is also necessary to notify a parent of the young person if an appearance notice or a summons is issued. Notice must also be given when the young person makes a promise to appear or enters into a recognizance. That notice must include the young person's name, the charge, the time and location of the appearance, and the fact that the young person has the right to be represented by counsel. It is the responsibility of the officer in charge to send that notice, in writing, as soon as possible. Again, when a parent cannot be located, the notice may be sent to another adult relative or to another adult who knows the young person and is likely to help him or her.

There will be situations where confusion exists as to whom a notice should be given. In these cases, subsection 26(5) allows a youth justice court judge (or a justice of the peace when a youth justice court judge is not available) to decide who the appropriate recipient of the notice is.

The failure to send proper notice under subsection 26(2) *may* invalidate any further proceedings against the young person. The *YCJA*, however, provides youth justice court judges a great deal of latitude in this matter. Several options available to youth justice court judges are outlined under subsection 26(11).

Under section 27 of the *YCJA*, judges can compel a young person's parents to appear at the hearing. Parents who fail to appear may be sanctioned.

PERSONS UNDER 12 YEARS OF AGE

In Ontario, young persons who are under 12 years of age are dealt with under the *Child and Family Services Act*. As we pointed out in the previous chapter, the *CFSA* is child protection legislation and not criminal legislation. The *CFSA* is used by the province to deal with some of the articles not included in the *YOA* when it replaced the *Juvenile Delinquents Act* in 1984. From a policing point of view, the key element of the *CFSA* is that it covers children who are under 12 years of age.

The duties of police officers are outlined in some detail under the *CFSA*. Most importantly, police officers must recognize the fact that no matter what a young person under 12 years may have done, *they are not offenders.* From the law's perspective, they are not, and must not be treated as, young criminals.

Perhaps the most important section of the *CFSA* for policing is section 42. Under subsection 42(1), the police may apprehend young people under the age of 12 years without a warrant if they "could be found guilty of an offence." Clearly, this section gives police officers a considerable amount of discretion. When discretion is allowed, there will be occasions when decisions that are not agreeable to everyone are made. In these cases, police officers are protected from personal liability under subsection 44(7) of the *CFSA* "for any act done in good faith in the execution or intended execution" of their duty.

Officers who apprehend a child must return the child to a parent or guardian as soon as it is practical. Where the child cannot be returned in a reasonable amount of time, a police officer may detain the child in a "place of safety" until returning the child becomes possible. Subsection 42(2) makes it clear that the parents must be notified as soon as possible whenever a child is in police custody.

There are other circumstances where the *CFSA* allows police officers to take the initiative when dealing with children. Police officers may apprehend young people they think have left or escaped the "lawful care and custody" of the Children's Aid Society. There are also times when it will become obvious that a child is being abused, neglected, or otherwise mistreated. These situations are most likely to arise when the police are called to investigate a domestic dispute. In these circumstances, police officers may apply to the courts under subsection 40(4) of the *CFSA* for a hearing to decide if the child is "in need of protection."

Other situations arise where police officers are asked to assist child protection workers. For example, the police may be called to help a child protection worker when a warrant authorizes the apprehension of a child. Police officers may also be called upon to execute warrants to "bring a child to a place of safety."

Exercise 3

DEFINITIONS

Please define the following term:

Notification:

_____

_____

_____

_____

_____

_____

_____

_____

_____

TRUE OR FALSE

1. T F Youth justice court judges can compel a young person's parents to appear at a hearing.

2. T F Legally, persons under the age of 12 years are never offenders.

MULTIPLE CHOICE

1. A police officer who keeps a young person in custody must contact the parents of the young person

   a) within 12 hours
   b) within 24 hours
   c) as soon as possible
   d) by registered mail

2. When a parent is given notification that a young person is being kept in custody, which of the following is information to which parents have a right?

   a) the reason for the arrest
   b) the names of the other young persons also under arrest

    c) the location where the young person is detained

    d) two of the above

3. If an appearance notice or summons is issued, the police officer in charge must notify the parents of the young person of

    a) the charges

    b) time and location of the appearance

    c) the right of the young person to be represented by counsel

    d) all of the above

4. If there is confusion over who is to receive notice, who is charged with deciding?

    a) a youth justice court judge

    b) the staff sergeant

    c) the Crown prosecutor

    d) all of the above

5. The *Children and Family Services Act*

    a) defines no role for the police with respect to children under 12 years

    b) allows the police to arrest some children under the age of 12 years if they escape from the Children's Aid Society

    c) allows the police to apprehend children under age 12 years in certain circumstances

    d) forbids the police executing warrants in cases of children under age 12 years

CHAPTER 6

Extrajudicial Measures

Learning Outcomes

Students who have mastered this chapter will have the ability to do the following:

- Distinguish *between judicial and extrajudicial measures.*
- Identify *the extrajudicial measures that the police must consider.*
- Explain *the conditions under which extrajudicial measures are presumed to be adequate.*
- Explain *the meaning of extrajudicial sanctions.*
- Identify *the conditions under which extrajudicial sanctions may be used.*

EXTRAJUDICIAL MEASURES

The cornerstone of the *Youth Criminal Justice Act* (*YCJA*) is its emphasis on extrajudicial measures. Many such measures were allowed under the *Young Offenders Act* (*YOA*), in the sense that it was silent about them, and the *YOA* provided for what it called "alternative measures." The *YCJA*, in contrast, requires that the use of **extrajudicial** (or noncourt) **measures** be considered in some circumstances and that nonjudicial measures be ruled out as inappropriate before judicial measures are used.

It is the clear intention in the *YCJA* that less formal means are to be preferred over more formal ones and that the burden falls to the police, the Crown, and the judges to determine why the nonjudicial measures are inappropriate in the given instance. There are two broad types of extrajudicial measures: (1) those that are used prior to a charge being laid, which are applied by the police; and (2) those that are post-charge, called Crown warnings and extrajudicial *sanctions*, which are applied by the Crown prosecutors and youth justice courts, respectively.[1]

In the sections that follow, we examine the requirements of the *YCJA* with respect to extrajudicial measures and their impact on the behaviour of the police, Crown prosecutors, and the Court.

POLICE

The police have always had the discretion to deal with those who come into conflict with the law in ways that stop short of laying a charge. The most obvious cases involve relatively minor incidents where the offender has not previously been in trouble. The police may take no further action, give the offender a warning that further infractions will lead to a charge, or take a young person home and speak to the parents about what happened in this instance and the implications for the future.

Generally speaking, the more serious the offence, the less police discretion is exercised. Similarly, the more prior involvements with the law and the more serious the offences, the less likely it is that a simple warning will be used.

The *YCJA*, in keeping with its general approach of first trying the least intrusive measures, makes specific provisions for warnings, cautions, and referrals to programs or agencies.

Warnings and cautions are not specifically defined in the *YCJA*, but their meaning can be inferred as follows. **Warnings** are informal notices (admonitions) issued to a young person by a police officer. They may be made at the point of contact, or they might take place as part of a discussion with the parents of the young person. Warnings are, therefore, a more serious intervention than "doing nothing further," but a less serious intervention than issuing a caution.

Cautions, as in the case of warnings, stop short of laying a charge, which could lead to judicial proceedings. **Cautions** are notices to young persons and his/her parents about the offence that has been alleged. The *YCJA* makes provisions that each province may establish a "program" to "administer cautions." Even without such a program, the police are still required, under the *YCJA*, to consider whether a caution would be an appropriate way of dealing with a given instance. Presumably, a program to administer cautions would require formal "paperwork," perhaps including a letter to the parents as well as a mechanism for tracking persons who have received a caution. Ideally, the information would not be restricted to a single police service but be available across jurisdictions.

It remains to be seen whether Ontario will establish such a "program" and the form that it will take. Some police services have sophisticated information management systems that could easily accommodate almost any program, while other police services would struggle to tie their local information management systems to a larger network.

The third option that a police officer must consider when a young person is alleged to have committed an offence is referral. **Referral to a program** or agency means referral to a service in the community that may help the young person to avoid committing offences. Such referrals are considered to be a more serious intervention than a caution, but still stop short of starting judicial proceedings. Referrals may only take place with the consent of the young person.

When no offence is alleged to have occurred, the police may decide to do nothing further. There are circumstances when an offence is alleged to have occurred, but in the judgement of the police, doing nothing further is the best way to deal with the situation. The *YCJA* requires that the police officer at least consider the appropriateness of doing nothing further. When an offence is alleged to have been committed by a young person, the *YCJA* requires that warnings, cautions, and referrals be considered as sufficient prior to starting judicial proceedings.

The *YCJA* provides that a police officer shall consider the use of such measures as warning, caution, and referral to a program before proceedings with a charge. The *YCJA*, however, provides no consequences for failure to consider these things. That is, failure to consider does not interfere with proceeding with a charge.

It does not end there, however, for the police officer. If called to testify, a police officer who did not consider extrajudicial measures can expect to face stiff cross-examination by defence lawyers. Failure to consider, when addressed on the witness stand, does have consequences, which may include embarrassment as well as a weakening of the Crown's case. It is important, therefore, that such alternatives be considered, even in situations where they may be quickly discarded as inappropriate.

Appropriateness of Extrajudicial Measures

The *YCJA* leaves it to the police to decide whether the use of an extrajudicial measure is appropriate, but the appropriateness must be determined in the context of the principles of section 4 of the *YCJA*, which were presented in Chapter 4. In this context, the police must recognize that the *YCJA* has a bias in favour of extrajudicial measures for a broad range of offences. The emphasis is on holding young persons accountable for their behaviour and not on punishing them. Further, there is a clear preference for interventions that are timely. A discussion with the young person's parents today is preferable to having it dealt with by the court in a month's time. Again, the police must consider the responses that they will have to produce under cross-examination by defence counsel if they consider the "timely" response to not be adequate and go ahead and charge the young person.

The *YCJA* is specific that extrajudicial measures are not to be restricted to first-time offenders. Young persons who previously received an extrajudicial measure must be considered for further ones. Even a previous finding of guilt does not preclude the use of extrajudicial measures.

The *YCJA* identifies circumstances where extrajudicial measures are "presumed to be adequate to hold a young person accountable for...offending behaviour." Extrajudicial measures are required if the offence is nonviolent *and* the young person has not been previously found guilty of an offence.

The use of police discretion is limited by the *YCJA*; it is not eliminated. The limits favour the use of noncourt measures and open the police to serious cross-examination on the reasons for not using an extrajudicial measure.

Warnings, cautions, and referrals issued by the police *require* that a young person is alleged to have committed an offence, but they *do not require* that the young person admit that the allegation is true. Referral to a program or agency requires the consent of the young person but does not require an admission of guilt.

Evidence about warnings, cautions, referrals or that the police took no further action in respect of an offence is not admissible for the purpose of proving prior offending behaviour.

Exercise 1

DEFINITIONS

Please define the following terms:

1. Extrajudicial measure:

_____

_____

_____

_____

_____

_____

_____

2. Warning:

_____

_____

_____

_____

_____

_____

_____

3. Caution:

_____

_____

_____

_____

_____

_____

_____

_____

_____

_____

4. Referral to a program:

_____

_____

_____

_____

_____

_____

_____

_____

_____

TRUE OR FALSE

1. T F Extrajudicial measures are penalties imposed by persons who are not judges.

2. T F The more serious the offence, the less discretion police have in dealing with it.

3. T F Warnings are to be used for situations where the young person is not alleged to have committed an offence, but where there is concern about what may happen in the future.

4. T F It makes little difference to Crown prosecutors or defence counsel whether the police have considered extrajudicial measures.

5. T F Referral to a program by the police requires that the young person admit responsibility for the alleged offence.

MULTIPLE CHOICE

1. Which of the following is not an extrajudicial measure under the YCJA?

    a) police warning
    b) Crown warning
    c) police referral to a program
    d) extrajudicial sanction

2. Warnings and cautions can only be used by the police if the young person

    a) admits to having been involved in an offence
    b) is alleged to have committed an offence
    c) is represented by counsel, a parent, or a responsible person
    d) all of the above

3. The YCJA provides that provinces may establish programs

    a) that would allow the police to use cautions
    b) to administer cautions
    c) that would eliminate warnings in favour of more formal cautions
    d) all of the above

4. Referral to a program or agency is for the purpose of

    a) a mild, rather than a severe, punishment
    b) assisting the young person to avoid committing offences
    c) easing the burden on parents
    d) all of the above

5. Under the YCJA, which of the following is a police officer NOT required to do when a young person is alleged to have committed an offence?

    a) consider using a caution
    b) lay a charge
    c) consider referral to a program
    d) consider taking no further action

CROWN PROSECUTORS

Crown prosecutors exercise discretion with respect to the cases that they prosecute. In the exercise of such discretion, a variety of factors are taken into consideration, such as the quality of the evidence, the availability of witnesses, the likelihood of a successful prosecution, and whether the goals of the criminal justice system are being served. None of this depends on the YCJA. The YCJA does provide new means for Crown prosecutors to deal with young persons in conflict with the law: Crown warnings and extrajudicial sanctions.

Crown Warnings

The YCJA makes provision for provinces to establish a program that authorizes prosecutors to administer cautions to young persons, rather than starting or continuing judicial proceedings. The YCJA does not explicitly give a name to such cautions, but it is implicit that they are **Crown prosecutor cautions.**[2]

Extrajudicial Sanctions

The *YCJA* provides that provinces may choose to implement a set of extrajudicial measures that take the form of a program of extrajudicial sanctions. **Extrajudicial sanctions** are formal interventions administered to a young person who has been accused of an offence but where the process is a noncourt (extrajudicial) one.

Several conditions must be met before extrajudicial sanctions may be used (s. 10):

1. The young person must be alleged to have committed an offence.
2. The young person cannot satisfactorily be dealt with by warning, caution, or referral because of the seriousness of the offence, the nature and number of previous offences, or any other aggravating circumstances.
3. The sanction must be part of a "program of sanctions" authorized by the province.
4. The person who is considering whether to use the sanction is satisfied that it would be appropriate, having regards for the needs of the young person and the interest of society.
5. The young person accepts responsibility for the alleged offence (this is not the same as pleading guilty).
6. The young person fully and freely consents to the sanction.
7. The young person has been advised of the right to be represented by counsel and given reasonable opportunity to consult counsel.
8. There is sufficient evidence, in the view of the Crown, to proceed with prosecution.
9. Prosecution is not barred by law.
10. The young person does not deny participation or involvement in the commission of the offence.
11. The young person does not express the wish to have the charge dealt with by a youth justice court.
12. The parents of the young person receiving the sanction shall be informed of the sanction.

Admissions as Evidence

Admissions, confessions, or statements accepting responsibility for acts or omissions that are made by young persons as a condition of being dealt with by extrajudicial measures are not admissible in evidence against any young person in civil or criminal proceedings [ss. 10(4)].

Right of Victim to Be Informed

When a young person receives an extrajudicial sanction, the victim has a right to request and to be provided with information as to the identity of the young person and how the offence was dealt with [ss. 10(4)]. This section does not provide a right for the victim to be consulted before the sanction is determined. The province will need to decide who the appropriate authority will be to provide the information; it could be the police.

It should be noted that while the *YCJA* allows victims to be informed of the identity of the young person when an extrajudicial sanction is used, there is no such provision when other extrajudicial measures, such as warnings, cautions, or referrals, are used.

COURT

A judge of the youth justice court can decide that a young person is best dealt with through extrajudicial measures and may order this be done. All the conditions for the use of extrajudicial sanctions must still be met if such sanctions are to be used.

Exercise 2

DEFINITIONS

Please define the following terms:

1. Crown caution:

_____

_____

_____

_____

_____

_____

_____

_____

_____

2. Extrajudicial measures:

_____

_____

_____

_____

_____

_____

_____

_____

_____

TRUE OR FALSE

1. T   F   Extrajudicial sanctions are applied in situations where the young person
             has been extra bad and failed at previous programs.

For each of the following indicate whether it is true or false that this is a condition that must be met before an extrajudicial sanction may be used:

2. T   F   The young person must have a previous finding of guilt.

3. T   F   Warning, caution, and referral were not considered by the police.

4. T   F   The young person pleads guilty to the offence.

5. T   F   Admissions of responsibility that are made by young persons as conditions of being dealt with by extrajudicial measures are admissible in criminal proceedings.

MULTIPLE CHOICE

1. Crown cautions, if they are to be used,

   a) must be part of a program established by the province
   b) require that the young person denies involvement with the alleged offence
   c) requires that the young person has already received two or more police warnings or police cautions
   d) all of the above

2. Extrajudicial sanctions are

   a) informal interventions
   b) to be considered when prosecution is otherwise impossible
   c) only used if the young person denies involvement in the alleged offence
   d) none of the above

3. Which of the following is NOT a condition for the use of an extrajudicial sanction?

   a) that the needs of the young person are addressed
   b) that the interests of society are addressed
   c) that the needs of the victim are addressed
   d) that the sanction is appropriate

4. In order for an extrajudicial sanction to be used, which of the following is true about the involvement of legal counsel?

   The young person

   a) must be advised of the right to be represented by counsel
   b) must consult with counsel
   c) must have counsel that is independent of the counsel of parents
   d) all of the above

5. When a young person receives an extrajudicial sanction, which of the following does the victim have a right to request?

   a) the address of the young offender
   b) to be consulted about the type of sanction to be used
   c) information on how the offence was dealt with
   d) all of the above

SHORT ESSAYS

1. Identify five conditions that must be met before an extrajudicial sanction may be used.

1) _____

_____

_____

2) _____

_____

_____

3) _____

_____

_____

4) _____

_____

_____

5) _____

_____

_____

2. Why do you suppose admissions or confessions that are made by a young person as a condition of receiving an extrajudicial measure are not admissible against the young person in civil or criminal proceedings?

_____

_____

_____

_____

_____

_____

_____

_____

_____

_____

_____

3. What rights does a victim have when a young person is dealt with by way of an extrajudicial sanction?

_____

_____

_____

_____

_____

_____

_____

_____

_____

_____

ENDNOTES

1. It is up to each province to decide whether and how programs of extrajudicial sanctions will be established. The *YCJA* does not exclude that such sanctions may be initiated at the level of the police, but it appears more likely that it would occur at the level of the Crown prosecutor mainly and at youth justice court.

2. Whether a program of Crown cautions is established in Ontario is to be decided by April 1, 2003. See www.youthinconflict2e.nelson.com.

Detaining and Processing Young Persons

Learning Outcomes

Students who have mastered this chapter will have the ability to do the following:

- Explain *the underlying philosophy of the* Criminal Code of Canada *with respect to the speed with which a detained person needs to be brought before a justice.*
- Explain *the presumption with respect to the detention of young persons.*
- Identify *the reasons for which a young person can continue to be detained.*
- Describe *what is involved in a Promise to Appear.*
- Explain *the requirement for release to a responsible person and the responsibilities of that person.*
- Explain *the circumstances under which young persons may be detained with adults.*
- Identify *the purpose of bail hearings.*
- Explain *the conditions under which it is permissible to fingerprint and photograph young persons.*
- Describe *who is covered by the ban on publication.*
- Identify *the time limits within which records of young persons must be destroyed.*
- Explain *the accessibility of records of young persons.*
- Explain *the appropriateness of conditions of release.*
- Describe *"reverse onus."*

Arrest and Detention

The *Criminal Code of Canada (CCC)* and the *Youth Criminal Justice Act (YCJA)* outline the basic rules of procedure for arresting and detaining a young person. The specifics of how those rules are implemented will vary from one location to another and, of course, will change over time. Nationally, some provisions of the *YCJA* differ from province to province. For example, Ontario and Nova Scotia have a two-tier system, where they handle young persons under 16 years of age in courts and detention facilities different from those for 16 years of age and older. Differences will occur from province to province in terms of programs that may be established for cautions, conferences, and precharge screening.

New police officers need to find out from their supervisors how local conditions have been adapted to meet the requirements of the *YCJA*. Some of those conditions will involve the physical layout of buildings; other conditions will relate to the availability of support personnel and the practices of local Crown prosecutors and judges. In some municipalities, for example, uniformed officers do not fill out much paperwork beyond a summons. Officers in an adjoining jurisdiction, however, may be responsible for filling out most of the necessary forms. Even experienced officers who transfer from one jurisdiction to another will take some time to get "the lay of the land."

When it comes to detention, the *YCJA* introduces specific considerations, different from those that apply to adults, which need to be taken into account. The general rules for arrest and detention are presented in sections 494 to 503 of the *CCC*.

The underlying philosophy of the *CCC* is that we should not detain an accused person any longer than necessary after their being arrested. This is consistent with the long history of *Writs of Habeas Corpus* that have been an integral part of English common law for several centuries. *Writs of Habeas Corpus* are used to ensure that an accused person is brought before the courts within a reasonable amount of time to examine the legality of the detention. Section 503 of the *CCC* requires that an arrested person be brought before a justice "without unreasonable delay." Where a justice is readily available, this means within 24 hours at most. Where a justice is not available, the person is to be brought before a justice "as soon as possible."

> Subsection 503 (4) also states that
>
> a peace officer or officer in charge having the custody of a person who has been arrested without warrant as a person about to commit an indictable offence shall release that person unconditionally as soon as practicable after he is satisfied that the continued detention of that person in custody is no longer necessary in order to prevent the commission by him of an indictable offence.

Sections 497 and 498 of the *CCC* detail the circumstances surrounding temporary detention. Section 497 deals with situations where a peace officer arrests a person without a warrant for an indictable offence, a hybrid offence, or for one punishable on summary conviction. This section makes it clear that normally and as soon as is practical, the officer shall "release the person from custody with the intention of compelling his appearance by way of summons" or by issuing an appearance notice. Section 498 outlines the situation for persons arrested and taken into custody without a warrant. Again, for offences that may be handled by summary conviction and for hybrid offences and less serious indictable offences, the officer in charge must normally release the accused. The accused person's appearance in court is assured through the issuance of a summons, a promise to appear, or by posting **surety** (that is, money or other action or promises to the court), depending upon the individual circumstances of the offence and the accused.

Exceptions to release provisions exist and they are specified in sections 497 and 498 of the *CCC*. These exceptions occur when it is necessary to establish the person's identity, preserve evidence, or prevent the continuation or repetition of this or another offence.

One of the objectives of the *YCJA* is to reduce the amount of time that young persons are incarcerated during the pretrial stage. As with the *CCC*, the *YCJA* provisions are based on the presumption that the young person will be released. Arrest and detention are measures to deal with exceptional circumstances.

Three principles are at the heart of this approach. First, it is the least restrictive means that should be used to ensure that the young person will appear in court. Second, the young person is presumed to be innocent until there is a finding of guilt. Third, the *YCJA* clearly specifies—what courts have previously decided—that pretrial detention is not to be used as a form of punishment.

To decide which procedure is most appropriate for releasing the accused, the officer needs to assess several factors. Clearly, the severity and circumstances surrounding the immediate offence need to be considered. It would be unwise, for example, to release a young man into his parent's custody if he was just charged with assaulting his mother or sister. There may, however, be another responsible person into whose custody the young person might be released without posing a threat to either the mother or the sister. The police are required to consider whether such options exist. On the other hand, releasing the same individual to a parent after his having committed a minor assault against an acquaintance or a stranger, might pose little danger to the victim or others. In order for a young person to be placed in the care of a "responsible person," two conditions must be met:

1. The "responsible person" agrees in writing to care for and be responsible for the attendance of the young person in court, as well as comply with any other conditions that the judge may specify.
2. The young person agrees, in writing, to comply with the arrangement as well as any other conditions that might be specified.

Another significant factor to consider is the young person's record. To assess the record, the officer should check with the Canadian Police Information Centre (CPIC) and with the local database for prior police contacts and convictions. An officer who is undecided about whether to release a young person may find the decision less difficult if the young person has a history of not appearing in court.

Except for the most serious crimes, the police officer must remember that the presumption is that release will take place, unless the police officer has reasonable grounds to believe that detention is in the public interest. The public interest has regard to all the circumstances of the situation, including the need to accomplish the following:

1. Establish the identity of the young person
2. Secure evidence about the offence
3. Prevent the commission of an offence
4. Ensure the safety of a victim or witness
5. Have reasonable grounds to believe that the young person will attend court

In addition to its emphasis on the use of the use of a "responsible person" as an alternative to pretrial detention and the presumption of release, the *YCJA* includes two other considerations:

1. It prohibits the use of detention as a substitute for mental health, child welfare, child protection or other social measures.
2. It has a presumption against detention, if the young person could not be sentenced to custody when found guilty of an offence.

Exercise 1

DEFINITION

Please define the following term:

Surety:

_____

_____

_____

_____

_____

_____

_____

_____

_____

_____

TRUE OR FALSE

1. T   F   In order to follow the *Criminal Code of Canada,* it is important to detain adults as long as possible.

2. T   F   The *Youth Criminal Justice Act* requires that young persons be detained for a lesser period of time than adults.

3. T   F   Accused persons are to be brought before a justice any time it is convenient for the police.

4. T   F   A young person's record can be consulted when making the decision of whether or not to release the young person.

5. T   F   Under the *YCJA*, arrest and detention are among the usual ways that a young person involved in an offence is dealt with.

MULTIPLE CHOICE

1. Accused persons are to be brought before a justice

a) before the end of the shift of the arresting officer

b) within three hours of arrest
c) without unreasonable delay
d) as soon as notification of arrest and detention is provided to parents

2. Which of the following is not a sufficient reason to not release a young person?

a) to establish the person's identity
b) to get him to give up the name of the other persons involved in the crime
c) to preserve evidence
d) to prevent the repetition of this offence

3. When deciding to release a young person, which of the following should the police officer be satisfied with?

a) that the accused will probably appear in court
b) that the accused is of no danger to a victim
c) that the accused is of no danger to others
d) all of the above

4. Which of the following must occur before a young person is released in the care of a "responsible person"?

a) The police officer must issue a warning to the young person.
b) The Crown prosecutor must give consent.
c) The "responsible person" must agree in writing to care for and be responsible.
d) The parents of the young person must consent.

5. Which of the following does not constitute grounds for the detention of a young person?

a) need to establish the identity of the young person
b) need to secure evidence about the offence
c) the parents of the young person are divorced
d) the safety of a witness is an issue

SHORT ESSAYS

1. Identify three pieces of information that should be found on a *Promise to Appear* form.

1) _____

_____

_____

2) _____

_____

_____

3) _____

_____

_____

APPEARANCE BEFORE A JUDGE

If a young person continues to be detained by the police in spite of the various provisions that require or allow release, the young person must be brought before a youth justice court judge or justice of the peace without unreasonable delay and within 24 hours of arrest. Here, too, there is the presumption that the young person brought before a judge should be released and that the release should be without conditions. It is the burden of the Crown to show cause why detention is justified.

If detention is not justified, the judge must release the young person *without conditions,* unless the Crown can show cause as to why conditions are justified.

Under the *YCJA,* the judge is required to presume that detention is not necessary for the protection of the public if the young person could not, on being found guilty, be sentenced to custody. The three criteria for the use of custody as a sentence require that the young person has done one or more of the following:

1. Committed a violent offence
2. Failed to comply with two or more custodial sentences
3. Committed an indictable offence for which an adult would be liable to imprisonment of more than two years and has a history that indicates a pattern of findings of guilt.

The *YCJA* requires that the judge inquire about the possible availability of a "responsible person" as an alternative to detention.

The release of the young person may be subject to the following:

1. An undertaking with conditions
2. A **recognizance**, which is a promise to do something, typically appear in court, that may be with or without sureties
3. A recognizance without sureties and with conditions

Conditions of Release

Conditions of release fall into three categories: those that shall not be used, those that should not be used, and those that are allowable.

Shall not. Conditions of release are not to be selected on the basis of their being punitive or therapeutic.

Should not. Conditions of release should not be vague, for example, "obey house rules," or so broad as to make successful compliance unlikely.

Allowable. Allowable conditions of release are specified in the *CCC,* subsection 515(4) and include the following:

1. Report at specified times to, for example, the police
2. Remain within a specified jurisdiction
3. Not communicate with persons or go to places specified in the order
4. Comply with "other reasonable conditions" specified in the order

With respect to "conditions," the *YCJA* is concerned that the nature of the conditions does not unnecessarily place the young person in the situation of "reverse onus." **Reverse onus** refers to the onus or burden shifting to the young person to show cause why release is justified. Reverse onus is created when there is a failure to meet a condition or recognizance. Conditions that are unnecessary or vague may elevate the risk of the young person becoming in a reverse onus situation. This is inconsistent with the *YCJA* where the dominant presumption is in favour of release.

As in many other areas, the *YCJA* augments the basic procedures that apply to adults. Those additional elements in the *YCJA* highlight the special status of young persons. The temporary detention of young persons is one area where adult and youth practices differ substantially, and it is to that issue that we turn next.

Exercise 2

DEFINITION

Please define the following terms:

1. Recognizance:

_____

_____

_____

_____

_____

_____

_____

_____

_____

_____

2. Reverse onus:

_____

_____

_____

_____

_____

_____

_____

_____

_____

_____

_____

TRUE OR FALSE

1. T   F   If a young person is detained by the police, the young person must be brought before a youth justice court judge or justice of the peace within six hours.

2. T   F   The judge must presume that detention is not necessary for the protection of the public if the young person could not, on being found guilty, be sentenced to custody.

3. T   F   Custody may be considered a sentence if the young person failed to comply with a noncustodial sentence.

4. T   F   Custody may be used as a sentence if the young person committed an indictable offence and would be liable to imprisonment of more than two years and has a history of findings of guilt.

5. T   F   Conditions for release should not be punitive.

MULTIPLE CHOICE

1. A young person who continues to be detained by the police must be brought before a youth justice court judge or justice of the peace

   a) without unreasonable delay
   b) within 24 hours
   c) both of the above
   d) none of the above

2. Which of the following apply when a young person is brought before a youth justice court judge or justice of the peace?

   a) the presumption that the young person will be released
   b) if released, the release should be without conditions
   c) the burden is on the Crown to show why detention is justified
   d) all of the above

3. A youth justice court judge is required to presume that detention is not necessary for the protection of the public, unless the young person

   a) has already received a police caution
   b) is assumed of having committed a theft under $1,000
   c) is accused of having committed a violent offence
   d) is accused of having committed a theft over $1,000

4. Which of the following is an appropriate condition of release under the *YCJA*?

   a) requirement to attend a treatment program
   b) requirement to obey the rules of the house of the responsible person
   c) regular attendance at church
   d) report at specific times to the police

5. Reverse onus, when it comes to young persons,

   a) should be encouraged
   b) should be avoided
   c) is highly desirable
   d) can only occur if the young person was previously referred to a program

TEMPORARY RESTRAINT, TEMPORARY DETENTION, SECONDARY CAUTIONS, AND BAIL

Temporary Restraint

The issue of detaining young offenders comes up both before and after their appearance in youth justice court. The *YCJA* has two major emphases on detention. The first is that there is a broad presumption against detention (covered in the previous section); the second is that if there is to be detention, young persons are to be kept separate from adults. The *YCJA* is clear that we are *not* to house young offenders with adults, whenever possible. Of course, circumstances do arise where complying with this restriction is impossible. Typically, one such set of circumstances arises when the young person is in temporary restraint. **Temporary restraint** is when the young person is in the custody of a police officer before a youth court justice can remand the young person to a regional detention centre [*YCJA* 30(1)(2)].

What are the issues surrounding the temporary restraint of young persons before their appearance in youth justice court? The *YCJA* outlines the basic rules underlying the detention of young persons. Young persons who are detained must be held in specially designated youth facilities, separate from adult offenders.

There are, however, some exceptions to this rule. Young persons may be held under the supervision and control of a peace officer while they are being transferred from one location to another. Normally, that transfer would be from a designated youth detention area to youth justice court. A youth justice court judge may also waive the location requirements if "the young person cannot, having regard to his own safety or the safety of others, be detained in a place of detention for young persons." Another exception occurs when "no place of detention for young persons is available within a reasonable distance" [*YCJA* 30(3)].

The general provision that young people must be held in special areas separate from adults does not apply at the point of arrest. Specifically, section 30(7) states that these provisions

> do not apply in respect of any temporary restraint of a young person under the supervision and control of a peace officer after arrest, but a young person who is so restrained shall be transferred to a place of temporary detention...as soon as is reasonably practicable, and in no case later than the first reasonable opportunity after the appearance of the young person before a youth justice court judge or a justice.

The need for the exemption from keeping young persons separate from adults becomes obvious when we examine the practicalities of policing. For example, if a police officer arrests a young person for committing an offence with an adult accomplice, it is often difficult for the arresting officer to arrange to have the two accused transported in separate cruisers. Consequently, if a 16-year-old and a 19-year-old are arrested for having just committed a break-and-enter, it is permissible for the arresting officer to place both persons in the back seat of the cruiser to transport them to the police station.

In summary, then, situations where the young person is considered in temporary restraint include the following:

1. Transportation to the police station after being arrested
2. Being held in the police station while waiting to be interviewed
3. Being in lockup while waiting to be released
4. Waiting to be taken before a youth court justice
5. All situations where the young person is transferred between the regional detention centre and the court

Of course, it is good practice to keep young offenders separate from adults, whenever possible. Some police services in larger centres, for example, have clearly separated areas for interviewing and holding young persons. Unfortunately, this degree of physical separation is not always possible in smaller centres or in situations where many young persons are arrested in a short period.

Temporary Detention

Temporary detention, on the other hand, normally refers to the period when the young person is in a detention centre before sentencing. Typically, this would occur if the young person has committed a very serious offence or has a history of nonappearance and was denied bail as a consequence. Temporary detention includes the periods the young persons spend waiting to be tried and any time they are detained while being tried. Two key provisions relate to temporary detention: first, the young persons *must* be kept separate and apart from adults. This provision includes separate washroom facilities. Second, the young persons must have, at least, all the benefits and privileges extended to adult offenders.

The only exception to the rule about separation from adults is when a youth justice court judge or a justice decides that the young person may pose a risk to his own or another person's safety, or a suitable place for detaining young people is not available within a reasonable distance.

Young persons who are detained must have their persons and clothing searched before they can be left alone. This includes temporarily locking a young person in an interview room. Young females must only be searched by a female officer.

While not strictly an issue of detention, it should be remembered that suspects and their counsels have the right to conduct their conversations in private. Normally, the officer in charge will provide an interview room for this purpose. Such facilities need not be extended to parents or other persons who may wish to converse with the suspect. The decision to extend such privileges is at the discretion of the officer in charge.

Secondary Caution to Charged Person

As we pointed out in the previous chapter, getting a young person's statement admitted as evidence during the trial is very difficult. Nevertheless, officers should attempt to obtain a statement, even if they expect that it will do little to convict the offender in court. Some statements do make it into the court record, and sometimes, the process of making a statement helps "convince" the young persons that accepting some sanction is the wisest solution. Statements also give the officer an opportunity to assess the offender's immediate physical and emotional conditions. The officer might also gain some insight into the young person's domestic situation. This is useful information when considering whether and under what terms to release the young person.

Interviews with the accused are occasionally useful in re-directing the investigation toward another perpetrator or an accomplice. At the very least, going through the process hones the officer's interview and questioning skills. Most formal statements are taken in rooms that are specially set aside for that purpose, and they are often equipped with a video recording device.

When the interview takes place, the officer should again advise the young person of his or her legal rights. At this point, it is also essential to give the young person what is known as a "secondary caution." This **secondary caution** is to help ensure that the young person has not been pressured or coerced into giving a statement. That is, the young person is giving the statement freely and voluntarily. Typically, a secondary caution would be worded in the following way:

> If you have spoken to any police officer or to anyone with authority or if any
> such person has spoken to you in connection with this case, I want it clearly
> understood that I do not want it to influence you in making a statement.

> Do you understand what I have just said?

As with the primary caution, the wording needs to be adjusted to fit the young person's ability to understand the points being made. Consequently, it is necessary to ask the question in different ways and to ask the suspect to explain what he or she thinks the caution means. The exact wording of the officer's caution and the young person's response should be copied into the officer's notes.

If a statement is given, the video tape of the statement will undoubtedly be played in court. Defence counsel will scrutinize the tape to ensure that there were no real or apparent inducements offered and that the young person was not being coerced. This scrutiny generally goes far beyond that for adult cases, and the interviewing officers' words, demeanour, and body language will all be called into question.

Bail

Young persons who commit particularly serious crimes, who are charged with multiple offences, or who have a history of nonappearance are generally detained by the police. Young persons are also not released where the *CCC* forbids the release of adults (e.g., charges of murder). In these instances, the decision of whether to release the young person or not is made at a bail hearing.

A **bail hearing** is a judicial process where it is decided whether and under what circumstances a person charged with an offence will be released. **Bail** refers to the financial conditions on which a person will be released with a promise to appear in court. Bail money may be forfeited if the defendant fails to appear.

Either a justice of the peace or a youth justice court judge may preside over a bail hearing. Justices of the peace, however, cannot preside when young persons are charged with offences under section 469 of the *CCC*: murder, conspiracy to commit murder, or being an accessory after the fact to murder.

Where a justice of the peace cannot preside, a youth justice court judge holds the hearing. A youth justice court judge can also review the order of a justice of the peace upon the request of the young person, the young person's counsel, or the Crown. Notice must be given two days ahead of time, and the hearing is made *de novo*. In other words, the second hearing is not an appeal of the decision made by the justice of peace; it is treated as a totally new or original application for bail.

Ontario has a two-tier system for dealing with young persons. Those who are 12 to 15 years of age generally have their bail hearing heard before the Provincial Court, Family Division, while those who are 16 and 17 years of age have their hearing in the Provincial Court, Criminal Division. The reason for this distinction is that different government ministries are responsible for the young person, depending upon the young person's age. With those different ministries come different facilities and programs.

Under the *YCJA*, if the matter involves an accused who is a young person, each court is a youth justice court, and each judge is a youth justice court judge.

The standard provisions outlined in section 515 of the *CCC* relating to surety apply to young persons as well as to adults. There is, however, one significant option of interest to police officers that is open to the youth justice court that does not apply to adults. A youth justice court judge or a justice may decide to place the young person in the care of a **responsible person** as outlined in section 31 of the *YCJA*. This provision is only used when other forms of release (such as a notice to appear) are not applicable and the young person would otherwise be kept in detention.

The section 31 provision is used when the responsible adult "is willing and able to take care of and exercise control over the young person, and…the young person is willing to be placed in the care of that person." The responsible person must indicate in writing that he or she will supervise the young person and assume the responsibility for making sure the accused appears in court. That person must also agree to whatever other conditions the judge may impose. If the young person breaks any of those provisions, or the responsible person can no longer supervise the young person, the supervising adult must notify the police of the situation.

If no responsible adult comes forward, the young person will be remanded in detention until the scheduled court appearance or until another bail hearing is requested.

The court can remove a young person from the care of the responsible person if that person becomes unwilling or unable to exercise care and control over the young person. The supervising adult, the young person, or "any other person" may apply to the youth court to have the responsible person relieved of their responsibility. In this instance, an arrest warrant is issued for the young person, who is then compelled to appear in court.

Exercise 3

DEFINITIONS

Please define the following terms:

1. Temporary restraint:

_____

_____

_____

_____

_____

_____

_____

_____

2. Temporary detention:

_____

_____

_____

_____

_____

_____

_____

_____

_____

3. Secondary caution:

_____

_____

_____

_____

_____

_____

_____

_____

_____

_____

4. Bail hearing:

_____

_____

_____

_____

_____

_____

_____

_____

_____

5. Responsible person:

_____

_____

_____

_____

_____

_____

_____

_____

TRUE OR FALSE

1. T   F   It is when the secondary caution is being given that it is acceptable for a police officer to offer to "go easy" on the young person in exchange for cooperation.

2. T   F   Bail hearings are only about money.

3. T   F   If a responsible person cannot be found, it may be necessary to keep a young person accused of a crime in detention.

MULTIPLE CHOICE

1. The police may house young offenders with adults
    a) never
    b) any time as long as it is during the day
    c) when doing otherwise is impossible
    d) for a maximum of 24 hours

2. Which of the following is not a consideration at a bail hearing?

    a) the seriousness of the offence
    b) the suffering of the victims

c) the family situation of the young person

d) the risk of flight

SHORT ESSAYS

1. Identify four circumstances under which it is permissible for a police officer to detain a young person with adults.

   1) _____

   2) _____

   3) _____

   4) _____

2. Why must young offenders who are detained and are about to be left alone be searched?

   _____

   _____

   _____

   _____

   _____

   _____

   _____

   _____

3. You are a police officer who is testifying in court. You are being asked by defence counsel about whether and how you provided the young person with a secondary caution. Identify three questions that might be put to you as a way of challenging whether you did it correctly.

   1) _____

   2) _____

   3) _____

4. What makes a bail hearing for a young person different from one that is for an adult?

   _____

   _____

   _____

   _____

_____

_____

_____

_____

_____

RECORDS

Fingerprinting and Photographing

Section 113 of the *YCJA* allows police officers to fingerprint and photograph young persons under the same general conditions that apply to adults under the *Identification of Criminals Act*. In other words, an officer may fingerprint and photograph young persons if the officer charges them with committing an indictable or a hybrid offence. Fingerprinting or photographing a young person is *only* permissible, however, if they have been charged or convicted of an offence. It is also *not* permissible to fingerprint or photograph a young person who has been charged with a summary offence only.

This situation is at odds with some practices involving adults. For example, adults are occasionally asked to provide fingerprints to aid in an investigation. A typical situation might be when unidentified prints are found at a crime scene and several possible suspects exist. Those suspects may be encouraged to exclude themselves from the investigation by providing fingerprints that can be compared with those found at the crime scene.

For less serious indictable offences, the young persons may be released from custody and given a notice requiring their appearance at a later date for the fingerprints and photographs to be taken. For more serious cases, the fingerprinting and photographing are usually done when charges are laid. If the young person accused is required to appear at a later date, notice of that must also be given to the young person's parents or guardian. Normally, failure to appear for fingerprinting is an offence under section 145 of the *CCC*. Bala (1997:135, fn. 7) notes, however, that in the case *R. v. K.(P.A.)*, Justice Scott ruled that a youth could only be convicted under this section if a copy of the notice to appear had been provided to the youth's parents.

Police Records

A police service that is involved in the investigation of any offence alleged to have been committed by a young person may keep a record of that offence as well as the original copy of fingerprints or photographs of the young person [ss. 115(1)].

When a young person is charged with committing an offence that could cause an adult to be photographed, fingerprinted, or otherwise measured, the investigating police service *may* provide a record relating to the offence to the Royal Canadian Mounted Police (RCMP). If the young person is found guilty of the offence, the record *shall* be provided to the RCMP.

The RCMP has a central repository, known as the Canadian Police Information Centre (CPIC), which holds information on offences where there has been a finding of guilt. In addition to CPIC, the RCMP central repository contains a number of specialized respositories, such as the following: the Criminal Intelligence Service of Canada (CISS); the national DNA data bank, which includes DNA profiles from unsolved crimes; a convicted offender index, which includes DNA profiles from young offenders;

and the "special records repository," which includes prohibition orders made under section 51 of the *YCJA* (prohibition from possessing certain weapons).

Government Records

A department or agency of any government in Canada may keep information that it obtains for any of the following purposes:

1. Investigation of an offence alleged to have been committed by a young person
2. Use in proceedings against a young person
3. Administering a youth sentence or other order
4. Considering whether to use extrajudicial measures
5. As a result of the use of extrajudicial measures to deal with a young person [ss. 116(1)].

Other Records

Persons or organizations may keeps records of information that they obtained as a result of the use of extrajudicial measures and/or for the purpose of participating in the administration of a youth sentence.

Period of Access

The length of time that the record of a young person can be accessed depends on the nature and result of the charge. These periods are summarized in Table 7.1.

Table 7.1: Period of Access to the Records of a Young Person [ss. 119(2)]

DISPOSITION	PERIOD OF ACCESS
Extrajudicial sanction	Two years after the young person agrees to be subjected to these sanctions
Acquitted	Two months after the expiry of time for an appeal
Charge dismissed	Two months after the dismissal
Charge stayed	One year if no proceedings taken against the young person for that period of time
Found guilty and receives an absolute discharge	One year after the finding of guilt
Found guilty and receives a conditional discharge	Three years after the finding of guilt
Found guilty of a summary conviction offence	Three years after the youth sentence has been completed
Found guilty of an indictable offence	Five years after the youth sentence has been completed
Subsequent convictions	Time extended
Presumptive offences	May be retained indefinitely
Violent offences (other than presumptive)	Additional five years
If over 18 years and commits subsequent offence and young person's crime-free period has not expired	Record becomes part of adult record and adult rules apply

Protection of Privacy

A major distinction between how we handle adult offenders and young offenders relates to the issue of privacy. It is permissible to publish the names of adults charged or convicted of an offence. It is also normal practice for local newspapers to assign a court reporter to cover the more interesting cases heard in court. In fact, the *right* to a public trial is a fundamental aspect of our legal system. Public and open trials, we believe, are one way of making sure that the power of the state is limited and that the courts do not engage in abusive and arbitrary procedures.

The *YCJA*, on the other hand, is written from a perspective that sees publicity as detrimental to the personal and social well being of the young person. Consequently, there are strict limitations on the public release of information (called **publication**) relating to the offence, hearing, adjudication, disposition, or appeal of a young person.

The prohibition in [ss. 110(1)] is clear: "No person shall publish the name of a young person, or any other information related to a young person, if it would identify the young person as a young person dealt with under this *Act.*" This includes not only young persons who are found guilty but also young persons who are under investigation or charged, as well as young victims or witnesses. The issues at hand may be sensitive for them, and they may be intimidated by the public attention to their testimony. The reputation of the witness or victim may also be adversely affected by publication.

Unlike the *Young Offenders Act,* the *YCJA* provides detailed exceptions to the general rule of nonpublication and these have to do with the following: receipt of adult sentences; conviction for presumptive offences; information made available in the course of the administration of justice; seeking public assistance in apprehending a young person; and where the young person is not over 18 years and not in custody and wants the information made public.

The first four of these exceptions are clarified below:

1. *Adult sentence.* The *YCJA* permits the publication of names of all young persons who have received adult sentences for murder, attempted murder, manslaughter, aggravated sexual assault, or repeat violent offences or any other criminal offences [ss. 110(2)(a)].

2. *Presumptive offence.* Young persons who have been convicted of a presumptive offence for which an adult sentence was sought but, nevertheless, received a youth sentence may be an exception. The Crown needs to make application for publication, but the youth court judge needs to balance the public interest with the importance of the rehabilitation of the young person.

3. *Administration of justice.* Publication made in the course of the administration of justice where the purpose is not to make the information known to the community is allowed.

4. *Seeking public assistance.* Publication of the name of a young person allows authorities to seek public assistance in apprehending a young person who is dangerous. An application needs to be made to a youth justice court judge, and counsel for the young person does not have to be informed. The order is operative for only any five days. The fact that the police must make application to a judge means that a clear process must be followed by the police and that they cannot simply take it upon themselves to publish the information.

In brief, the ban on publication does not mean that records cannot be kept, and identifying information regarding young persons and witnesses cannot be passed from one person to another. The *YCJA* exempts situations where the information is used for the administration of justice. In other words, it is permissible for police officers and other justice personnel to identify young persons when they are engaged in standard investigative practices. They may also provide information in the young person's file to court workers, corrections' personnel, or youth workers, who may, for example, provide extra-judicial measures.

Nothing in the *YCJA* prevents an officer from inadvertently identifying young offenders by arresting them in a public place. For example, arresting a young person at school in the view of other students is not considered a violation of privacy. The decision about when and where to arrest a suspect rests with the individual police officer.

Accessibility of Records

Sections 119 of the *YCJA* allow a broad range of people access to young persons' records before the expiry of the time limits placed on the records. Young persons and their counsel, for example, are granted automatic access to the young persons' youth justice court records.

The *YCJA* has a list of persons, groups, or institutions who may seek access to youth records and a list of the purposes of such access. That is, information requirements vary under individual circumstances of individual cases. Subsection 119(1) recognizes access by the following:

1. Young persons, their counsel, parents, or adults the court permits to assist them
2. Crown prosecutor
3. Any judge, court, or review board
4. Justice officers to assist in an investigation
5. Persons administering extrajudicial measures or sanctions or prepares reports under the *Act*
6. Provincial director
7. Those participating in a conference
8. Victim
9. Coroner, privacy or information commissioner, ombudsman or child advocate
10. Government officials
11. An accused person or his counsel who needs it to make a defence
12. Official agents of the federal government for statistical or security and other purposes

Unlike youth court records, however, police and other government records relating to the young person are made available at the discretion of the agency keeping the records. Thus, police officials *may* allow victims access to all or parts of the record of a young person who has been charged or convicted of an offence, if, in their judgment, it will help the victim.

The counsel of the young person who is accused will often request access to the police file. This file will likely contain the names and addresses of witnesses. As a matter of courtesy, some departments routinely ask witnesses (or more likely their parents) if they mind having their names and addresses revealed when such requests are made. Many police officers will also inform witnesses that they are under no obligation to speak with the offender's counsel if they do not wish to do so. It is also standard procedure to inform the Crown's office when these requests are made.

In addition to the individuals and agencies cited above, the *YCJA* provides for the sharing of information with other entities. Access is given for particular circumstances or specific purposes so it is expected that the custodian of the records, for example, the police, will exercise discretion, as will the court, when an application is made. Insurance companies may be granted access to investigate a claim arising out of an offence. School authorities may receive a portion of a record that is relevant to ensure compliance with a court order or ensure the safety of staff, students, or other persons or to facilitate the young person's rehabilitation. On the other hand, in the 2000 decision *Re: F. N.*, the Supreme court of Canada upheld an appeal forbidding the Roman Catholic School Board of St. Johns' from routinely distributing the youth court docket to local school boards. Fundamentally, the supreme court agreed that this practice violated the nondisclosure provisions of the what was then *YOA*. The distribution of "tailored" information, however, with respect to specific offenders, is acceptable.

Exercise 4

DEFINITIONS

Please define the following term:

Publication:

_____

_____

_____

_____

_____

_____

_____

_____

_____

TRUE OR FALSE

1. T F Young person may be fingerprinted, but not photographed, by the police.

2. T F The preferred procedure under the *Youth Criminal Justice Act* is to fingerprint young persons before they are charged.

3. T F It is a violation of the *Youth Criminal Justice Act's* prohibition on publication if a police officer tells her husband that one of the youths in the neighbourhood was charged with assault.

4. T F In order to publish the name of a young person the police must apply to youth justice court for permission.

5. T F Records of young offenders are generally kept for a shorter period of time than the records of adults.

MULTIPLE CHOICE

1. Once fingerprints and photographs of young persons are taken, they may be retained

   a) for no longer than 12 months
   b) until the young person reaches the age of 18 years

   c) forever
   d) none of the above

2. To which categories of people who fall within the legal age that defines a young person does the *Youth Criminal Justice Act's* ban on publication apply?

   a) offenders
   b) victims
   c) witnesses
   d) all of the above

SHORT ESSAYS

1. Describe the procedure that applies for fingerprinting a young person charged with a summary offence.

   _____

   _____

   _____

   _____

   _____

   _____

   _____

   _____

   _____

   _____

   _____

2. Identify three circumstances in which it may be appropriate to publish the name of a young person.

   1) _____

   _____

   _____

   _____

   _____

   2) _____

   _____

   _____

3) _____

_____

_____

_____

_____

3. Why do you suppose the *Youth Criminal Justice Act* has provisions for the destruction of records of young persons?

_____

_____

_____

_____

_____

_____

_____

_____

_____

_____

_____

SUMMARY—PUTTING IT TOGETHER

There is no one typical criminal event: Crimes differ, offenders differ, and circumstances differ. How police officers deal with a young person who commits a minor act of vandalism or shoplifting will be very different from how they handle a serious assault or drug offence. To illustrate the many steps an officer might follow in arresting a young offender, however, we will consider an example of a call to investigate a theft under $5,000. The steps in this example are charted in Figure 7.1.

In this example, two male suspects are caught trying to steal some electronic appliances from a discount store. The total value of the goods is approximately $1,900. One suspect is 17 years of age, and the other is 19 years of age. The manager of the store observed the suspects, and the store's security camera recorded the act. The manager

Figure 7.1: Example Arrest

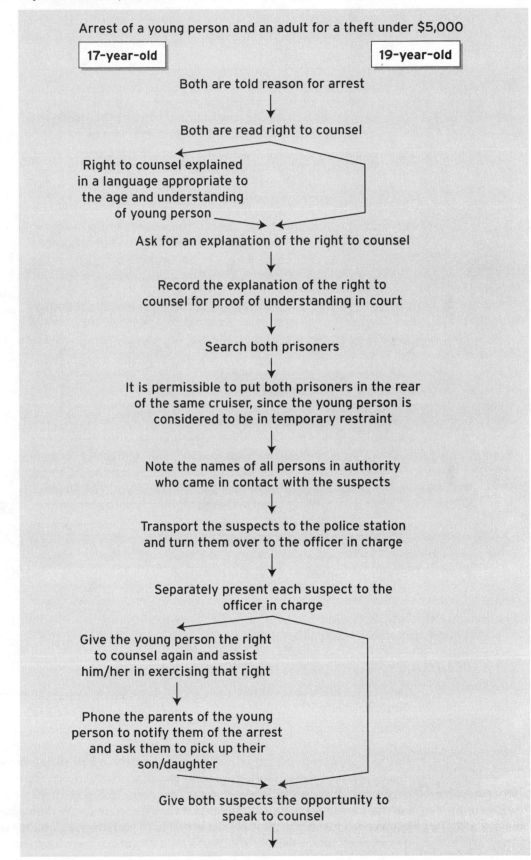

Figure 7.1: Example Arrest (Cont'd)

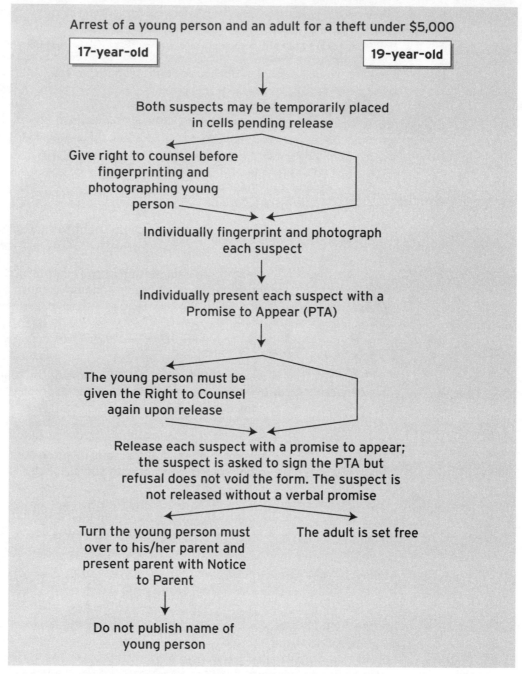

Arrest of a young person and an adult for a theft under $5,000

17-year-old   19-year-old

Both suspects may be temporarily placed
in cells pending release

Give right to counsel before
fingerprinting and
photographing young
person

Individually fingerprint and photograph
each suspect

Individually present each suspect with a
Promise to Appear (PTA)

The young person must be
given the Right to Counsel
again upon release

Release each suspect with a promise to appear;
the suspect is asked to sign the PTA but
refusal does not void the form. The suspect is
not released without a verbal promise

Turn the young person must
over to his/her parent and
present parent with Notice
to Parent

The adult is set free

Do not publish name of
young person

Source: Adapted and used with permission of John Grime, Coordinator and Professor, Law and Security
Administration, Mohawk College.

and two salespeople detained the suspects as they exited the store. We will focus on
those aspects of the arrest that illustrate the difference between the handling of a young
person and that of an adult.

After arriving on the scene and discussing the matter with the store manager and the
salespeople, the police officers responding to the call decide that they should charge the
two suspects under section 322(1) of the *CCC* (simple theft). Although one suspect is a

young person as defined by the *Youth Criminal Justice Act*, the officer decides to charge the individual, rather than not take further action or issue a warning or caution. This decision is based on the young person's age and the seriousness of the offence. If the young person had been much younger and the property stolen had been a couple of compact discs worth $30, the officers might have decided that it was in the best interests of the young persons not to charge. This might have been the officers' decision, even if the store manager pressed for charges to be laid. The officers may consider the victim's wishes, but it is up to the individual officer to decide what is appropriate for a young person under the circumstances.[1]

Once the officers have decided to arrest the two suspects, they tell both suspects the reason for their arrest. They read both suspects their right to counsel. The officer reading the right to counsel to the young person decides that the young person's level of comprehension seems to lag somewhat. The officer repeats the right to counsel using simpler language. Both suspects are asked for an explanation of the right to counsel. If either suspect shows a misunderstanding, the right is restated. The officers detail the reading of the right to counsel and the suspects' responses in their notebooks. By writing down the responses verbatim, the officers' notes will be of value in providing proof of understanding in court. Simply noting down that "the suspects understood the right to counsel" is not sufficient.

The officers search both suspects. Putting both suspects in the back seat of the cruiser is permissible, since the young person is considered in temporary restraint. Just before leaving the crime scene, one officer takes notes and records the name of any person in authority with whom the suspects might have come into contact.

The suspects are taken back to the police station where they are presented individually to the officer in charge. Once the adult offender is turned over to the officer in charge, the officer in charge asks him if he would like the opportunity to speak with a lawyer. However, the right to counsel is again explained to the young person. The young person explains that he "knows the drill" and declines the offer to contact a lawyer. At this point, the officer phones the young person's home. The parents are contacted, notified of the arrest, and asked to pick up their son at the police station.

Both suspects are now placed in holding cells while waiting to be released. In this instance, the police station has a separate corridor just for young offenders, and this is where the 17-year-old is held. The 19-year-old is placed in the general holding area used for adults.

Since the theft is a hybrid or dual offence under section 334(b) of the *CCC*, both suspects will be taken for fingerprinting and photographing. While the 19-year-old is processed in the standard manner, the young person is once again explained his right to counsel and given the opportunity to call counsel. Although the suspects were involved in the offence together, they are kept separate while the fingerprints and photographs are taken.

In this case, the identity of the suspects is known, the issue of protecting evidence is not an issue, and neither suspect appears to pose a threat to others. A check of the records and the immediate demeanour of the suspects do not suggest that they will fail to appear in court. Consequently, the officer in charge decides to release both suspects with a Promise to Appear. Again, both suspects are processed separately. In the instance of the adult suspect, the suspect and the officer in charge simply sign the appearance form. After the paperwork is completed, the adult offender is set free.

A few minutes later, the young person's parents arrive at the station. The officer in charge uses this opportunity to explain the situation to the parents and to explain the right to counsel again. While the officer is explaining the availability of legal aid's 1-800 number, the 17-year-old explains that he "knows the drill" and will speak with Ms. Blackstone of the law firm of Winnem and Luzem when he gets home. The young person agrees to sign the Promise to Appear form in the presence of his parents. Once done, the officer in charge presents the parents with a Notice to Parents. When that is completed, the officer in charge turns the young offender over to his parents, and they leave the station.

As a last point, a reporter from the local newspaper enters the station and thinks he recognizes the two suspects. When asked if these are "the two characters" who were involved in the theft at the discount electronics store, the officer in charge explains that one suspect is an adult and the other is a young offender. The reporter then asks for and receives the full name of the adult suspect for possible publication but is reminded by the officer in charge that he cannot publish the name of the young offender.

Exercise: You Be the Judge

Here is a set of facts which the Supreme Court of Canada had to work with. Each of the cases that follow was heard when the *Young Offenders Act* (*YOA*) was in place. The legal issues involved in these cases are the same in the *Youth Criminal Justice Act* (*YCJA*) as they were under the *YOA*. Therefore, these decisions will continue to apply fully. Given your knowledge of the *YCJA*, the principles on which it is based, and the *Charter of Rights and Freedoms*, answer the following questions about how you would have decided the case. The Court's decision is summarized on pages 146 and 147, but answer the questions first, and look at the answers after that.

> A young person was charged with second-degree murder of a cab driver. His great-aunt, a First Nations band elder with little formal education, accompanied him on his arrest to the police station. The young person regarded her as his mother. The police informed her that there would be time to look for a lawyer on their arrival at the police station, but on their arrival, both were taken to an interview room, where the investigating constable began taking a statement over the course of four and a half hours. Prior to taking the statement, a "Statement to Person in Authority Form" was completed. The officer tried to explain the right to counsel, the right to have an adult present, and the fact that any statement could be used in proceedings against the accused. A statement was made without the advice of a lawyer. Later, the young person, at his request, met with his lawyer for half an hour. The next day, the young person informed the investigating constable that he had information to add to his statement. After the young person finished speaking with his lawyer, he and the constable went through the process of completing the "Statement to Person in Authority" form. The young person indicated that he did not want a lawyer or other adult present. The second statement included an exchange about the plan the young person and his co-accused had to murder a cab driver.

1. Should the *first* statement have been admitted as evidence? _____ Yes _____ No

   Indicate the reasons for your decision:

   _____

   _____

   _____

   _____

   _____

_____

_____

_____

_____

_____

_____

2. Should the *second* statement have been admitted as evidence? _____ Yes _____ No

Indicate the reasons for your decision:

_____

_____

_____

_____

_____

_____

_____

_____

_____

_____

3. Does it make a difference to you that the same police officer was involved in taking the first and second statements in terms of the admissibility of the second statement?

Indicate the reasons for your decision:

_____

_____

_____

_____

_____

_____

_____

_____

_____

_____

_____

4. Does it make a difference if the police officer used information contained in the first statement in the questions posed to the young person at the time the second statement was taken?

Indicate the reasons for your decision:

_____

_____

_____

_____

_____

_____

_____

_____

_____

_____

THE DECISION

The trial judge excluded the first statement, but not the second. The Supreme Court [in *R.v. I. (L.R.) and T. (E.)*] ruled that the second statement must be excluded as well. The following are edited excerpts of the reasoning provided by the Supreme Court.

With respect to the first statement, neither the young person nor his great-aunt appreciated the consequences of his act of confession, despite the fact that young person had had previous dealings with the police. If waiver had been in issue, the young person would not have had sufficient information concerning the extent of his jeopardy to make an informed and valid decision as to whether or not to speak with a lawyer. Accordingly, neither section 56 of the *YOA* nor section 10(b) of the *Charter* were complied with, and the first statement was inadmissible on this ground as well.

The admissibility of the second statement was affected by the grounds for exclusion of the first statement. A parent is not an alternative to counsel, unless the right to counsel is waived. Section 56 of the *YOA*, which appears to provide that a parent or other adult may be an alternative to counsel, must be interpreted in a manner consistent with both the section 10(b) of the *Charter* right to counsel and the provision in section 11 of the *YOA* requiring that counsel be available.

The determination of whether or not a young person validly waived his or her section 10(*b*) of the *Charter* right to counsel is not to be based simply on what the police told the young person but upon the young person's actual awareness of the consequences of his or her actions. The police need not advise an accused, as a matter of course, of the maximum penalty he or she might face. The phenomenal difference in potential consequences faced by the young person in youth court as opposed to adult court, however, mandates that a young person be aware of the possibility (where it exists) that he or she will receive an adult sentence, and the potential result of this in terms of stigma and penalty. The particular characteristics of young offenders make extra precautions necessary in affording them the full protection of their *Charter* rights.

Under the rules relating to confessions at common law, the admissibility of a confession which had been preceded by an involuntary confession, involved a factual determination, based on factors designed to ascertain the degree of connection between the two statements. These included the time span between the statements, reference to the previous statement during questioning, the discovery of additional incriminating evidence subsequent to the first statement, the presence of the same police officers at both interrogations and other similarities between the two circumstances. A subsequent confession would be involuntary if either the tainting features that disqualified the first confession continued to be present or if the making of the first statement was a substantial factor contributing to the making of the second statement. An explanation of one's rights either by a police officer or counsel may not be of use in the face of a strong urge to explain away incriminating matters in a prior statement.

Here, there was not only a close temporal relationship between the statements but also the second statement was a continuation of the first, and the first statement was a substantial factor leading to the making of the second. The statements were taken less than a day apart by the same officer. There was no evidence that the police, in the interval between the two statements, had gathered further evidence tending to incriminate the appellant to which the appellant might be asked to respond. There was also continuous reference by the police officer throughout the second statement to information given in the first statement. All the evidence leads to the conclusion that the second statement was a continuation of the first. Communication with counsel did not make this conclusion unnecessary.

Exercise: You Be the Judge

Here is a set of facts which the Supreme Court of Canada had to work with. Given your knowledge of the *YCJA*, the principles on which it is based, and the *Charter of Rights and Freedoms*, answer the following questions about how you would have decided the case. The Court's decision is summarized on the following page, but answer the questions first, and look at the answers after that.

> The accused was charged under the *Young Offenders Act* with theft. He was 17 years old at the time of the alleged offence. He voluntarily made an inculpatory written statement to a person in authority after having been cautioned and advised of his rights under the *Canadian Charter of Rights and Freedoms*. He was 18 years old when he made the statement. The police treated him as an adult and did not advise him that he had a right to have an adult person in attendance when he made the statement. Section 56(2) of the *Act* provides that a statement given by a young person

to a person in authority is not admissible unless certain conditions are met, including the requirement that the young person be advised of his right to have an adult person in attendance when making the statement.

1. Should the statement have been admitted as evidence? _____ Yes _____ No

Indicate the reasons for your decision:

_____

_____

_____

_____

_____

_____

_____

_____

_____

_____

_____

_____

THE DECISION

The Supreme Court [in *R.v. Z. (D.A.)*], as reflected in the edited version of the ruling provided below, decided the following:

The section 56(2) of the *Young Offenders Act* does not apply to statements made by an accused 18 years of age or older. Both the express words used by Parliament and the overall scheme and purpose of the *Act* support this conclusion. The term "young person" is defined in section 2 as a person at least 12 years old but under 18 years. The definition is further extended to include any person charged under the *Act* with having committed an offence while between the ages of 12 and 18 years.

The concern over ensuring that all accused are similarly held accountable for the mistakes of their youth does not dictate that all the special protections afforded under the *Act*, regardless of the age of an accused. In enacting certain of the *Act's* special protections, Parliament has sought to address concerns specific to a youth, rather than an adult.

There is clearly nothing underlying the purpose of section 56(2) requiring its application to an adult accused. The aim of section 56 is to protect adolescents who, by virtue of their lack of maturity, are not likely to fully appreciate their legal rights and the consequences of making a statement to the police. These concerns do not arise with respect to an accused over the age of 18 years. No further protection beyond that already afforded under the *Charter* and common law is necessary to ensure that any statement made by an adult accused is truly voluntary. As such, the context of section 56(2) does not require that the term "young person" therein be interpreted to include a person over the age of 18 years.

ENDNOTES

1. Of course, the manager and the store owner have the option of laying a private information.

The Youth Justice Court

Learning Outcomes

Students who have mastered this chapter will have the ability to do the following:

- *Describe* the difference in the roles of defence counsel and Crown prosecutors.
- *Distinguish* between a pre-sentence report and a pre-sentence assessment.
- *Describe* the role of a youth justice court judge.
- *Understand* what goes on at a youth justice court trial.
- *Understand* the purposes and principles of youth sentences.
- *Describe* a range of youth sentences.
- *Explain* the circumstances under which a young person may receive an adult sentence.

JURISDICTION: YOUTH JUSTICE COURT

Adult court is for persons 18 years of age and older. When young persons, that is those between the ages of 12 and 17 years, are in court, the court is always a youth justice court and the judge is always a youth justice court judge. It makes no difference what the name of the court is or the level of the court [ss. 13(2)]. Under the *Youth Criminal Justice Act (YCJA)*, there is no such thing as the transfer of a young person to adult court. Young persons may be given adult sentences, as we will see later, but this occurs in a youth justice court.

THE MAIN PLAYERS

While the *YCJA* recognizes the unique status of young persons, the youth justice court is basically modelled after the ordinary courts. That is to say, they are fundamentally adversarial, and the requirement of due process that forms the basis of the ordinary courts also forms the basis of the youth justice court. Structurally, this means that professional lawyers—a Crown counsel, and a defence counsel representing the accused—will present the two sides of the case. The youth justice court judge must apply the requirements of the *YCJA*. Many of these requirements are different from the rules that apply to adults with respect to a wide range of issues, including frequency of instructions about right to counsel, publication of information, and type and length of sentence. Fundamentally, however, the youth justice court judge plays the same role as a judge in adult court, with one important exception. The major departure for the youth justice court judge is that the judge has to consider whether the matter at hand is best dealt with through extrajudicial measures, including an extrajudicial sentence. That is, the *YCJA* requires that the youth justice court judge consider the merits of dealing with the young person in a non-court manner. Such considerations do not apply in adult court.

Defence Counsel

Section 25 of the *YCJA* states that "a young person has the right to retain and instruct counsel without delay." That right can be exercised "at any stage of proceedings against the young person." Thus, even if a police officer obtains a written waiver, the waiver is voided once the young person requests counsel. Once the young person has passed through police custody, the *YCJA* requires the youth justice court to remind the young person of their right to counsel at several stages in the proceedings. As listed in [ss. 25(3)], they are the following:

- Pretrial detention hearings
- Adult sentence hearings
- Trials
- Hearings to consider the application for a continuation of the custodial portion of youth sentence
- Hearings to determine whether the young person has breached condition(s) of community supervision
- Hearings to set the conditions of conditional supervision
- Hearings to determine whether the suspension of conditional supervision is appropriate
- Reviews of a youth sentence
- Reviews of the level of custody

The *YCJA* is clear that young persons need to be notified of their right to legal counsel and that they need to be given the opportunity to retain such counsel. Young persons do not have to exercise this right.

If the young person is not represented by counsel, the youth justice court may not accept a plea, unless the following occur:

1. The youth justice court judge must ensure that the young person understands the charge.
2. If it applies, the youth justice court judge must explain the consequences of being liable to an adult sentence and explain the process for applying for a youth sentence.
3. The youth justice court judge must explain the options available to the young person.

If the court is not satisfied that the young person understands these things, then the court must direct that the young person be represented by counsel.

Despite emphasis on, and many references to, the "best interests" of the young person and society in the *YCJA*, the primary role of the defence counsel is to represent the legal interests of the accused. The job of the young person's lawyer is to ensure that the young person's legal rights are preserved and respected. Defence lawyers do not represent society, or even young persons' parents; their sole client is the young person.

The centrality of legally trained personnel (particularly defence counsel) in court to deal with young people is relatively new in Canada. Under the *Juvenile Delinquents Act*, young people were entitled to legal representation, but the participation of lawyers was not encouraged. Legal representation was the exception, rather than the rule. Legal representation of young persons was really introduced with the *Young Offenders Act*, and it continues with the *YCJA*.

As we indicated in the previous chapters, the *YCJA* requires the police to inform young persons of their right to consult and to retain counsel at almost every step in the legal process. This right is also printed on summonses, warrants, notices, and other documents given to the young person. If the police wish to question the young person, counsel must be present or the young person must sign a legal waiver. Even young persons whom the police bring into the station for a breathalyzer test must be given the opportunity to consult counsel before the test can be given. If the young person is not able to contact or obtain private counsel, the *YJCA* requires the court either to refer the young person to the provincial legal aid plan or to appoint a counsel. In some larger centres, duty counsel will often provide initial advice to young persons if they appear in court without a lawyer.

The ability of young persons to request counsel for even relatively minor offences has raised concerns about cost in many jurisdictions. The *YCJA* indicates that the provinces are not prevented from establishing rules to recover costs of appointed counsel from young persons or their parents. The *YCJA* considers that a conflict of interest might exist for lawyers whom the young person's parents have hired and paid to represent the young person. In situations where a youth justice court judge sees "the interests of the young person and his parents are in conflict," the judge "shall ensure that the young person is represented by counsel independent of his parents" [*YCJA* 25(8)].

The first advice that most defence counsel will likely give their clients is to remain silent and not to cooperate with the police beyond providing their full name and age. Some counsel take the advocate role to the extreme and will challenge any evidence or testimony presented, even if they believe their client is guilty. This is a legitimate aspect of a defence counsel's job, particularly if their client advises them to do so.

Under the *YCJA*, there are even more options available to defence counsel than under previous legislation. The emphasis on the use of extrajudicial measures in the *YCJA* means that defence counsel have multiple points in the criminal justice system where they can attempt to have their clients dealt with in a more or less formal manner. These points occur at the level of the police (warning, caution, referral to program or agency), the Crown prosecutor (Crown cautions), and the youth justice court (extrajudicial sanctions).

The Crown Prosecutor

As in ordinary court, the primary role of the Crown prosecutor is to represent the government's (Crown's) case before the court. The Crown, in youth justice court, also carries out most of the same functions as in adult cases. Thus, Crown prosecutors often advise police officers about the specific charges to lay. They also screen cases to ensure that there is sufficient evidence to proceed with a charge. Usually, the Crown will review both the substantive case against the young person and the procedure followed by the police in the arrest.

An additional feature is added by the *YCJA*. The Crown now needs to satisfy itself that the police considered the options of taking no further action, warning, caution, and referral to a program and that the circumstances of the case warrant is being raised to their level. The Crown must also consider whether a Crown caution would be the appropriate disposition of this matter.

It is common for individual police officers to get annoyed with Crown prosecutors who choose not to proceed with a particular case. We must remember that the Crown is responsible for presenting the case in court, and poor evidence or faulty procedure will only lead to both the Crown and the arresting officer being embarrassed in court. Experienced Crown attorneys are usually good judges of what the local courts will or will not accept. In some circumstances, the Crown will drop the immediate charges but will ask the police to lay them again after the proper procedures are followed.

It is sometimes difficult for new officers to understand that different rules of professional conduct govern Crown and defence counsel. The primary role of defence counsel is to follow the client's instructions. Thus, many counsel believe that questioning every element of evidence and pursuing every technical defence open to them is their ethical obligation—even if they know that their client has done the deed. Their job is not to second guess what might be in the "best interests" of their client, their client's parents, or society. Crown counsel, on the other hand, are restrained professionally from taking a "win at all costs" approach. Their role is to present the government's case to the court and allow the court to judge its merits. Crown counsel are also expected to use their professional judgment about what is in society's best interests.

It is this obligation—to consider the best interests of society—that will lead the Crown to drop charges if the offence is a minor one and the cost to the participants is high. For example, the Crown may choose not to proceed with the case if witnesses are required to travel long distances or will otherwise be severely inconvenienced. The Crown will also use its judgment when agreeing to reduce charges if the offender agrees to enter a guilty plea to a lesser offence. The **plea bargain** is a tradeoff, where both attorneys weigh the likelihood of conviction against the cost of conviction to the accused and the cost of prosecution to the community.

In cases concerning young persons, however, the Crown has additional duties beyond screening charges and conducting prosecutions. In Ontario, it is the role of the Crown to decide whether the young person might be eligible for an extrajudicial measure. This can successfully divert the case from the court entirely. Where an extrajudicial measure is possible, the Crown will often discuss the case in more detail with the arresting officer. The goal here is to obtain as much information as possible about the officer's knowledge of the accused, the victim, and any witnesses.

Another duty of the Crown is to decide how to proceed with hybrid or elective offences. Until otherwise elected, hybrid offences are treated as indictable offences in both adult and youth justice court proceedings. Many consequences of proceeding by indictment are the same for young persons as for adults. The potential sentence associated with an indictable offence is more severe than if the case is handled summarily. The main difference between adult court and youth court, however, is that the youth court handles indictable offences *procedurally* the same way as summary offences. Section 143 indicates that indictable offences and offences punishable on summary convention "may be charged in the same indictment and tried jointly."

In many situations, the police charge offenders with more than one offence. Because of the uniformity of procedure in youth court, listing both indictable and summary offences on the same information is possible.

Yet another obligation of the Crown is to provide **disclosure**. The basic rules of disclosure that apply to adult cases also apply to those of young persons. In general, the Crown must disclose its case—including evidence and the names of potential witnesses—to the young person's counsel before the trial. The defence, on the other hand, is under no obligation to disclose anything to the Crown. Because of the confidentiality rules surrounding young persons, the range of persons who may be privy to disclosure is generally more restricted in cases involving young persons than in cases of adults.

The Judge

Judges in youth justice court have the same general rights and responsibilities as judges in ordinary courts. It is the primary role of the judge to "manage" the proceedings in the courtroom. The judge is also responsible for the following:

1. Determining that proper procedure was followed in laying the charges, including that all requirements identified in section 146 on the admissibility of evidence were followed
2. Determining that the young person is aware of, and has had opportunity to, obtain and consult with counsel
3. Resolving disputes between lawyers over the admissibility of evidence
4. Determining guilt or innocence
5. Determining the advisability of an extrajudicial sentence
6. Sentencing the offender after a finding of guilt

Youth court judges also intervene in the trial process more frequently than a judge would in the case of an adult. The *YCJA* mandates part of this intervention. For example, it is the responsibility of the judge to ensure that young defendants are aware of the nature of the charges against them, even if counsel represent them. Youth court judges also have more latitude in intervening if they suspect the young person is suffering from a mental deficiency or a mental disorder.

Judges intervene most actively, however, when they believe that the young person's counsel is not doing an adequate job of representing the client. In these situations, the judge may be more proactive in assessing the value of evidence and in questioning witnesses. Judges are loath, however, to become too involved in the "nonjudicial" aspects of the trial, since doing so can place them in seriously conflicting roles. Furthermore, instances of too much judicial activism provide ready grounds for appeal. Fortunately, the availability of duty counsel, in most courts, and the provisions of the *YCJA* that allow a judge to direct that the young person be provided with legal counsel remove the need for much judicial intervention.

In larger centres, the youth justice court judge who presides over the bail hearing may not preside over the trial. Once a trial starts, however, the same judge who hears the trial must be the one who passes judgment. If this is not possible, then under section 131, the replacement judge may proceed with the sentencing if an adjudication has been made or "if no adjudication has been made, recommence the trail as if no evidence had been taken."

The Police

The arresting officer is usually present in court to act as a witness and to review the evidence with the Crown prosecutor. Officers are typically not present when the young person has negotiated a plea beforehand. Police officers are also able to provide other information to the Crown about the victim, the witnesses and, occasionally, the accused. This extended role of the police is important because a broader range of evidence is admissible in youth justice court than in adult court. If the court continues or postpones the case, the Crown might also confer with officers over available dates.

Exercise 1

DEFINITIONS

Please define the following terms:

1. Plea bargain:

_____

_____

_____

_____

_____

_____

_____

_____

2. Disclosure:

_____

_____

_____

_____

_____

_____

_____

_____

_____

TRUE OR FALSE

1. T F   In adult court, it is professionals who present the two sides of the case, but in youth justice court, there are no professionals.

2. T F   When a parent or another responsible adult is present, it is not necessary to remind a young person of right to counsel; having said it once is enough.

3. T F   Young persons are eligible to apply for legal aid.

4. T F   A young person who is brought into the police station for a breathalyzer test has a right to consult counsel before the test can be given.

5. T F   When the case of a young persons gets to court, there is no longer a role for the police.

MULTIPLE CHOICE

1. Defence counsel must be mindful that their job includes representing
   a) the young person who is their client
   b) the society
   c) the criminal justice system
   d) two of the above

2. Under the rule of "one lawyer per family," young persons are represented by
   a) the lawyer of their parents' choosing
   b) the lawyer who represents their parents
   c) both of the above
   d) none of the above, because there is no such rule

3. In youth justice court, the role of the Crown Prosecutor is
   a) very different from what it is in adult court
   b) not much different from what it is in adult court
   c) is focused on the needs of the young person because of the *YCJA*
   d) two of the above

4. Which of the following is *not* a responsibility of the judge in youth justice court?
   a) determining that proper procedure was followed in laying the charges
   b) resolving disputes over the admissibility of evidence
   c) determining guilt or innocence
   d) ensuring that defence counsel has made full disclosure to the Crown

SHORT ESSAYS

1. Identify two advantages to the Crown for entering into a plea bargain.

   1) _____

   _____

   _____

2) _____

_____

_____

2. Identify two advantages for the defence in entering into a plea bargain.

1) _____

_____

2) _____

_____

3. Describe the responsibility of the Crown and of the defence counsel with respect to disclosure.

Crown:

_____

_____

_____

_____

_____

_____

_____

_____

Defence Counsel:

_____

_____

_____

_____

_____

_____

_____

_____

_____

4. What do you consider to be the most important difference between the responsibility of a judge in a youth justice court and a judge in an adult court?

_____

_____

_____

_____

_____

_____

_____

_____

_____

5. Why is it so important?

_____

_____

_____

_____

_____

_____

_____

_____

_____

THE TRIAL

Perhaps the main difference between youth justice court and ordinary court is that the youth court follows summary procedures whatever the offence. Thus, even if charged for an indictable offence, the young person does not have the right to elect a jury trial, with two exceptions: first, if the young person is alleged to have committed first- or second-degree murder, even if the Crown is seeking a youth sentence, the young person may elect trial by jury; and, second, if the young person is alleged to have committed a "presumptive offence" and the Crown has not given notice of intent to seek a youth sentence. A **presumptive offence** under [s. 2(1)] is one that is committed by a person who has attained at least the age of 14 years and the offence falls into one of the following categories: first-degree murder or second-degree murder; attempt to commit murder; manslaughter; aggravated sexual assault; or a serious violent offence for which an adult is liable to imprisonment for more that two years, after having had at least two judicial determinations at different proceedings that the young person has committed a serious violent offence.

Another significant difference is that all young persons *must* appear before the courts, whatever the charge. For many offences, particularly the less serious ones, adults who are charged may decline to appear personally in ordinary court if they are represented by counsel.

For the most part, the rules of procedure that govern cases tried in ordinary or adult court apply to the youth court. Formality in the youth justice courts varies more than one would find in the ordinary courts. One area where this is most apparent is in the "openness" of the court. We expect ordinary court proceedings to be public affairs and it is only under exceptional circumstances where judges will exclude spectators. Indeed, the *Canadian Charter of Rights and Freedoms* enshrines the *right* to a public hearing.

In the youth justice court, judges are freer to decide who should be allowed in the court and under what circumstances. They may allow only those immediately concerned with the offence or those who are legally entitled to participate in the trial in court. It is also common for judges to exclude witnesses from the courtroom when others are giving testimony. This is done to minimize witness "contamination," where one witness is influenced by the testimony of another. In other instances, some judges will exclude children (those under 12 years of age) from viewing the proceedings, even if they are siblings of the accused. For many judges, the protection of the young person's privacy is a prime consideration, but the protection of victims and witnesses is also to be considered.

Judges who hear cases of 16- and 17-year-old youths, however, are often likely to retain public access to the proceedings. While the *YCJA* does not permit anyone to publish the names of any young person who may appear before the courts, many judges do not consider awareness of the case by individual members of the community to pose a serious problem.

Youth justice court judges also differ considerably with respect to the decorum they expect in their courtrooms. Some judges will not allow participants to appear before the bench in T-shirts, shorts, or sandals. Others are less concerned with dress and will only draw the line when offensive logos are displayed. Judges can enforce decorum in the courtroom through statutory references to contempt. They can exclude young persons who are disruptive in court under section 650 of the *Criminal Code of Canada*. Section 15 of the *YCJA* give youth justice court "the same power, jurisdiction, and authority to deal with and impose punishment for contempt against the court as may be exercised by the superior court of criminal jurisdiction."

As with ordinary court, the actual trial may follow one of several routes. Both defence and Crown counsel have the right to ask for an adjournment. Defence counsel are likely to ask for an adjournment if they are late coming to the case or if they need further disclosure from the Crown. Crown counsel usually ask for an adjournment if the case is serious and there are problems relating to witnesses. When the Crown makes such a request, most defence counsel will move for a dismissal of the charges. The decision of whether to proceed or not rests with the judge.

Because the *YCJA* requires the police to consider warnings, cautions, and referrals to programs, it is rare that the young person will be in court for a first offence or a nonserious alleged offence. Similarly, the requirement that the Crown consider a Crown caution as an extrajudicial measure should keep less frequent and less serious alleged offenders out of court. This is precisely in keeping with the intent of the *YCJA*, which seeks to reserve court proceedings for the more serious cases.

Another difference between adult court and youth justice court proceedings occurs when the trial starts. After the charges are read, the judge must be satisfied that the young person understands the charge. If, in the judge's opinion, the young person does not understand the charge, then the *YCJA* obliges the judge to enter a plea of not guilty for the accused and a full trial must go on. Where the judge is satisfied that the young person does understand the charges, the judge may accept a plea of guilty or not guilty.

While it is rare, young offenders have the same option as adults in entering a plea of not guilty by reason of insanity. Section 34 of the *YCJA* also allows the youth court, "at any stage in the proceedings," to ask for a medical or psychological assessment of the young person. This assessment can be requested by the defence counsel or the Crown. It is the judge's decision as to whether it will be ordered. The court alone can also require it if

- "the court has reasonable grounds to believe that the young person may be suffering from a physical or mental illness or disorder, a psychological disorder, an emotional disturbance, a learning disability or a mental disability";
- the young person shows a pattern of repeat offending; or
- the charge is one involving serious violent offence.

Section 34 assessments, however, are more often called for at the disposition stage.

Fortunately for the administration of justice, most young offenders enter into a plea bargain even when they enter an initial plea of not guilty. Even a small increase in the proportion of young offenders who appear before the courts entering a plea of not guilty would soon clog the court system. The high proportion of guilty pleas is perhaps a testimony to the efficiency and good judgment of most police officers and Crown prosecutors. It remains to be seen as to the number of cases that start in court and end with an extrajudicial measure.

Where the accused enters a plea of not guilty, the court proceeds in a manner similar to that observed in adult cases. As in a criminal trial, the evidence must show guilt "beyond a reasonable doubt." The civil law criterion of a "balance of probabilities" is not sufficient for conviction. A main difference one observes in the youth justice court is the higher percentage of young witnesses. This should come as no surprise, given the age of the defendants. The law has long recognized that the testimonies of youthful and, particularly, child witnesses need to be handled differently from those of adult witnesses. Consequently, special provisions exist in the *YCJA* for handling both young witnesses and their testimonies.

Witnesses

Witnesses serve the same function in the youth court as they do in the adult court. Because witnesses are more likely to be children or young persons, there are some special provisions relating to them. For example, under section 151 of the *YCJA*, the trial judge must instruct children (those under 12 years of age) "as to the duty of the witness to speak the truth and the consequences of failing to do so." They also give this instruction to witnesses who are young persons if the judge believes it is necessary. Failure to give these instructions to a child can form grounds for appeal.

We have already noted that the identity of young persons who are witnesses is subject to the standard ban on publication. One advantage of this ban is that it protects young witnesses from having their own records publicized.

Exercise 2

DEFINITION

Please define the following term:

Presumptive offence:

_____

_____

_____

_____

_____

_____

_____

_____

TRUE OR FALSE

1. T   F   It is for any of the most serious offences that a young person can elect to have trial by jury in youth court.

2. T   F   Trial by jury is a right of all Canadians as long as the charge against them involves a violation of the *Criminal Code of Canada*.

3. T   F   Typically, the youth justice court is held in private without any member of the public allowed to be present.

MULTIPLE CHOICE

1. In the youth justice court, a young person may elect to have a trial by jury

   a) for any serious offence
   b) only when both parents consent
   c) for first- or second-degree murder if the Crown is seeking a youth sentence
   d) none of the above

2. Young persons must personally appear before the youth justice court

    a) only for charges of presumptive offences
    b) only for charges of serious offences
    c) only if their lawyer is not present
    d) for all charges

3. In the youth justice court, judges may consider the protection of the privacy of all but which of the following?

    a) the police
    b) the young person who is charged
    c) victims
    d) witnesses

4. The *YCJA* seeks to reserve court proceedings for

    a) more serious cases
    b) young persons who have already received two or more warnings
    c) young persons who are second-time offenders
    d) two of the above

5. In the youth justice court, the standard for a finding of guilt is

    a) the guilt is "beyond a reasonable doubt"
    b) the guilt is "on the balance of probabilities"
    c) the standard changes with the merits of each individual case
    d) there is no formal finding of guilt

SHORT ESSAYS

1. Identify three features of a trial of a young person that may be different from a trial for an adult.

    1) _____

    _____

    _____

    2) _____

    _____

    _____

    3) _____

    _____

    _____

2. Identify two ways in which witnesses who are young persons are treated differently from adult witnesses.

1) _____

2) _____

SENTENCES

Under the *YCJA*, court trials are reserved for the more serious cases. It is unlikely, therefore, that many judicial sentences will be announced immediately at the end of the trial. Extrajudicial sentences will likely be handled at this time. Where judicial sentences are involved, the court may adjourn while awaiting for a pre-sentence report or a pre-sentence assessment to be prepared.

The Pre-sentence Report

Under subsection 39(6) of the *YCJA*, the court must ask that a **pre-sentence report** be prepared the sentencing process if the judge is contemplating a custodial disposition. The youth justice court may request a pre-sentence report in other circumstances when the court believes it is advisable. Practically, this has come to mean that the court will order pre-sentence reports if the young person's counsel insists on one. Defence counsel are generally of the opinion that an outlining of the youth's problems in a pre-sentence report can moderate the sentences that the court might impose. Furthermore, they believe these reports can result in a disposition that is more likely to be helpful to the young person.

Pre-sentence reports are usually prepared and written by probation officers or "youth workers." The report can be presented to the court either in writing or, if defence counsel provide a waiver, orally. Copies are made available to the judge, the young person and his or her counsel, the prosecutor, and the young person's parents. Once sentenced, a copy of the pre-sentence report will be forwarded to the custodial facility along with the young offender. Subsection 40(2) details what needs to be included in the report. Among the items mandated are the following:

- Results of interviews with the young person, the young person's parents and, where possible, members of the young person's extended family
- Results of interviews with the victim, where possible
- Information on the young person's age, maturity, character, attitude, and willingness to make amends
- Information on the relationship between the offender and the offender's family, including how much control the parents might have over the young person
- Any plans the young person might have to get his life back on track
- Any history of offending
- A history of any extrajudicial sanctions and their outcome
- A history of the young person's school attendance and performance

Pre-sentence Assessments

As with adults, the process of sentencing is separate from the process that determines guilt. Once the young offender is found guilty of the charge, the question becomes one of what the appropriate sentence should be. The range of available sentences is broad and includes extrajudicial sanctions and judicial sanctions that extend from absolute discharge to custodial requirements.

Before handing down a sentence, the judge may request additional information that could help the court in ensuring that the twin objectives of the young offender system are met: (1) the protection of the community, and (2) the needs of the young person in conflict with the law. The community needs protection from future victimization, and young persons' needs are met when an intervention is provided that reduces their likelihood of coming into further conflict with the law.

The court requests a pre-sentence report when the young person is already involved with probation services. A probation officer prepares the report. The report is a narrative of the young person's involvement with the law, the family history as far as the probation officer knows it, and the person's progress while on probation.

In some situations, there is concern that the young person may be suffering from disturbances that are severe enough for the court to consider them when making a disposition. Section 34 of the *YCJA* indicates the conditions under which the court can order **pre-sentence assessments** of the medical, psychological, or psychiatric condition of the young person. The relevant parts of that section are the following:

> A youth justice court may, at any stage of proceedings against a young person,
>
> a) with the consent of the young person and the prosecutor; or
> b) on its own motion or on the application of the young person or the prosecutor, where
>
> > i) the court has reasonable grounds to believe that the young person may be suffering from a physical or mental illness or disorder, a psychological disorder, an emotional disturbance, a learning disability, or mental disability
> > ii) the young person's history indicates a pattern of repeated findings of guilt under this *Act*, or
> > iii) the young person is alleged to have committed a serious violent offence,
>
> The order for an assessment shall not lead to the young person being retained in custody except in the following circumstances:
>
> c) the youth justice court is satisfied that on the evidence custody is necessary to conduct an assessment of the young person, or that on the evidence of a qualified person detention of the young person in custody is desirable to conduct the assessment *and* the young person consents to custody; or
>
> d) the young person is required to be detained in custody in respect of any other matter or by virtue of any provision of the *Criminal Code of Canada*.
>
> When a youth justice court receives a report made in respect of a young person pursuant to subsection (1),
>
> a) the court shall, subject to subsection (9), cause a copy of the report to be given
>
> > i) to the young person,
> > ii) any parent of the young person, if the parent is in attendance at the proceedings against the young person,
> > iii) counsel, if any, representing the young person, and
> > iv) the prosecutor, and

b) the court may cause a copy of the report to be given to a parent of the young person not in attendance at the proceedings against the young person if the parent is, in the opinion of the court, taking an active interest in the proceedings.

The purpose of a section 34 assessment under the *YCJA* is to make available to the youth justice court, including Crown and defence counsel, recommendations about sentences. Those recommendations are based on a clinical understanding of the emotional, cognitive, and social functioning of the young person who has come into conflict with the law, along with the needs of that person, the individual and social risk posed, and the need for intervention.

A full court-ordered assessment consists of four stages:

1. *Information gathering,* which consists of a clinical case history and a battery of cognitive, personality, and diagnostic tests that may be administered over a period of days or weeks. Interviews are also conducted with parents and others who may have information on the youth's functioning
2. *Interpreting* the various dimensions of assessment (e.g., cognitive functioning, personality, emotional functioning, social functioning, and risk of recidivism)
3. *Integration* of the information
4. *Recommending* options that provide direction and are reasonable

The court orders section 34 assessments in only a minority of cases, probably less than 5 percent. There seems to be considerable variation from area to area, and from judge to judge, about how extensively they are used. Avison and Whitehead (1997) and Whitehead and Avison (1998) examined their use in London, Ontario, and found that there was a high level of satisfaction with the assessments and the purpose they serve. Judges as well as Crown and defence counsel found them useful in reaching agreement on what kind of sentence would be appropriate. Defence counsel also found them helpful in dealing with the young person's parents on the question of what they should request.

None of the parties saw the assessments as a means of "getting the kid a free ride." Indeed, it was widely acknowledged that a defence counsel who might be looking for a noncustodial sentence would be least likely to initiate such a request because if a custodial sentence were recommended, it would carry much weight.

According to Whitehead and Avison, such assessments have two major advantages. First, as mentioned above, they increase the likelihood of reaching agreement on what an appropriate sentence should be. The parties express confidence that they are meeting the needs of the young person while they protect the community.

Second, section 34 assessments make it possible to avoid custodial sentences in some cases and, in other cases, to have shorter custodial periods than would have been likely without an assessment. The clinical judgments of psychologists and, sometimes, but less often, psychiatrists about the potential for violence or recidivism make a significant difference. In addition, the recommendations made by these professionals for courses of intervention that involve a series of steps (some custodial, some noncustodial, and some therapeutic) allow for a more comprehensive approach to addressing the needs of the young person.

SENTENCING

There are three broad types of sanctions available to the youth justice court under the *Youth Criminal Justice Act*: extrajudicial sanctions; youth sentences; and adult sentences. Youth sentences and adult sentences are judicial sanctions.

Extrajudicial Sanctions

Extrajudicial sanctions are a part of extrajudicial measures that are decided by a youth justice court judge. Under the *YCJA*, a judge must consider whether the one of extrajudicial sanctions would be satisfactory to meet the needs of the young person, the protection of society and the administration of justice.

Youth Sentences

Purpose

Section 38 indicates the purpose of youth sentences. The purpose actually has multiple parts with multiple objectives:

1. To hold a young person accountable for an offence
2. To do so through the imposition of just sanctions
3. That these sanctions have meaningful consequences for the young person
4. That the sanctions promote the young person's rehabilitation and reintegration into society
5. That this contributes to the long-term protection of the public

Principles

When a youth justice court imposes a youth sentence, it shall determine the sentence in accordance with the following principles:

1. The punishment should not be greater than would be appropriate for an adult.
2. Sentences should be similar in a "region" (the *YCJA* does not define region).
3. The sentence must be "proportionate" to the seriousness of the offence and the degree of responsibility of the young person.
4. All available sanctions other than custody should be considered for all young persons, with particular attention to the circumstances of aboriginal young persons.
5. The sentence must be the "least restrictive" that is capable of achieving the purpose outlined above.
6. The sentence must be the "one" that is "most likely" to rehabilitate and re-integrate the young person.
7. The sentence must promote a sense of "responsibility" and an "acknowledgement" of harm done to the victims and the community.
8. The sentence must consider the degree of participation in the commission of the offence.
9. The sentence must consider the harm done to the victims and whether it was intentional or reasonably foreseeable.
10. The sentence must consider whether reparations have been made to the victim or the community.
11. The sentence must consider the time spent in detention.
12. The sentence must consider the previous findings of guilt.
13. The sentence must consider any other aggravating or mitigating circumstances.

Section 39 stipulates that a young person shall not receive a custodial sentence as a youth sentence, unless one or more of the following apply:

1. The offence was violent.
2. There was previous failure to comply with noncustodial sentences.
3. It is an indictable offence for which an adult would have been liable for a term of imprisonment of more than two years and the young person has a history that indicates "a pattern of findings of guilt."

Sentencing Options

To carry out those principles, youth justice court judges have available a range of sentences. The dispositions that are available to the court are listed under section 42 of the *YCJA*:

- Reprimand
- Absolute discharge
- Conditional discharge
- Fine, not exceeding $1,000
- Restitution order for specific (not general) damages
- Prohibition or seizure order
- Community service order
- Probation
- Intensive support and supervision
- Nonresidential programs
- Custody and supervision
- Intensive rehabilitative custody and supervision

Since substantial flexibility surrounds these options, considering them in detail is worthwhile.

In-court Sanctions

A **reprimand** is a statement by the youth justice court judge that indicates to the young person that law has been violated. The statement may indicate the severity with which it could be dealt and the reasons why, on this occasion and in these circumstances, the judge considers that the young person should have learned the appropriate lesson.

An **absolute discharge** is just what it implies. The court releases a young person with no obligations or restrictions on their freedom. As Platt (1991:142) points out, however, an absolute discharge in the youth justice court does not have the same impact as one given in an ordinary court. Platt points out that "it is incorrect to request that an absolute discharge be granted to a young person so that he or she can avoid a *criminal* record." The fact is, an absolute discharge carries the same implications for the retention of a youth justice court record as any other sentence. Consequently, if a young person re-appears in court on another charge, the fact that he or she has been given an absolute discharge is admissible at the sentencing stage.

The judge must also be assured that this disposition is "in the best interests of the young person and not contrary to the public interest." Absolute discharges cannot be combined with any other disposition.

Police officers who believe a young offender is worthy of this disposition can improve the young offender's chances of obtaining an absolute discharge. To do so, they must make their views known to the Crown or give evidence in support of the defendant. Experienced defence counsel can often improve their client's chances of obtaining a discharge by involving the young person in a pretrial regimen. This will likely include giving an apology to the victim, paying for damages, and getting involved in some positive community activity.

While the *YCJA* makes provisions for reprimands and absolute discharges, it remains to be seen whether they will be used. Most of the situations in which they have been applied in the past, for example, in cases of first offences and nonviolent offences, are now to be dealt with through extrajudicial measures.

A **conditional discharge** allows for the young person "to be discharged on any conditions as the court considers appropriate." A typical condition imposed by the court would be that the offender remain at work or return to school and be supervised. Once the young person fulfills the conditions imposed, the sentence has the consequences of an absolute discharge.

A **fine** is a financial penalty. The young person can be fined an amount no larger than would be required of an adult for a similar offence. The maximum fine under the *YCJA* is $1,000 [*YCJA* 42(1)(d)], and the mandatory minimum fines stated in the *Criminal Code of Canada* do not apply to young offenders. In fining the defendant, the judge must consider the young person's ability to pay the fine. If the young person has no savings and no source of income (such as a part-time job), the court will not use this option. Often, small fines are used with another disposition.

For more significant fines, youth justice court judges will usually allow the young offender to make periodic payments. Some jurisdictions also allow offenders to work off fines by becoming involved in some form of community service. Youths who do not meet their fine obligations must explain the situation to the court. Failure to appear can result in an arrest warrant being issued, and judges can always substitute a more severe sentence. Young persons who default on a fine, however, cannot be incarcerated.

The courts can order the young person to make restitution or pay compensation for any property taken or damaged during the commission of the offence. **Restitution** involves returning any property that may have been taken to its rightful owner. **Compensation** usually involves a monetary payment when the offender cannot make restitution or it is inappropriate in the circumstances. It can also involve "compensation in kind" by way of personal service.

Subsections 50(4) and 50(6) indicate, however, that the person to be compensated needs to be consulted and must agree to the compensation. One difference between compensation orders for young persons and adults is that compensation must be for specific damage and not general damages [*YCJA* 42(2)(e)]. Otherwise, the same basic conditions that apply to fines apply to compensation orders. Thus, the judge must consider the offender's ability to pay. As with fines, restitution and compensation orders are often used with other sentences, such as probation.

Prohibition means that the youth justice court can also prohibit or forbid a young person from owning something that they could otherwise legally possess, if it were not that they had been involved in the commission of the offence. For example, the court may disallow a young person from having any of the following in his or her possession: firearm, cross-bow, prohibited weapon, restricted weapon, prohibited device, ammunition, or explosive substance. Property may also be forfeited and seized. A young computer hacker may find that he is no longer in possession of his personal computer.

As with fines, the youth court is not bound by mandatory minimums attached to some prohibitions identified in the *Criminal Code of Canada*. The court is obliged, however, to provide a maximum time up to a period of two years after the completion of a custodial portion of a sentence [*YCJA* 51(4)].

Community-Based Sanctions

Community service orders (CSOs) are used increasingly in the youth justice system. A judge may require the young person to perform up to 240 hours of community service. The community service cannot be extended beyond one year. Furthermore, the judge must determine that the young offender "is a suitable candidate for such an order" and "the order does not interfere with the normal hours of work or education of the young person" [*YCJA* 54(7)(b)].

Most communities have a community service coordinator who works out of a local probation office. Community service is generally sponsored by a nonprofit or service organization, such as a youth club, native centre, or service club. Often, the John Howard Society plays a significant role in coordinating and supervising young people serving CSOs.

Community service orders are a means for young offenders to "pay off" property damage that resulted from acts of vandalism. Judges generally use CSOs to make young offenders more aware of the consequences of their actions and to make them "give something back" to their communities. Thus, the court may require a young person who has victimized an elderly person to perform work around a retirement home.

Occasionally, the judge may impose a personal service order where the offender must work directly for the victim. This is most often used when the victim is a corporate entity, such as a store in which the offender shoplifted, or a car dealer where the young offender was caught slashing tires. The same time limits for a CSO apply in these situations.

Young persons who fail to abide by a CSO may be charged with the offence of failure to comply. This is a summary offence, and the young person is liable to a maximum sentence of six months in open custody.

The youth court may impose a **probation** order on the young person for a period not exceeding two years for most offences. This is extended to three years where the sentence for an adult would be life sentence. If the young person commits another offence while on probation, the court can extend the period of probation. Young persons may serve probation orders either continuously or intermittently, and they generally include subsidiary conditions. In Ontario, a professional probation officer usually supervises probation orders.

Subsection 55(1) of the *YCJA* indicates the conditions that must appear on the probation order. These are that the young person must "keep the peace and be of good behaviour" and must "appear before the youth justice court when required to do so." Subsection 55(2) specifies conditions that the judge *may* impose on the order. These possibilities include the provisions that the young person

- is bound by the probation order and must report to a designated probation officer, must notify the court or probation officer of any change in address, employment or education status,
- must remain in a specific locality or jurisdiction,
- must try to obtain and maintain employment,
- must attend school or a suitable training program,
- must reside with a parent or other designated adult who is willing to take responsibility for the young person,
- must reside at a specific location, and
- must comply with any other reasonable conditions set out by the court.

The courts tailor probation orders to suit the particular circumstances of the offender. They may require offenders from homes with little supervision to report to their probation officer regularly. In extreme situations, the courts may ask the young person to reside in a specific home. In more stable circumstances, the order may not require reporting beyond the initial contact. Some probation officers are excellent at finding an effective "program" for a troubled young offender. Others, for workload reasons and otherwise, do little more than see the young person biweekly for a 20-minute chat.

The schooling provisions may pose particular problems for a community. Many young offenders are "problem cases" for school officials and have long histories of suspensions and expulsions. Many judges correctly perceive the young person's need for schooling, but most schools do not have adequate facilities for handling tough cases. Often, calls from school officials to the police involve problems with young people who are already on probation. For many young offenders on probation, there is constant conflict with their probation officer, school officials, and the police. Ultimately, many of the worse cases report back to court, where the only viable alternative becomes custody.

Most young offenders complete their probation orders successfully. Some clearly do not. Where the young person consistently breaks a probation order or has no intention of complying with it, the probation officer may charge the young person with a "failure to comply with a court order." A breach of probation is the only offence relating to non-compliance with a sentence that can lead to a sentence of secure custody.

A young person may be sentenced to an **intensive support and supervision program** if the provincial director has determined that a program to enforce the order is available. Such programs would have to be seen to address the needs of the young person and contribute to rehabilitation and re-integration without placing the society at risk.

The judge's order may be for the young person to **attend a nonresidential program,** if the provincial director has determined that a program to enforce the order is available, for a maximum of 240 hours over a period of not more than six months.

The *YCJA* does not specify the specific conditions that "intensive support" or "non-residential" programs must have. As with all else in the *YCJA*, however, the expectation is that the programs will assist young persons in areas of their life where they have needs. Some such programs may well focus on life skills, others on anger management, and still others on rehabilitation from alcohol or drug abuse. The *YCJA* leaves it to individual communities to put in place the programs that may be of the greatest assistance to young persons and to provincial directors and judges to determine their appropriateness in given circumstances.

Custody and Supervision

Judges may also sentence young persons to periods of custody and supervision. It needs to be recalled that we are still dealing with youth sentences, not adult sentences that young persons may qualify for. Under the *YCJA*, orders are for **custody and supervision**; that is, a period of incarceration plus a period of supervision. The supervision period is to be one-half as long as the custody period. The idea is that the supervision part of the sentence will assist in the young person's rehabilitation and re-integration into society.

The length of these custody and supervision orders varies by the severity of the offence. The total of the periods is not to exceed two years, unless the offence is a serious or presumptive one.

> *Serious offences.* If the offence is one for which the punishment under the *Criminal Code of Canada* is imprisonment for life, the maximum is three years.
> *Presumptive Offences.* The youth sentences for presumptive offences fall into three categories.

For the following offences the length of the order may not exceed three years (two years of custody and one year of supervision): attempt to commit murder; manslaughter; and aggravated sexual assault or a serious violent offence when combined with two previous judicial determinations in different proceedings [YCJA 2(1)(a)(ii)(iii)(iv)].

1. For first-degree murder, the sentence may not exceed 10 years (six years of custody and four years of supervision).
2. For second-degree murder, the sentence may not exceed seven years (four years of custody and three years of supervision).

The youth justice court may make an order for **intensive rehabilitative custody and supervision** [*YCJA* 42(7)]. Such orders may only be made when the following conditions are met:

1. The young person has been found guilty of a presumptive offence.
2. The young person is suffering from a mental illness or psychological disorder.
3. A plan of treatment and intensive supervision has been developed.
4. The program has been determined to be available and appropriate for the young person.

From the above, it can be seen that the number of sentencing options available under the *YCJA* to deal with the most serious cases has increased in comparison with the *Young Offenders Act*. Again, this is in keeping with the objective of the *YCJA* to focus court (i.e., judicial) responses on the most serious cases and to use extrajudicial measures for the rest.

The *YCJA* also makes provision for young persons to receive "adult sentences."

Adult Sentences

An important feature of the *YCJA* is that it identifies a category of offences that are presumed to carry an adult sentence if committed by a young person over the age of 14 years; these are called **presumptive offences.**

The presumptive offences are the following:

1. First- or second-degree murder
2. Attempt to commit murder
3. Manslaughter
4. Aggravated sexual assault
5. Serious violent offences combined with two previous convictions for serious violent offences under subsection 42(9)

When it is alleged that a young person who has reached the age of 14 years has committed one of these offences, it is presumed that the young person will be liable for an adult sentence. It then becomes the responsibility of the defence to make an application for an order that the young person should, if found guilty, be subjected to a youth sentence instead.

The Crown may make an application for an order that a young person be liable to an adult sentence if found guilty of an offence for which an adult is liable to imprisonment for a term of more than two years. If the Crown intends to seek an adult sentence, either by making an application or by establishing that the offence is a presumptive offence, the Crown must give notice to the young person and to the youth justice court prior to the young person entering a plea [*YCJA* 64(2)].

If the young person does not oppose the application by the Crown, an adult sentence shall be imposed [*YCJA* 64(5)].

If the Crown gives notice that an adult sentence will not be sought, the court shall order that the young person is not liable to an adult sentence and order a ban on publication.

The decision as to the merits of the application for a youth sentence or for an adult sentence is made at a **sentencing hearing.** This hearing takes place after the issue of guilt has been decided. At the sentencing hearing, the Crown, the defence, and the parents of the young person are given an opportunity to be heard [*YCJA* 71].

In making its decision on applications, the youth justice court must consider the following:

1. The seriousness and circumstances of the offence
2. The age, maturity, character, background, and previous record of the young person
3. Other factors the court considers relevant
4. Whether a youth sentence is of sufficient length to hold the young person accountable for the offending behaviour
5. A pre-sentence report

The **onus,** or burden of proof, is on the applicant. When the court makes a decision, it "shall state the reasons for the decision." When a young person who is subject to an adult sentence is sentenced to imprisonment, that incarceration must be in a youth custody facility separate from adults or in a provincial correctional facility for adults or a penitentiary [*YCJA* 76(1)]. If the young person is under the age of 18 years, however, the placement should be in a youth custody facility [76(2)(a)], and if the person is aged 18 years or over, in a provincial correctional facility [76(2)(b)]. Usually, no young person would remain in a youth facility after attaining the age of 20 years [76(9)].

Adult sentences, while provided for in the *YCJA*, are meant to be used in exceptional cases, where it is clearly demonstrated that a youth sentence is not long enough to hold the youth accountable. When an adult sentence is considered necessary it should still be lighter than the average sentence imposed an adults in order to reflect the greater dependence and reduced maturity of youth.

Exercise 3

DEFINITIONS

Please define the following terms:

1. Pre-sentence assessment:

_____

_____

_____

_____

_____

_____

_____

_____

_____

2. Reprimand:

_____

_____

_____

_____

_____

_____

_____

_____

_____

3. Absolute discharge:

_____

_____

_____

_____

_____

_____

_____

_____

4. Community service order:

_____

_____

_____

_____

_____

_____

_____

_____

_____

5. Presumptive offence:

_____

_____

_____

_____

_____

_____

_____

_____

_____

TRUE OR FALSE

1. T F Pre-sentence reports are usually prepared by the police officer who made the arrest.

2. T F Once a young person receives an absolute discharge, that discharge cannot be admitted again in court.

3. T F The purpose of a youth sentence is to appropriately punish the young person for the harm done.

4. T F A youth justice court judge may require a young person to perform up to 240 hours of community service.

5. T F Community service orders are reserved for those 16 and 17 years old and never used for those 14 and 15 years old.

MULTIPLE CHOICE

1. Which of the following is not a concern of the *Youth Criminal Justice Act* when it comes to sentencing?

   a) protection of society
   b) holding young persons accountable for their behaviour
   c) ensuring that young people show respect for the judge and officers of the court
   d) the mental and emotional health of the young person

2. Which of the following is not likely to be found in a pre-sentence report?

   a) results of interviews with the young person
   b) results of interviews with the accomplices of the young person
   c) information on the young person's age and attitude
   d) plans the young person might have about the future

3. There is no reason to believe that pre-sentence assessments are found to be useful by

   a) judges
   b) defence council
   c) Crown prosecutors
   d) young persons

4. Which of the following may not be used as a condition of probation?

   a) report to a probation officer
   b) try to obtain employment
   c) attend school
   d) love, honour, and obey parents

5. Which of the following conditions is not permitted in a probation order?

   a) must remain in a specific city
   b) must try to obtain employment
   c) must reside in a specific location
   d) all of the above are permitted

SHORT ESSAYS

1. What are the principal differences between pre-sentence reports and pre-sentence assessments?

   _____

   _____

   _____

   _____

   _____

   _____

   _____

   _____

   _____

2. Discuss the following statement: "There is no reason to believe that the *Youth Criminal Justice Act* is interested in the protection of society."

   _____

   _____

   _____

   _____

   _____

   _____

   _____

   _____

3. You are a police officer who has questioned and arrested a young person. You are going to be a witness if the case goes to court. On the basis of your discussions with the young person and her family, you form the view that an absolute discharge could be the right disposition in this case. What would you do next?

_____

_____

_____

_____

_____

_____

_____

4. What value do you suppose a restitution or compensation order has as part of a disposition for a young offender?

_____

_____

_____

_____

_____

_____

_____

5. You are a police officer who is asked to speak to a community group. Its members are upset about community service orders because they think that it is simply a way of going soft on young offenders. They ask you, "What use are they anyway?" Your response is:

_____

_____

_____

_____

_____

_____

_____

_____

_____

_____

6. Several things are to be taken into consideration when a youth justice court imposes a youth sentence. Identify seven of them.

1) _____

_____

2) _____

_____

3) _____

_____

4) _____

_____

5) _____

_____

6) _____

_____

7) _____

_____

7. Under what conditions may an adult sentence be imposed on a young person?

_____

_____

_____

_____

_____

_____

_____

_____

_____

_____

_____

_____

_____

_____

CHAPTER

9

Custodial Sentences

Learning Outcomes

Students who have mastered this chapter will have the ability to do the following:

- Describe *the difference between "least degree of restraint" and "higher degree of restraint."*
- Identify *the things to be taken with consideration in deciding the appropriate degree of restraint in a custodial decision.*
- Distinguish *between "reintegrative leave" and "day release."*
- Explain *the role of conditional supervision in dealing with young persons.*
- Describe and explain *the difference between mandatory and nonmandatory conditions involved in orders of conditional supervision.*
- Explain *the circumstances under which a police officer may arrest a young person under an order of conditional supervision.*
- Describe *some of the types of custodial facilities that exist in Ontario.*
- Explain *why a range of service options is useful in dealing with young persons.*

CUSTODIAL PROVISIONS

Levels of Custody

The purpose of the system of custody is the protection of society through "safe, fair, and humane" restraints that will assist the rehabilitation and reintegration of young persons into the community [*YCJA* 83].

The *Youth Criminal Justice Act* [*YCJA* 85] requires that there be at least two "levels" of custody. Formerly, these were referred to as "open custody" and "secure custody," but the *YCJA* does not use these words. The two levels of custody in the *YCJA* are distinguished by the "degree of restraint" they impose on the young person. One level of custody is referred to as the one with the "least degree of restraint," and the other level is referred to variously as "more than a minimal degree of restraint," "a higher degree of restraint," and "increased degree of restraint." We will use the expression **higher degree of restraint** to refer to the level of custody that is greater than the **least degree of restraint.**

Ontario has decided to use the more well known terms "open custody" and "secure custody." The practical implication is that both sets of terms will be used. It needs to be kept in mind that **open custody** means a facility with the least degree of restraint, while **secure custody** means a facility with more than a minimal degree of restraint.

Among the principles to be applied in using custody to achieve its purposes are the following [*YCJA* 83(2)(a)(c)]:

1. The "least restrictive measures" should be used that are consistent with the protection of the public, of personnel working with young persons, and of young persons.
2. The system of custody and supervision should facilitate the involvement of members of the public and the families of young persons.

The *YCJA* leaves it to each province to determine the nature and types of facilities that will provide the two levels of restraint. It is up to the provincial director to determine which facility and which levels of restraint best serve the needs of the young person and the community under the *YCJA*.

Provincial director is a term found often in the *YCJA*. The term applies to a fairly broad category of persons. It means a person, a group or class of persons or a body appointed by a province who performs functions under the *YCJA*. Persons in charge of probation services as well as persons in charge of provincial correctional facilities, for example, are "provincial directors." There is not, therefore, a single provincial director of Ontario; there are many individuals and groups who hold that designation.

Degree of Restraint

The types of facilities that are *likely* to be considered as providing the **least degree of restraint** that may be suitable for a custodial sentence are a community residential centre, group home, child care institution, or forest or wilderness camp. Although it is considered to have the least degree of restraint, residents are not permitted to leave the facility, unless staff accompanies them or they have an authorized temporary release. Whenever possible, such facilities should be close to the community in which the young person lives. This would help with the reintegration of the young person into the community by making it easier for the young person to remain in contact with parents and local schools.

Some least degree of restraint facilities resemble adult halfway houses in that they do not have an "institutional look," thus allowing them to blend into their neighbourhood. In these residences, young persons are expected to perform some typical household duties, such as keeping their sleeping areas tidy, occasionally helping to cook meals, washing dishes, and taking out the trash. Some facilities have classrooms and teachers who are available daily; many use temporary absence provisions to allow residents to attend local schools.

Higher degree of restraint facilities are places that afford a higher level of containment of young persons. In Ontario, such facilities are locked settings surrounded by a security fence. This gives them the look of an "adult prison." Staff supervision is greater than in least degree of restraint facilities, and movement within the facility is also restricted. Typically, the residents' rooms have locks on the doors so that they can be "locked down" at night.

Higher degree of restraint facilities have regular classrooms, and most have segregation rooms for those who have serious behaviour problems or who commit violations of the rules of the institution. Young persons who are placed in higher degree of restraint facilities are those who pose a significant risk to themselves or to others.

We can expect that what constitutes "least" as compared with "higher" degree of restraint will vary both within and across jurisdictions. There are limits, however, on how these definitions can be applied. Bala (1997:241) reports a Nova Scotia case, where the government attempted to use a former adult jail as a youth facility. It was classified as an open as well as closed custody facility, with "open custody" meaning that the cells were unlocked. The courts did not share the Nova Scotia government's view of what open custody meant.

Terms of Custody

Many readers would undoubtedly have seen television broadcasts and movies that depict the system of justice in the United States. It is common for American judges to impose indeterminate sentences where they sentence the offender from, say, seven to 10 years in prison. Indeterminate sentences do not form part of the legal landscape in Canada.[1] Nearly all periods of incarceration are determinate—that is, a definite time limit is assigned.

Each province will have to decide whether judges will determine level of restraint for custodial sentences or whether an administrative approach will be taken, and it will be decided by the provincial director. If it is to be done by the provincial director, then there will be provision for an independent Custody Review Board. Subject to review would be cases where a young person would be placed in a facility that has more than a minimal degree of restraint or where there is to be a transfer of a young person to a higher or increased degree of restraint. The *YCJA* leaves it to the provincial director to decide the appropriate level of custody, unless the province decides otherwise.

Regardless of who makes the decision, subsection 85(5)(a) identifies the "appropriate level of custody" as the one that is "least restrictive" to the young person, having regard to the following:

1. The seriousness of the offence and the circumstances in which that offence was committed
2. The needs and circumstances of the young person, including proximity to family, school, employment, and support services
3. The safety of other young persons in custody
4. The interests of society
5. That the level of restraint should allow for the best possible match of programs to the young person's needs and behaviour
6. The likelihood of escape

Review of Sentences

When young persons are committed to periods of custody beyond one year, they must be automatically returned to the youth criminal justice court for a review of the sentence at the end of the first year [*YCJA* 94(1)]. The *YCJA* [s. 94] also provides for reviews "on request." Reviews may be initiated by the provincial director and will take place if requested during the period of incarceration by the young person, the young person's parent, or the Attorney General. To be eligible for a review, the youth sentence must be for less than one year, and meet the following criteria:

1. The young person must have served at least 30 days in custody from the date of the sentence.
2. The young person must have served at least one-third of the period of the sentence.
3. At any point in time, "where a youth justice court is satisfied that there are grounds for the review."

If young persons receive sentences of more than one year, then they are eligible for a review, if they have served six months after the date of the most recent sentence.

A young person's sentence can be reviewed on any of the following grounds:

1. The young person has made sufficient progress to justify a change in sentence.
2. The circumstances that led to the youth sentence have changed materially.
3. New services or programs are available that were not available at the time of the sentence.
4. The opportunities for rehabilitation are now greater in the community.
5. On such other grounds as the youth criminal justice court considers appropriate.

This mandated review assessment is, what we might call, asymmetrical. That is, the courts can shorten the young person's period of custody; they cannot lengthen it, unless the young person commits another offence. No review will be heard if the young person's case is being appealed.

A major distinction between how adults and young persons are handled while in custody relates to release provisions. Adult correctional officials have the authority to modify the offender's term in custody significantly by granting parole. Provincial officials in charge of young persons do not have that authority. Any change to the young person's custody can only be made by the youth justice court. Thus, the youth justice court is far more involved in the young person's sentence and treatment than are ordinary courts with adult offenders.

Reintegrative Leave Provisions

The *YCJA* [s. 91] allows for reintegrative leaves and day releases. Reintegrative leaves may be allowed for not more than 30 days. **Reintegrative leave** is at the discretion of the provincial director and allows the young person to be absent from custody with or without an escort. It is used for medical, compassionate, or humanitarian purposes or for the purpose of rehabilitation or reintegration into the community. For example, such leaves may be given when a close relative of the young person is ill or if he or she requests to attend a relative's funeral. Corrections officials may also allow a young person a reintegrative leave when they require some medical service that cannot be provided at the institution.

Another form of reintegrative leave is generally known as **day release**. Day releases usually allow the young person to leave the institution during the day to perform some duty and then return at night. The exact days and time for these releases are at the discretion of the provincial director. The *YCJA* identifies several reasons for allowing a day release. These include the following:

1. Attending school
2. Continuing employment, or performing domestic or other duties for the family
3. Participating in employment or training related programs
4. Attending outpatient treatment programs.

The appropriate authority may revoke these leaves at any time. Young persons who do not return once their reintegrative leave has been revoked or who fail to follow any conditions applied to the absence may be arrested without a warrant and returned to custody.

Conditional Supervision

Section 96 provides that a young person being held in custody may be released from custody and placed under conditional supervision if the provincial director is satisfied that the needs of the young person and the interests of society would be better served. The provincial director must make such a recommendation to the youth justice court. Further, all youth sentences imposed under subsection 42(2)(n) contain provision for a portion of their sentence (one-third) to be served under supervision in the community.

An order for **conditional supervision** allows a young person to serve part of their sentence in the community with a set of restrictions or "conditions" which they must abide by. Conditional supervision is meant to allow for a more gradual release of the young person from custody back to the community. Conditional supervision orders are generally more restrictive than probation orders, so they give the youth justice court a greater degree of control when dealing with sentences.

The *mandatory* conditions to be imposed on the young person are outlined in subsection 97(1) and require that the young person do the following:

a) Keep the peace and be of good behaviour.
b) Report to the provincial director and be under the supervision of the provincial director.
c) Inform the provincial director immediately on being arrested or questioned by the police.
d) Report to the police, or any named individual, as instructed by the provincial director.
e) Advise the provincial director of the young person's address of residence and report immediately to the provincial director any change

   i) in that address,
   ii) in the young person's normal occupation, including employment, vocational or educational training, and volunteer work,
   iii) in the young person's family or financial situation, and
   iv) that may reasonably be expected to affect the young person's ability to comply with the conditions of the sentence.

g) Do not own, possess, or have the control of any weapon, as defined in section 2 of the *Criminal Code of Canada*, except as authorized by the order.
h) Comply with additional conditions set by the provincial director that address the needs of the young person and promote reintegration into the community and offer adequate protection to the public.

When the conditions are for young persons who have been found guilty of presumptive and other serious offences, the youth justice court may also impose other, *nonmandatory*, conditions [ss. 105(3)], such as the following:

a) On release, travel directly to the young person's place of residence, or to any other place that is noted in the order.
b) Make reasonable efforts to obtain and maintain suitable employment.
c) Attend school or such other place of learning, training, or recreation, as is appropriate, if the court is satisfied that a suitable program is available.
d) Reside with a parent, or such other adult that the court considers appropriate, who is willing to provide for the care and maintenance of the young person.

e) Reside in such place as the provincial director may specify.
f) Remain within the territorial jurisdiction of one or more courts named in the order.
g) Comply with other reasonable conditions set out in the order, including conditions that address the needs of the young person and promote reintegration into the community while securing the good conduct of the young person and preventing the commission of other offences.

A prime difference between probation orders and conditional supervision orders is the ability of the authorities to apprehend the young person who breaks a condition of the order. Young persons are in violation of a probation order if they actually breach a condition and adequate evidence exists to prove the breach. Under a conditional supervision order, however, it is sufficient to revoke the order, if there are "reasonable grounds to believe that a young person has breached or *is about to breach* a condition of an order."

Once the young person's order is suspended by the provincial director, the young person may be remanded to custody if the provincial director believes it is appropriate. Once the young person is in remand, the correctional authorities have 48 hours to either cancel the suspension or refer the young person to the youth justice court for a review.

The provincial director may also have a warrant issued for the apprehension of the young person [ss. 107(1)]. Any police officer may execute those warrants anywhere in the country. Police officers have the authority under subsection 107(3) to arrest a young person without a warrant if they have reasonable grounds to believe that a warrant is outstanding. Once a young person has been arrested, the young person is to be brought before the provincial director "without unreasonable delay" and, in any event, within 24 hours [ss. 107(4)(a)].

Exercise 1

DEFINITIONS

Please define the following terms:

1. Least degree of restraint:

_____

_____

_____

_____

_____

_____

_____

_____

_____

2. Higher degree of restraint:

_____

_____

_____

_____

_____

_____

_____

_____

3. Provincial director:

_____

_____

_____

_____

_____

_____

_____

_____

4. Reintegrative leave:

_____

_____

_____

_____

_____

_____

_____

_____

_____

_____

5. Day release:

_____

_____

_____

_____

_____

_____

_____

_____

_____

_____

6. Conditional supervision order:

_____

_____

_____

_____

_____

_____

_____

_____

_____

TRUE OR FALSE

1. T F "Least degree of restraint" when applied to a custodial facility means that the residents are allowed to come and go as they please, but only during the day.

2. T F A facility with a "higher degree of restraint" means that the extent of restraint or control is greater than in a facility with a "lower degree of restraint."

3. T F In contrast to the United States, the practice in Canada is to have indeterminate sentences.

When a custodial disposition is made, the following are to be taken into account:

4. T F The highest level of restraint available

5. T F The safety of the young person

MULTIPLE CHOICE

1. Which of the following is least consistent with a facility in a higher degree of restraint?

   a) community reintegration
   b) "lock down"
   c) classrooms
   d) segregation cells

2. If a young person turns 18 years while serving a term of custody,

   a) the term of custody ends
   b) the offender is automatically transferred to a correctional facility for adults
   c) the term continues
   d) the term of custody is automatically extended so that custody will last for at least 12 additional months

3. Changes to a young person's custody can be made by

   a) correctional officials
   b) the provincial director
   c) the youth justice court
   d) the Crown prosecutor

4. Young persons who do not return once their reintegrative leave has been revoked may be

   a) arrested only with a warrant and returned to custody
   b) arrested without a warrant and returned to their parents' home
   c) arrested without a warrant and returned to custody
   d) arrested and subjected to treatment

5. Conditional supervision orders allow young persons to

   a) serve dispositions to secure custody in open custody
   b) hold a job or go to school while living in a secure custody facility
   c) serve the remainder of their sentence in the community

d) serve the remainder of their custodial disposition with almost no conditions imposed on them, except for staying out of trouble

SHORT ESSAYS

1. Describe the underlying reasons for having facilities that provide custody with the least degree of restraint.

_____

_____

_____

_____

_____

_____

_____

_____

_____

_____

2. Identify five factors that are to be taken into account when a sentence is to be served in a facility with a higher degree of restraint.

1) _____

2) _____

3) _____

4) _____

5) _____

3. Identify four purposes for which reintegrative leaves may be granted.

1) _____

2) _____

3) _____

4) _____

4. Identify five mandatory conditions to be imposed as part of a conditional supervision order.

1) _____

_____

2) _____

_____

3) _____

_____

4) _____

_____

5) _____

_____

5. Identify five nonmandatory conditions that may be imposed as part of a conditional supervision order.

1) _____

_____

2) _____

_____

3) _____

_____

4) _____

_____

5) _____

_____

6. Identify four purposes for which day release may be granted.

1) _____

2) _____

3) _____

4) _____

7. Under what conditions may a police officer arrest a young person who is under an order of conditional supervision?

_____

_____

_____

_____

_____

_____

_____

_____

_____

CUSTODIAL SENTENCES

In Ontario, young persons who are between the ages of 12 and 15 years when they commit an offence are known as **phase I offenders**. These young persons become the responsibility of the Ministry of Community, Family, and Children's Services. On the other hand, young persons who are between the ages of 16 and 17 years when they commit an offence are known as **phase II offenders**. These young people become the responsibility of the Ministry of the Solicitor General and the Ministry of Public Safety and Security.

Generally, institutions for phase I offenders have a more extensive range of programs available for the young persons. Phase II facilities, on the other hand, often have fewer programs and are a step closer to what we would normally see in an adult facility.

As indicated, the *YCJA* requires two levels of custody for young offenders—open and secure. In Ontario, there are both custodial levels for phase I and phase II offenders. The majority of phase II facilities in Ontario are operated by agencies. For the past two decades, it has been the policy of the Ontario government to allow agencies to play an increasingly larger role in providing residential services for young offenders.

Several of the major centres that fall under the Ministry of Community, Family and Children's Services are listed in Table 9.1. It is not unusual for some facilities to be at capacity and for young persons to be transferred to institutions in other parts of the province. Table 9.2 lists phase II facilities operated by the Ministry of Public Safety and Security.

Table 9.1 Phase I (12–15 years of age) Centres under the Ministry of Community, Family, and Children's Services

Facility	Location	Security	Details
Crossroads, Sound Learning Program	Newmarket	Open Custody & Detention	
Cedar Grove Transitional Living	Newmarket	Open Custody & Detention	
Mckinnon House	Oshawa	Custody & Detention	10 beds; co-ed
Morton House	Barrie	Open Detention	
Douglas House	Orillia	Open Detention	
New Path	Cookstown	Open Detention	
Cerminara's Boys' Residence	Niagara Falls	Custody & Detention	9 beds; male only
Victoria St. Residence	Brantford	Custody & Detention	8 beds; co-ed
David S. Horne	Fonthhill	Custody & Detention	10 beds; co-ed
Bernhardt House	Hamilton	Custody & Detention	9 beds; co-ed
George R. Force	Hamilton	Custody & Detention	12 beds; co-ed
Peninsula Youth Centre	Hamilton	Secure Custody & Secure Detention	30 beds; co-ed
Arrell youth Centre	Hamilton	Secure Custody & Secure Detention	22 beds; co-ed
Achievement St. Lawrence	Kingston	Custody & Detention	10 beds; co-ed
Corbyville Children's Home	Corbyville	Custody & Detention	10 beds; co-ed
Ventures Group Home	Gananoque	Open Custody & Detention	8 beds; male only
Anago Resources	Parkhill	Custody & Detention	5 beds; female only
Anago Resources, King St. Detention	London	Custody & Detention	12 beds; co-ed
Community Homes, Adelaide St.	London	Custody & Detention	8 beds; co-ed
Community Homes, Sylvan St.	London	Custody & Detention	8 beds; co-ed
Craigwood Youth Services, Midway Unit	Ailsa Craig	Secure Custody & Detention	10 beds; co-ed
Craigwood Youth Services, Woodview	Ailsa Craig	Secure Custody & Detention	
Maurice H. Genest Detention Centre for Youth	London	Secure Custody & Detention	18 beds; co-ed
Bluewater Centre	Goderich	Secure Custody & Detention	
Forest Youth Centre	Forest	Open Custody & Detention	8 beds; co-ed
Hoe Manor	Peterburg	Open Custody & Detention	16 beds; co-ed
Maryvale Good Shepherd Centre	Windsor	Secure Custody & Detention	16 beds; co-ed

Facility	Location	Security	Details
Renaissance Homes Inc., Dover Youth Home	Dover	Custody & Detention	10 beds; co-ed
Renaissance Windsor	Windsor	Custody & Detention	10 beds; co-ed
Pine Hill York	Chesley	Open Custody & Detention	10 beds; co-ed
CASATTA/Burlington	Burlington	Custody & Detention	8 beds; co-ed
McMillan Centre for Youth	Milton	Custody & Detention	16 beds; co-ed
Sprucelane	Acton	Custody & Detention	10 beds; co-ed
Stuart Farms	Oakville	Custody & Detention	9 beds; co-ed
CASATTA/ Cambridge	Cambridge	Custody & Detention	9 beds; co-ed
CASATTA/ Wellington	Guelph	Custody & Detention	8 beds; co-ed
Crisis Centre Nipissing Detention	North Bay	Custody & Detention	10 beds; co-ed
Crisis Centre – Custody Residence	North Bay	Custody & Detention	10 beds
Near North Youth Centre	North Bay	Secure Custody & Secure Detention	10 beds; co-ed
Nee-Gi-Nan	Cochrane	Custody & Detention	10 beds; co-ed
Terra-Firma	Monteith	Custody	5 beds; co-ed
Pinegar Youth Services	Kirkland Lake	Secure Custody & Secure Detention	12 beds; co-ed
Payukotayno	Moosonee	Detention & Custody	5 beds; co-ed
Alpha House	Pembroke	Open Custody & Open Detention	4 beds; co-ed
Cornwell Youth Residence	Cornwall	Open Custody & Open Detention	12 beds; male only
Sherwood Observation and Detention Centre	Ottawa	Secure Custody & Secure Detention	9 beds; co-ed
William E. Hay Centre	Ottawa	Secure Custody & Secure Detention	24 beds
The Boy's Home Site #1	Bridgeway	Open Custody & Detention	8 beds; male only
The Boy's Home Site #2	Toronto	Open Custody & Detention	8 beds; male only
The Boy's Home Site #3	Withrow	Open Custody & Detention	8 beds; male only
The Boy's Home Site #4	Toronto	Open Custody & Detention	8 beds; male only
CASATTA/Rexdale	Rexdale	Custody & Detention	10 beds; co-ed
CASATTA/Warrendale	Rexdale	Custody & Detention	10 beds; co-ed
Fernie House – Cedar Brook I	Toronto	Open Custody & Detention	6 beds; male only
Fernie House – Cedar Brook II	Toronto	Open Custody & Detention	6 beds; male only
Dellcrest Logan	Toronto	Open Custody & Detention	8 beds; male only

Facility	Location	Security	Details
Fernie House	Scarborough	Open Custody & Detention	9 beds; male only
Kennedy House Youth Services, Site #3	Scarborough	Open Custody & Detention	8 beds; male only
Kennedy House Youth Services, Site #4	Scarborough	Open Custody & Detention	8 beds; male only
Turning Point Services – Humberview	Rexdale	Custody &Detention	10 beds; co-ed
Turning Point Services – Yorklea	East York	Custody & Detention	10 beds; co-ed
York Detention Centre Detention PD: Donna Hansplant	Toronto	Secure Custody & Detention	28 beds; co-ed
Syl Apps Youth Centre	Oakville	Secure Custody & Detention	52 beds; co-ed
St. John's	Uxbridge	Secure Custody & Detention	80 beds; male only
Sault Ste. Marie Observation and Detention	Sault Ste. Marie	Custody & Detention	8 beds; co-ed
Sudbury Youth Services	Sudbury	Custody & Detention	10 beds; co-ed
Bruce J. McKitrick	Thunder Bay	Custody & Detention	8 beds; co-ed
Jack McGuire Centre	Thunder Bay	Custody & Detention	7 beds; co-ed
S.T.E.P. (Short Term Emergency Placement)	Kenora	Custody & Detention	8 beds; co-ed
Young Starr House	Kenora	Open Detention	
William W. Creighton Youth Services S.T.E.P.	Longbow Lake	Open Custody & Detention	8 beds
Kenora District Jail Young Offender Unit	Kenora	Secure Custody & Secure Detention	4 beds
J.J. Kelso Centre	Thunder Bay	Secure Custody & Secure Detention	18 beds

Table 9.2 Phase 2 (16–17 years of age) Facilities under the Ministry of Public Safety and Security

Facility	Location	Security
Eagle Rock Youth Residence	Sarnia	Open
Community Resources of Halton	Burlington	Open
Newcombe House	Hamilton	Open
Patterson House	Hamilton	Open
Dovercourt Youth Home	Toronto	Open
Dowling Youth Home	Toronto	Open
Durhamdale House	Pickering	Open
Marjorie Amos House	Brampton	Open
Gifford Contract Homes	Toronto	Open

Facility	Location	Security
Fairbairn House	Ottawa	Open
Maison de Mon Pere	Cornwell	Open
Talitha House	Ottawa	Open
Mee-Quam Youth Residence	Cochrane	Open
Ivik Youth Residential Centre	Fort Frances	Open
Kairos Youth Residential Centre	Thunder Bay	Open
Yonge House	Kingston	Open
Butch Collins Residence	Windsor	Open
Onesimus House	Belleville	Open
Art Eggleton House	Toronto	Open
Blue Jays Lodge	Toronto	Open
Gord Saunders House	Sault Ste. Marie	Open
King Clancey Residence	Toronto	Open
St. Paul Street West Residence	St. Catherines	Open
Terry Fox House	Toronto	Open
Phoenix House	Navan	Open
Pine Hill Youth Residence	Chesley	Open
Portage Ontario for Drug Dependencies, Inc.	Elora	Open
Hope Harbour Home	Kitchener	Open
Revelations House	Kingston	Open
Roebuck Home	Peterborough	Open
Calvert House	Hamilton	Open
Cuthbert House	Brampton	Open
Harmony House	London	Open
Wycliffe Booth House	Ilderton	Open
Cedar Youth Residence	Sudbury	Open
Chaudiere House	Ottawa	Open
Peter Willis Residence	Brantford	Open
William Street Residence	Brantford	Open
St. Leonard's Home	Trenton	Open
St. Vincent de Paul Home	Peterborough	Open
Kenora Youth Home	Kenora	Open
Wenonah & Cherokee House	Gravenhurst	Open
Carrefour Jeunesse	Sturgeon Falls	Open
Bluewater Youth Centre	Goderich	Secure
Brockville Jail Young Offenders Unit	Brockville	Secure
Brookside Youth Centre	Cobourg	Secure
Cecil Facer Youth Centre	Sudbury	Secure
Hamilton - Wentworth Detention Centre, Young Offenders Unit	Hamilton	Secure

Facility	Location	Security
Kenora Jail, Young Offenders Unit	Kenora	Secure
Project Trunaround	Moonstone	Secure
Quinte Detention Centre Young Offenders Unit	Napanee	Secure
Sault Ste. Marie Jail, Young Offenders Unit	Sault Ste. Marie	Secure
Sprucedate Youth Centre	Simcoe	Secure
Thunder Bay Correctional Centre	Thunder Bay	Secure
Toronto Youth Assessment Centre	Etobicoke	Secure
Vanier Centre for Women, Young Offenders Unit	Brampton	Secure
Windsor Jail, Young Offenders Unit	Windsor	Secure

It is current practice to assign a case manager (usually a probation officer) to every offender who receives a disposition resulting in custody or probation. Probation officers are responsible for putting together a risk/needs assessment and a case management plan within 30 days of the young offender receiving a disposition from the youth court. A plan of care is also provided for young persons who are in a custodial facility for more than 30 days. The plan of care outlines the services to be provided to the young person and the young person's response to treatment.

The Ontario Ministry of the Solicitor General through its correctional services division is responsible for offenders who are aged 16 and 17 years. According to the Ministry, facilities currently available for phase II offenders include the following:

- Four secure youth centres
- Ten detention units with 250 bed spaces for pretrial detention and 200 bed spaces for shorter-term custody dispositions
- One privately operated strict-discipline facility providing 32 bed spaces
- Fifty community residences for open custody dispositions, operated by nonprofit community agencies under contract to the Ministry, providing 530 bed spaces with a broad range of community programs
- One hundred and thirty probation officers providing community supervision, counselling and referral for youth receiving noncustodial sentences.

The province has taken a "strict discipline" approach to young offender custody. This model is one that emphasises earned privileges, self-control, respect for self and others, rewards and punishments, education, and positive work habits. Young offender services, accommodation, and programs are delivered using a case-management model, which is designed to address the individual needs of each young person. Treatment services vary across the facilities, but within the system, there is a broad range of programs available including the following:

- Psychological and psychiatric therapy
- Education, literacy and life skills
- Employment counselling
- Chaplaincy services
- Counselling for alcoholism, substance abuse, and anger control
- Recreation
- Discharge planning

ALTERNATIVES

While most custodial facilities follow a traditional design, there have been experiments with alternative arrangements. Project DARE, for example, is based on the Outward Bound wilderness program located in Ontario at Algonquin Park. This program stresses the value of meeting physical challenges in order to enhance the young person's self-confidence.

Ontario has been experimenting with a "boot camp" variant called Project Turnaround. Project Turnaround is based on a paramilitary model with a strong focus on discipline and structure. The project is based on several programs that have been introduced in the United States.

At present, Project Turnaround is used for males who are high-risk, repeat offenders. The program consists of a primary secure custody facility and a secondary "intense community supervision facility" that are run on a strict-discipline regimen. Offenders selected for the program serve sentences of four to six months in the primary facility and three to six months in the secondary facility. The primary objectives of the program are to teach self-discipline, personal responsibility, and respect by learning how to cooperate while living with others.

Strict discipline is defined by "highly-structured, 16-hour days that stress mandatory education and life skills development, earned privileges, rigorous physical activities, community service work projects, and minimal idle time" (Ontario Minister of the Solicitor General, 1996). Staff and residents dress in uniforms.

CONCLUSION

Custody, whether open or secure, is more of an opportunity than an intervention. Given the *YCJA* preference for noncustodial dispositions, custody occurs in circumstances that are serious enough to warrant having young offenders live apart from their families. Being in a custodial facility means that varying degrees of control are imposed on the comings and goings of young persons.

In the case of open custody, the conditions of its continuation are clear, and there is the threat that violation of these conditions (e.g., stay in school, stay out of trouble) can lead to re-appearance in court and a more restrictive custodial sentence.

Secure custody is also an opportunity. Some stimuli that may trigger problem behaviour may be removed and there is the opportunity to expose the young persons to programs and services that may help them learn ways of dealing with problems in living without engaging in law-violating behaviour. Some of these programs and services are educational, others are vocational, and still others are therapeutic. For example, some institutions offer anger management, addictions counselling, and a variety of brief interventions of the mental health variety.

Young offenders have the right to refuse treatment. This a controversial provision that is not favoured by some professionals, including the present authors. Nevertheless, what it means is that while young people are in custody, there is the opportunity to expose them to the option of such services. They may also meet the people who would deliver them and even begin one or the other of these programs, with the option to drop out at any point of their choosing.

When the system works well, staff members who work in custodial facilities use the information in the predisposition reports and the recommendations from predisposition assessments to formulate a plan of action for dealing with the young person during custody. Mental health issues are frequently prominent, and there is considerable variation in the extent to which custodial facilities have access to support services from trained clinicians (Avison and Whitehead, 1998).

It is paradoxical that, on the one hand, custody is used to deal with the needs of the young offender and the community, while, on the other hand, we allow young offenders to decide whether they will participate in treatment. The very mental health issues (e.g., aggression, poor impulse control, immaturity, depression) that contribute to their receiving custodial dispositions can only be addressed programmatically if the young offender agrees. By virtue of their age, let alone their emotional state, they are, arguably, in a poor position to judge their own needs for treatment.

Consequently, except for the physical control provided by a custodial disposition, the success of interventions depends heavily on those who work in these facilities. The extent to which they can earn the trust and respect of the young people in their care influences the likely success of various programs and services in making a difference in the life—and, later, career—of each young person.

Exercise 2

DEFINITIONS

Please define the following terms:

1. Phase I offender:

_____

_____

_____

_____

_____

_____

_____

_____

2. Phase II offender:

_____

_____

_____

_____

_____

_____

_____

_____

_____

_____

TRUE OR FALSE

1. T F   The distinction between phase I and phase II offenders is based on the seriousness of the offence.

2. T F   Facilities that provide custody for young persons in conflict with the law in Ontario are all privately operated.

3. T F   All facilities are required to have the same treatment services.

MULTIPLE CHOICE

1. Which of the following is not consistent with the "strict discipline" approach to custody for young offenders?

   a) earned privileges
   b) respect for self and others
   c) extend periods of leisure time to teach the need for structure
   d) education

SHORT ESSAYS

1. Identify two things that a probation officer must do within 30 days of a young person receiving a sentence.

   1) _____

   _____

   _____

   2) _____

   _____

   _____

2. Discuss critically the following statement: "Defence counsel and the police cannot help but disagree strongly on the need to provide so many different types of services to young persons in conflict with the law."

   _____

_____

_____

_____

_____

_____

_____

_____

_____

_____

_____

_____

_____

_____

ENDNOTES

1. An exception being sentences for dangerous offenders [*CCC* 753(4)].

CHAPTER

10

Interaction: Young People and the Police

Learning Outcomes

Students who have mastered this chapter will have the ability to do the following:

- Discuss *the complicated relationship between youthful offending and adult criminality.*
- Explain *the factors that appear to make a difference in the perception of the police by young people.*
- Identify *things that the police can do in an effort to enhance their image in the community.*
- Identify *strategies that can be used in interaction with young people.*
- Identify *the responsibility of police officers when they perceive child endangerment occurring.*
- Identify *some common characteristics of victims of child abuse and child neglect.*
- Identify *some common characteristics of perpetrators of child abuse and child neglect.*
- Explain *the responsibilities and options available to the police in dealing with young people who are "out of control."*
- Identify *the indicators of gang presence.*
- Explain *the advantages of having a police service whose composition reflects that of the larger community.*

YOUNG PEOPLE AND THE POLICE

Most adult criminals start their careers as young persons; most young persons who come into conflict with the law do not become adult criminals. In their classic study of delinquency in a birth cohort, for example, Wolfgang et al. (1987) discovered that only about 20 percent of those people they studied without a juvenile record became adult criminals, while almost half of those with chronic criminal records as young people became chronic adult offenders. This paradox underlies one of the biggest challenges facing the criminal justice system. The "key" to much adult crime, it seems, is to identify the chronic offenders and devise some successful strategy for getting them off the crime track. Unfortunately, it is often difficult to identify those who will become chronic offenders until they become chronic offenders. By that time, as much research suggests, it is already too late to change their behaviour.

While those results might suggest a strong element of pessimism, we should not forget that most young people who come in contact with the authorities do not become chronic or hard-core offenders. It is the goal of the *Youth Criminal Justice Act (YCJA)* to handle both these categories. The lighter side of its philosophy is to recognize that the majority of young persons who come into conflict with the law need little, if any, intervention. Indeed, many argue that if we are too heavy handed with these youngsters, we may reinforce the very behaviour we wish to prevent. On the other hand, the *YCJA* recognizes that some young people pose a significant danger to themselves and to their communities and need serious intervention if they are to be rehabilitated and re-integrated into society.

The police officer is the generally first point of contact with the criminal justice system for both categories of young people. Because of this wide range of "clientele," the police officer must show great flexibility in responding to the problems posed by young persons. At the same time, the law places some restrictions on that flexibility.

In this chapter, we will provide some insights and advice that might make the task somewhat easier. The first part of the chapter reviews some of what we know about how young people view the police and why they react to them as they do. The second part of the chapter focuses on some strategies that might be useful in handling different types of young miscreants.

ATTITUDES TOWARD THE POLICE

During the past 30 years, several studies have been conducted that shed some light on the views of young people toward the police. There has also been some research on the effectiveness of various efforts to improve the image of the police in the community, in general, and with young people, in particular.

When we ask the question, what is the "attitude" of one or another group toward the police, we must recall what we mean by attitude. An **attitude** is an emotional predisposition to react in a particular way toward a particular stimulus. Toward a given stimulus (e.g., person of a particular race or person who does a particular kind of work), one may have a generally positive attitude or a generally negative attitude, but not both at the same time.

Existing research suggests that police officers and various symbols associated with police officers, for example, uniforms and squad cars, are for few people neutral stimuli. Rather, they tend to evoke in some sectors of the population negative sentiments, and, in other sectors of the population more positive sentiments. It is useful to know what it is that seems to generate more or less positive attitudes toward law enforcement officers and whether anything can be done to change those attitudes.

The major items that relate to attitudes toward the police are age, social class, misunderstanding, and adversarial contact. The principal findings that relate to each are identified below.

Age

Public opinion polls in Canada and the United States show that young people have more negative attitudes toward the police than have older people. They are also less likely to rate the performance of the police as satisfactory than are adults. Interestingly, younger children rate police work as more prestigious than do older children.

No one can say for sure what is the cause of less favourable attitudes toward the police as young people move through adolescence, but some perspectives appear quite reasonable.

- Adolescence is naturally a time of opposition to the *status quo* and a time of idealism and sympathy for the underdogs of society. The idealism and sympathy may be expressed as antagonism toward those in power and their representatives.
- There is a change in the perception of authority as children grow up. Younger children generally view authority as a positive personal characteristic; power is equated with personal goodness.
- Young people who come into contact with the police because of their having violated the law have less positive attitudes toward the police than those who have not had that type of contact.

Social Class

The relationship between social class and perception of the police is complicated. If only socioeconomic status is considered, it frequently appears that less positive attitudes toward the police are closely associated with lower levels of income. However, such a simple analysis misses important features that make a difference. Commonly, if one takes into account contacts with the police because of misbehaviour, much of the apparent relationship disappears. Across all social classes, the greater the contact with police because of official contacts involving arrest and citations for misbehaviour, the more negative are the attitudes toward the police.

Young people who have been arrested, young people who self-report more, rather than fewer, acts of law-violating behaviour, and young people who define themselves as delinquents have much more negative attitudes toward the police than have young people who do not have those experiences. It is not surprising, therefore, that because members of the lower class have more official contact with the police that their attitudes tend to be more negative.

Misunderstanding

It is not unusual that there is misunderstanding about the nature of police work by the public. Neither is it unusual for the police to misunderstand how the public perceives them. Perception of the police is shaped by the result of personal contacts with the police, but beyond that, many people do not understand the nature of police work or the environment in which police officers have to function. Stereotypes about the police are transmitted culturally from one generation to another. Experiences judged to be negative by some people are told to others and can shape the views of those who have not had the contact. Wrongdoing by individual police officers may be easily generalized to all members of the group.

Police are often viewed as "the bearers of bad news," since they present people with traffic tickets, arrest warrants, and the like. The fact that the police are only doing their duty, that is, the job they are assigned, is easily missed, and the charge is made that they "should have something better to do with their time, by catching real criminals, such as murderers and rapists."

It has been noted that some contacts between the police and the community go poorly because both sides have expectations that they will go badly. Whether it is a mutual expectation of violence or a mutual expectation of insolence, there is little opportunity for the interaction to go well or be perceived positively. This is, of course, the reason that some communities have worked hard to alter the perceptions of the community about the police and sensitize the police to the needs and concerns of the community.

Adversarial Contact

Not all contact with the police is adversarial, but it is adversarial contact that is associated with the more negative attitudes toward the police. People who seek and receive assistance from the police tend to have more favourable attitudes toward the police. They are the ones who are most apt to feel served and protected.

Few people the police arrest are likely to consider the contact as favourable; indeed, it is likely to be seen as adversarial. There are, however, many other circumstances where contact takes place that has an unfortunate element in it for a member of the public, but where the event does not have to be perceived as adversarial. While no one is happy about being cited for a traffic violation or being stopped at a roadside check for those who drink and drive, the *manner* in which persons are treated by the police can make the contact not seem adversarial. Tone of voice, politeness, and professional demeanour can create an atmosphere of mutual respect, and the contact need not foster a negative view of either the police or the citizen.

Enhancing the Image

Police services devote resources to making contacts with the community that will increase the likelihood of the police being perceived as those who serve and protect. Addressing groups of seniors about ways of increasing their personal safety and avoiding scams does this among members of the public who already hold positive attitudes toward the police.

School visits by the police are used in many communities. They are part of the school's effort to "street proof" kids, and they are part of the police emphasis on humanizing the police officer to young people. Opportunities are taken to provide a perspective on the nature of police work and to encourage young people to see the police officer as, if not a friend, certainly a protector and someone who is not to be feared but who can be approached in times of need.

Studies produce contradictory results on the question of whether such programs make a difference in how the police are perceived. With the youngest children, the visits seem successful, but as these children become adolescents, the impact disappears.

Much police work is reactive, and the police depend on the cooperation of the community to be able to do what the community expects them to do. We can expect, therefore, that police services will continue to take steps to forge individual and collective alliances with the communities, their diverse groups, and individual citizens. In this sense, each police officer, besides having a wide range of other responsibilities, is also an ambassador who has a chance to make a difference in the amount of good will that prevails between the local police service and the citizenry.

Exercise 1

DEFINITIONS

Please define the following term:

Attitude:

_____

_____

_____

_____

_____

_____

_____

_____

_____

_____

TRUE OR FALSE

1. T F Most adult criminals start their careers as young offenders.

2. T F Most young persons do not become adult criminals.

3. T F Once young persons in conflict with the law come into contact with the authorities they are bound to be chronic offenders.

4. T F Among young people positive attitudes toward the police tend to decrease overtime.

5. T F An attitude is an emotional predisposition.

MULTIPLE CHOICE

1. Which of the following is true about the attitude of young people toward the police?

   a) Attitudes are more positive as young people move through adolescence.
   b) Attitudes are more positive among younger kids.
   c) Attitudes are remarkably stable over time.
   d) Attitudes are little affected by personal experience.

2. Which of the following is related to young people's attitude toward the police?

   a) having been arrested
   b) self-definition as delinquent
   c) self-reported law-violating behaviour
   d) all of the above

3. Which of the following are more likely to think of police work as having prestige?

   a) younger children
   b) young offenders
   c) older children
   d) they are all about the same

4. Which of the following types of contact with the police is least likely to generate a positive image of the police?

   a) making a 911 call
   b) being arrested
   c) asking the police for directions
   d) reporting a robbery

5. Which of the following appear to play some role in determining people's attitude toward the police?

   a) culture
   b) age
   c) experience
   d) all of the above

SHORT ESSAYS

1. Identify five symbols associated with police work.

   1) _____

   2) _____

   3) _____

   4) _____

   5) _____

2. Assess the following statement: "All kids want to grow up to be cops."

   _____

   _____

   _____

   _____

   _____

_____

_____

_____

_____

3. Why is it that lower socioeconomic parts of the population tend to have less favourable attitudes toward the police?

_____

_____

_____

_____

_____

_____

_____

_____

_____

_____

4. Identify three possible sources of negative stereotypes about the police:

1) _____

2) _____

3) _____

5. What sorts of attitudes, if they are held by a police officer, are unlikely to be helpful in dealing with young persons?

_____

_____

_____

_____

_____

_____

_____

_____

_____

6. Identify four things that an individual police officer could do in an attempt to improve the image of the police in her/his community:

1) _____

_____

_____

2) _____

_____

_____

3) _____

_____

_____

4) _____

_____

_____

DEALING WITH YOUNG PEOPLE

How we interact with others is determined by a combination of factors, including our personalities, our social roles, and the specific circumstances in which we find ourselves. Being a police officer, particularly an officer in uniform, predefines how an exchange is going to take place even before you speak to someone. This situation is not unique to being a police officer. People react to *what* we are as much as to *who* we are. Consequently, people have views of how they should behave when interacting with any professional groups, including members of the clergy, teachers, physicians, social workers and, of course, the police.

Most young people have ambivalent feelings when interacting with the police. On the one hand, their parents and teachers have told them that if they are lost or in trouble, the police are a source of assistance. On the other hand, the authority of the police causes many young people to approach them with a certain level of fear and trepidation. The uniform and the physical equipment carried by an officer—a gun, handcuffs, and, possibly, a night stick— reinforce those feelings. Some children of immigrants to Canada come from cultures where the primary role of the police is repression, and their interaction with the "authorities" cannot have a positive outcome.

Officers should keep in mind that the uniform will shape their relationship with a young person before any personal interaction takes place. As with most things in life, this can have both positive and negative consequences. The uniform can sometimes be a hindrance when an officer is attempting to build interpersonal rapport. On the other hand, the uniform can help maintain a necessary amount of respect, authority, and interpersonal distance.

All officers have their own personality characteristics and their own ways of dealing with people. With time, each of us develops strategies that work for us. There are, in addition, some guidelines that are helpful, whatever the specific strategies we use when we interact with young people. We offer the following points:

• Be firm but fair. Avoid giving young people a reason for being suspicious of or hating the police more than they already do.
• Do not overreact to the "punk-like" attitude of many young people. Be aware that much of the bravado and anti-establishment attitude expressed by many young people is put on for the benefit of their peers or to cover personal insecurities. Even more than adults, young people feel the need to "keep face" in front of their friends. Speaking to them one-on-one is usually more helpful than talking to them in groups.
• Remember that adolescence can be an extremely emotionally volatile time for many young people. As Bart Simpson says, "Making an adolescent depressed is as easy as shooting fish in a barrel." Unfortunately, this emotional volatility can sometimes put both the young person and others around them in danger.
• Remain approachable and understanding. Remember, however, you are not one of their "buddies" and that you do represent authority. Young people expect cops to be straight with them. Many young people justify their misbehaviour by taking an "everybody does it" attitude. "Everyone," for example, "is on the take" or "cuts corners," including the police. Do nothing to reinforce this view.
• Sweat the small stuff. Intervene in minor events—even if you decide to do nothing further. It sends a message that you are aware of what is going on, and this can often prevent more significant events.
• Maintain a good relationship with youth workers, particularly street workers. They are invaluable resources for handling young people in crises. Cross-referencing information from street workers and young people can also be useful in identifying adults who prey on vulnerable young people, such as drug pushers, pimps, and pedophiles.
• Talk with young people. Information and "street awareness" are major assets in police work. While the basic problems of adolescence change little from one generation to the next, pop culture (music, interests, dress, street language) has a way of changing overnight. Some of these elements are simply expressions of normal rebellion and attempts to express "individuality." Others are signs of trouble, such as gang membership or drug use.

SPECIAL CIRCUMSTANCES

There is no need to comment on the fact that the primary role of the police is law enforcement. Yet, law enforcement takes up only a small portion of an individual officer's day. Treger (1981), for example, indicates that over 90 percent of police services are social service interventions and not strictly law enforcement interventions. Most of those interventions are of a minor sort, where an officer provides information or general assistance. There are, however, some grey areas that arise where the police are asked to intervene in problems that may not quite fit under the category of law enforcement. It is to some of those that we turn our attention.

Child Endangerment

While the primary focus of this text is on the young offender, there are many situations in policing where the police encounter a young person who is a victim. In some situations, the same legislation that requires the police to intervene when a young person offends also requires the police to intervene when the young person is a victim.

A typical situation relates to what is called **child endangerment**. According to Brown et al. (1990:50), "Child endangerment is synonymous with child maltreatment, neglect, and physical, emotional, and child abuse. It is a generic term that also includes sexual molestation." Ironically, many children who are endangered eventually become young offenders. For example, a high proportion of young offenders are victims of dysfunctional families, where alcohol and drug abuse, violence, and parental conflict are common. These are many of the same factors that place a young person in immediate risk of being a victim. Brown et al. (1990:53) report that studies of prison inmates indicate that up to 90 percent claim to have been abused as children.

The police are often called to intervene in domestic disputes. While spousal violence may be the precipitating element behind the call for service, child endangerment is often a secondary aspect of the call. Clear cases of child endangerment are usually easy to spot. Abused children will often display signs of physical assault, such as bruises on their backs and faces (eyes and cheeks). Normal, robust children, typically have bruised knees, shins, elbows, and foreheads that result from falls and horseplay. Abused children's behaviour will often be atypical for the circumstances; for example, they may exhibit extreme shyness or cower when spoken to by an adult. In Ontario, officers have the option of intervening under the *Child and Family Services Act (CFSA)* if they think that the child is in immediate danger. Less obvious situations, where a case for abuse or neglect cannot be made, can be handled by contacting the Children's Aid Society officials and asking for a follow-up.

Unfortunately, many cases of child endangerment are not easy to detect. Adults who abuse or neglect children will often go to great lengths to cover their activities. They also tend to threaten and intimidate their young victims so that it may be difficult to elicit cooperation from a young person. Sadly, the chances are that when the officer becomes aware of a problem of abuse or neglect, it will have been ongoing for a considerable time.

Child abuse and neglect seem to span most social and economic groups in society so targeting high-risk groups is difficult. Carson and Macmurray (1996:116–117) identify some common characteristics of victims and perpetrators. Among victims, they note the following:

- As children get older, they are more likely to be victims of physical abuse, although younger children are more likely to require medical attention.
- Generally, children between the ages of eight and 12 years are most vulnerable to sexual abuse.
- Overall, females are more likely to be victims of physical abuse than are males.
- Ethnicity has almost no relationship with sexual abuse.
- Sexual abuse victims tend to be more isolated from peers.
- Females who live *without* their natural mothers or fathers are more vulnerable, and mothers being employed outside the home is more characteristic of these families.
- Victims generally have poor relationships with their parents.
- Sexual abuse victims are particularly likely to have parents who do not get along well or are in conflict with each other.

Among the characteristics of perpetrators, they note the following:

- Parents are typically the perpetrators of child abuse, and younger parents are more likely to be involved than older ones.
- Mothers are more likely to be perpetrators of physical abuse than are fathers (since mothers typically spend more time with children).
- There are higher rates of abuse in families where the father is disabled or not currently employed.
- Perpetrators of child maltreatment tend to be socially isolated.
- Presence of a stepfather (or nonbiologically related father) is more often related to sexual abuse.
- Most perpetrators of sexual abuse are related and/or known to the victim.
- Males are overwhelmingly responsible for sexual abuse.

The role of the police in less serious cases is complex. Clearly, the police officer cannot ignore situations of obvious neglect and abuse. Often, however, the intervention of a "disinterested" outsider can be successful in preventing future occurrences. Recognizing the situation and putting adults "on notice," particularly if no history of a problem exists, can serve the same purpose as intervening with young offenders without charging them.

While instances of child endangerment can evoke strong emotional responses, police officers responding to such calls should only serve as crisis mediators. The police have neither the mandate nor the resources to maintain the ongoing contact essential to change the causes of the behaviour. Thus, the individual officer's best response is to intervene, remove any child who is in *immediate* danger, document the situation, and act as a liaison with other agencies. As (Brown et al. 1990:59) point out,

> police officers should not attempt to assume dual roles: police and social worker. To attempt to assume dual roles is to minimize their effectiveness as police officers. They must know the boundaries of their roles…the police are charged by law to prevent crimes and to arrest criminals….In contrast, social workers are guided by civil statutes…and view their responsibility as providing assistance to these families so that they can remain intact.

Officers must keep in mind, however, that persons in domestic crises often suffer from **secondary victimization**. This usually happens after the police or social service agents leave the scene. The offender retaliates for the victim either calling or being responsible for calling the police. This risk of secondary victimization is one reason some jurisdictions have set up mandatory charge policies. Under these policies, police officers lay charges on their own initiative and do not rely on the victim for a formal complaint. Even where the police subsequently drop charges, this process allows for a cooling-off period.

Although the implication in this discussion is that the perpetrator is an adult, this is not always the case. Sometimes, young persons (particularly older teens) may not be the victims but the causes of domestic abuse. Older teens may victimize younger siblings, their parents, or other vulnerable relatives.

Children Who Are out of Control

Police officers generally deal with two categories of "problem" young people. The first category consists of those who have or appear to have clearly committed an offence under the *Criminal Code of Canada* or another statute. The second category consists of "youths identified as incorrigibles, runaways, habitual truants, involved in sexual and alcohol experimentation, and who refuse to obey the reasonable directives of parents, legal guardians, or custodians" (Brown, 1990:93). Often, parents, teachers, and others responsible for this latter group turn to the police for help.

Domestic and other calls resulting from the noncriminal misbehaviour of young people are a nuisance to many officers, since they are not trained or mandated to deal with such problems. On the other hand, the problem of out-of-control youngsters is a major challenge for most people, and they are unsure of where to turn for help. As Brown (1990:98) tells us,

> a general view held of the police by the general public is that they are mental health practitioners and the police agency is a social service agency. This view probably results from the fact that the police operate 24 hours a day, seven days a week, and respond as quickly as possible to calls for services. These telephone calls requesting assistance are frequently viewed as emergencies. When faced with problems beyond their control, particularly in the area of mental health, families may first turn to the police for assistance.

Intervention is important in these cases because many of these young people are straddling the fence between becoming full-fledged offenders and basically "good kids" who are going through a rough time. If the intervention is not effective, there is a good chance the young persons may hurt either themselves or someone else, or the behaviour may escalate into outright criminality.

Out-of-control kids are difficult for police to deal with for a couple of reasons. They have often not committed a statutory offence, or, while their behaviour may be a problem, the particular act or offence they commit is one that warrants "no action" or some similar minor intervention under the *YCJA*. In this latter situation, police officers essentially have three options, depending upon the circumstances. They may (1) invoke a minor intervention, such as speaking to the young person and the youth's parents to see if they can resolve the immediate situation, (2) take action under the *CFSA*, or, (3) refer the parents, the young person, or both, to another agency.

While the police wear many hats, it is the case that police officers are *primarily* law enforcement officials and not social workers. It is the role of police in these situations to ensure that the young person does not pose any immediate harm to himself or to others. The longer term responsibility for intervention resides with other professionals. Some police services make it easier for uniformed personnel by having "domestic intervention" specialists whose role is to deal with such situations. Uniformed police officers, however, cannot and should not take primary responsibility for solving these problems.

On the other hand, effective police practice involves follow-up. Sometimes, a phone call or in-person visit the next day to make sure that an appointment or a contact with a social service professional has been made can help. Out-of-control children can be immensely frustrating to parents and others who have to deal with them. Sometimes, that frustration can lead adults supervising those young people to lash out and commit acts of violence for which they can be charged. This creates the ironic situation where the person who is often responsible for the problem becomes the victim and the original "victims" become the offenders.

Police intervention in these situations is, at best, a band-aid approach. The objective of officers called to these occurrences is to defuse the situation by getting people to regain control of themselves or to restrain individuals so that they do not pose an immediate risk. The causes of out-of-control behaviour are complex and may range from dysfunctional child–parent relationships resulting from substance abuse and physical or psychological abuse, to normal adolescent boundary testing that has gone a little too far, to problems of raging hormones. These and other factors may be at play within the context of the young person having difficulties at school, being subjected to negative peer pressure, and having feelings of inadequacy and social marginality.

It is important that police officers know that this range of causes exists, not because they are responsible for sorting out those that apply in a given instance but because they need to recognize the complexity of human behaviour and not rely on simplistic solutions.

Dealing with Gangs

Gang behaviour is common in most large cities and even in many smaller centres. Even well-to-do suburban communities are not immune to gangs. For example, a recent phenomenon in some Canadian cities is "swarming." Groups of young people encircle (swarm) another young person or an adult in a shopping mall and often assault or rob the victim. At its worst, swarming is a very dangerous activity and, at best, it is a nasty form of harassment.

Traditional gang behaviour can include gang "rumbles," selling drugs, extortion, and running protection rackets. Gangs can be a significant problem in schools when they "shake down" other kids for their lunch money or their designer clothes. Adults sometimes use young gang members to distribute drugs in the belief that since their distributers fall under youth legislation, the consequences will be minimal if those young people are caught. Gangs can also be distribution networks for illegal weapons. Violent gang behaviour in many American cities has resulted in numerous deaths of gang members and many bystander shootings. While gang problems in Canada are not as prevalent as in the United States, many groups of Canadian kids pattern themselves after gangs found in Los Angeles, Chicago, or New York.

Typically, males make up gangs; few females are core members of gangs, and there are few all-girl gangs. Gang members vary considerably in their level of attachment to the gang as a unit and to other individuals in the gang. Some gangs are very short-lived, while others have a permanence and a neighbourhood reputation that passes down from one generation to the next. It is this variability that can make working with gangs difficult. It is also the case that a substantial gang mythology has grown over time, based on the experiences of a few inner city gangs in the United States and Hollywood's myth-making machine. Most gangs do not have the direction and coherence that either the gangs or the mass media would like you to believe.

Gangs often do not have an all-dominant leader and a clearly defined command structure. Membership is often in considerable flux with many people drifting in and out over time. Different individuals may take on leadership roles depending on what the gang is doing. On the other hand, some gangs revolve around one or two core members and simply disappear when those members are arrested, grow up, or move away.

This does not mean, however, that gangs are not a problem in some areas. Even if they are not engaged in serious crimes, neighbourhood gangs often pose a problem for local businesses and residents. Gang members who "hang" or "chill" in the front of stores or in shopping malls can intimidate customers and reduce a merchant's business. On neighbourhood streets, they can be a serious nuisance to both adults and other young people who live there. Gangs are also responsible for a considerable amount of vandalism. While it is the occasional serious, violent act that gains press attention, most crime-related gang behaviour involves petty offences, often fuelled by alcohol or drugs.

Young people find criminal gangs attractive for the same reasons they find membership in other social groupings attractive. Gang membership offers identity, companionship, peer acceptance, status, and a source of entertainment. Being a gang member may also mean access to illicit goods and services, such as drugs, alcohol, and pornography, as well as stolen or bootlegged property.

The first task of police officers in dealing with gang behaviour is determining whether serious gang activity exists in their community. Because of the ages of the people involved, most gangs have school connections. Kenney et al. (1989:321) provide seven indicators or signs that might be useful for identifying gang presence in schools:

1. Graffiti, the fist indicator of gang activity at school, contains numbers, names, secret codes and messages
2. Identifiable clothing, wearing of colours, hats or baseball caps, flags, insignias, bandanas
3. Hand signals among students
4. Specific slang
5. Street nicknames
6. Presence in school of sophisticated weaponry
7. Information on gang activity from fellow students

Not all gangs, however, are criminal gangs. It is part of human nature to form groups, and most of those groups—whether we call them gangs or clubs—are not part of the crime problem. The key to good police work is intelligence. For gangs, intelligence not only involves identifying gangs but going to the next step of deciding whether these gangs are a problem. In some circumstances, victims provide this information; in others, informants provide it.

Gangs are often grouped by ethnicity or neighbourhood, although not always. Most often, we become aware of gangs from lower-income areas, but "middle-class" gangs are not unheard of. Many Canadian gangs pattern themselves after American gangs they see in the movies or on TV or read about in the media (for example, in the case of Reena Virk, a young woman who was savagely beaten on Vancouver Island, the kids modelled themselves after the Bloods and the Crips, a gang that started in California).

Ethnic gangs have always been an element of the streetscape and have paralleled successive waves of immigration. Yesterday's newspapers carried stories of Irish or Italian gangs; today's papers carry stories of Black or East Asian gangs. The fact that gangs often group by ethnicity should not be surprising. Immigrants often cluster in certain neighbourhoods until they move up the socioeconomic ladder and integrate into the broader cultural matrix. Meanwhile, young people who live in those areas share common bonds defined by language, race, and customs that set them apart from the rest of their peers. They also share similar hassles in dealing with parents who are "still living in the old country."

Once gangs spring up in an ethnic community, calls will appear for police services to hire more officers from those communities. Invariably, there will be a time lag between the appearance of the problem and when officers can be recruited. Twenty-five years ago, Toronto had a "shortage" of officers of Italian, Greek, or Portuguese origin; today, the shortage is of those of East Indian, Black, Chinese, and other Asian ancestries.

Clearly, there are advantages of having officers who reflect the social mix of their community. In the case of ethnicity, language and cultural barriers can be formidable impediments to effective police work. Young people, those who are in trouble and those who are not, *may* find it easier to interact with a constable who is from a similar cultural background. On the other hand, simply being a coethnic does not necessarily make the job of policing easier. Indeed, it can make it more difficult at times. Young people will sometimes view coethnic officers as "sellouts," representatives of their parents' generation, or persons who they expect will give them "a break."

The key to successfully interacting with young people from ethnic communities is the same as interacting with a young person from any other group. Maintain a fair, honest, and professional demeanour while being sensitive to the problems that are faced by the children of immigrants.

Dealing with major gang situations is not something for an individual officer. An effective response to gang problems usually involves a coordinated effort of the police service, schools, community groups, and other social agencies. Individual police officers are invaluable sources of information on gang membership and local practices. Uniformed officers may also be assigned to work as police/school liaison personnel in crime prevention programs.

Exercise 2

DEFINITIONS

Please define the following terms:

1. Child endangerment:

   _____

   _____

   _____

   _____

   _____

   _____

   _____

   _____

2. Secondary victimization:

   _____

   _____

   _____

   _____

   _____

   _____

   _____

   _____

   _____

TRUE OR FALSE

1. T   F   The best advice for a police officer is to not talk to young people they encounter, unless they have something official to say to them.

2. T   F   Victims of child endangerment often become young offenders.

3. T   F   Police officers are not only law enforcement officers but social workers as well.

4. T   F   Gang behaviour is found only in the largest cities of Canada.

5. T   F   There are some clues as to whether gang behaviour exists in a community.

MULTIPLE CHOICE

1. Many young people have feelings when interacting with the police that can best be described as

   a) enthusiastic
   b) pitiful
   c) ambivalent
   d) joyful

2. What is the role of the police uniform in influencing the relationship with a young person?

   a) it can be positive
   b) it can be negative
   c) both (a) and (b) above
   d) it has no effect

3. Which of the following is probably NOT good advice to give a police officer on how to deal with young people?

   a) be firm but fair
   b) don't let them beat you to the punch
   c) sweat the small stuff
   d) talk with kids

4. Which of the following is a form of child endangerment?

   a) neglect
   b) emotional abuse
   c) sexual molestation
   d) all of the above

5. Which of the following is least likely to be true of victims of child abuse and neglect?

   a) children between eight and 12 are most vulnerable to sexual abuse
   b) sexual abuse victims have a dense web of peer relationships
   c) victims have poor relationships with their parents
   d) victims of sexual abuse have parents who do not get along well

SHORT-ESSAYS

1. A police officer walks up to a youngster on the street. Identify three things that might influence the exchange that takes place next:

1) _____

_____

2) _____

_____

3) _____

_____

2. The text identifies seven guidelines with respect to interaction with younger people. As far as you are concerned, what are the three most important ones, and why did you select each of these?

1) _____

_____

2) _____

_____

3) _____

_____

3. Explain the fundamental truth in the following statement: "Policing young people involves a lot of social work, but the police officer should not become a social worker."

_____

_____

_____

_____

_____

_____

_____

_____

_____

4. You are a police officer who goes to a home as a result of a domestic dispute in progress. You observe a house in physical disarray, quarrelling parents who have been drinking, and a young child (about three years old) who is dirty, thin, and scarred. Identify five things that you would do:

1) _____

_____

2) _____

_____

3) _____

_____

4) _____

_____

5) _____

_____

5. What does it mean to say that good police work with respect to gangs involves "intelligence"?

_____

_____

_____

_____

_____

_____

_____

_____

_____

_____

_____

_____

11

Future Directions

Learning Outcomes

Students who have mastered this chapter will have the ability to do the following:

- Identify *provisions in the* Youth Criminal Justice Act *that may be the subject of controversy.*
- Indicate *why there may be controversy over the presumption in favour of less intrusive interventions.*
- Indicate *why there may be disagreement over the presumption against custody.*
- Appreciate *the importance of the YCJA for the police.*

FUTURE DIRECTIONS

Criminal legislation generally evolves slowly. The *Young Offenders Act (YOA)* was in the works for over two decades before it finally replaced the 70-year-old *Juvenile Delinquency Act*. Some amendments to the *YOA* that Parliament passed in 1995 were still not proclaimed when the *YCJA* came into force. While frustrating to many, the slowness with which legislation moves does provide us with one advantage; it generally gives us substantial time for debate about what set of rules is in the best interests of society.

Time and debate do not necessarily result in consensus. Under any set of rules, youth crime continues to be a problem. That "problem" will be blamed, at least in part, on the *YCJA* as it was on the *YOA* and on the *Juvenile Delinquents Act*. Sometimes, an act is blamed for what it does or requires and other times on what it does not do or does not require.

Our best guess is that the greatest criticisms of the *YCJA* will be over three of its provisions: (1) maintaining 12 years as the lower age limit; (2) presumptions in favour of least intrusive interventions; and (3) presumptions against custody.

Twelve Years as the Lower Limit

Twelve years as the lower limit of age for defining a young person who would be subject to the *YCJA* is considered by some to allow 10- and 11-year-olds to "get away with murder." A relatively small number of very serious and high-profile crimes by 10- and 11-year-olds has created an outcry for "tougher laws" that in one way or another would allow the *YCJA* to "reach down" to the age of 10 years. Some would prefer that the definition of young person would start at age 10 years. Others would favour that Crown prosecutors have the option to show cause as to why a 10- or 11-year-old should be treated as a young person. Still others would favour a presumption that a 10- or 11-year-old would be treated as a young person, depending on the seriousness of the offence and/or the history of past offences and their seriousness. None of these prevails under the *YCJA,* so criticism should be expected, and it will even take the form of blaming the law for the behaviour of young people.

Presumptions in Favour of Least Intrusive Interventions

Many people firmly believe that if offending behaviour is dealt with swiftly and severely, it is less likely to recur than if it is dealt with slowly and mildly. The *YCJA* favours responses that are prompt and considers, for a broad range of offences, promptness more important than severity. The advantage of police warnings, cautions, and referral to programs or agencies is that they can be put in place quickly enough and that they are linked, in time, to the alleged offending behaviour. They do not even require that the young person admit guilt. Formal processing, through the youth criminal justice court, may be a more severe intervention, but it take much more time and resources. Its application is temporally removed from the incident that gave rise to police action in the first place.

The *YCJA* does not limit the number of warnings, cautions, or referrals for which a young person is eligible. These provisions are not about providing a "second chance" or giving someone "three strikes." It is possible that young persons may receive numerous warnings, cautions, and referrals and still be found eligible for more when a police officer eventually charges the young person. Case law will have to develop to identify, in a practical sense, the outer limits, especially in situations where the offences are not only nonviolent but, relatively, not serious as well.

Victims and, in some cases, parents of young persons may consider warnings and cautions to be futile and inadequate interventions. This may come to try the patience of the police as well. The question that will be asked is, why do we repeatedly have to find and deal with these young persons if, at the end of the day, all that they are going to get from us is a warning or caution? There is, of course, an answer. *That is the job of the police.* If the *YCJA* is to be effective, the principles on which it is based need to be respected. Interventions, even multiple interventions, that are put in place as close as possible to the alleged offence and that involve others in the community, for example, parents, programs, and agencies, who may help the young person not to commit other offences, are to form part of the extrajudicial way of dealing with young people who come into conflict with the law.

The criticism will be that there are too many chances and not a stern enough response to violations of the law: young people who refuse to obey will only learn to obey if they are dealt with more severely. More serious interventions, such as Crown cautions, will be called "too little, too late."

Presumptions against Custody

The third area where we expect criticisms of the *YCJA* is with regard to the use of custody, generally, and, more specifically, the presumptions against the use of custody.

In order to appreciate why the *YCJA* might be considered to be "soft on custody," it is important that we consider our use of custody, more generally. Canada is, and has been for some time, one of the more imprisoning countries in the world. "Locking people up" is considered an appropriate reaction to a broad range of offences, and we do not just mean as a result of a conviction. Pretrial detention has much appeal, even if such detention is not necessary to ensure appearance at trial.

In North America, far more than most other places in the world, we consider incarceration an important feature of our societal response to crime. We see it as an appropriate form of punishment, consider that it may have therapeutic/rehabilitative value, and view sentences that stop short of incarceration as a "slap on the wrist" that makes it unlikely that the offender will take the sentence seriously.

The *YCJA* reserves custodial sentences as the appropriate response to the most severe occurrences and for persons who have clearly demonstrated that a range of noncustodial interventions have not been adequate to deter offending behaviour. It is important to understand the basis of this approach, even if it does not "sit well" with one's personal view. The *YCJA* does not focus on punishing young persons. Its purpose is to provide responses that will be rehabilitative of young persons and lead to their reintegration into society. The more easily and the more quickly that can be done, the better off will be the community. Custody has certain advantages, such as restraining the person and making the person available for court proceedings. Custody also has some disadvantages. It cuts off people from some or all of the pro-social influences in their lives. It puts young persons with others who have committed crimes and may lead to their identifying themselves in terms of their unlawful acts, rather than in terms of other, more favourable characteristics that they have.

It should be noted that the idea of incarceration as a punishment is a quite modern one of the past 100 years or so. Previously, incarceration was used for two purposes: (1) to ensure that the person was available for trial; and (2) to hold the convicted person until sentence could be meted out (e.g., flogging or death). Today, we have many adults incarcerated because they would not be considered by society to be properly punished, without time in provincial jail or federal prison. Similarly, custody has been used on young persons even in situations where the protection of society is not an issue. The *YCJA* tries to change this practice that we see as rooted in cultural tradition, rather than the necessity of administering a criminal justice system. It is of interest to note that Quebec uses custody of young persons only about half as much as Ontario, without any apparent effects on the rates of offending behaviour among young persons.

IMPACT ON THE POLICE

The *YCJA* has an impact on the police that is clearly a matter of degree, if not totally a matter of kind. The exercise of police direction has been discussed in earlier sections. The police have a long history of interventions in the case of misbehaviour that are informal; these interventions are clearly intended to bring the misbehaviour to the attention of a young person's parents so that they might address it. The *YCJA* now *requires* that such interventions be considered and that they be considered multiple times. It also requires that the police bring to bear programs and agencies that may be available in the community to assist in appropriate interventions with young persons. Successful implementation of the *YCJA* places a premium on the ability of police officers to deal with young persons through means that stop short of arrest and detention. Officers are expected to talk with parents about the alleged offences of their children and make them aware of how the system now works and be familiar with the programs and agencies in the community to which referrals may be made. Because these are not one-time events, police officers will need to be able to weigh measures that have been tried in the past against current alleged offences to determine the most appropriate action in the given circumstance.

Police services will need to provide training as well as information packages on how to best handle some of these situations and the types of resources which police officers may avail themselves of. The *YCJA* expects the police to do more than was previously expected in dealing with offending behaviour at the level of the street. There are formal expectations that the police will do more informally, so the job of the police is even more complex than it was previously.

IMPLICATIONS FOR THE COMMUNITY

The *YCJA* allows provinces to implement a wide array of extrajudicial measures, including extrajudicial sentences. It is to be expected that different provinces will make different choices. These choices will likely reflect differences in past practices in dealing with young persons in conflict with the law as well as different political and social philosophies and the perceived preferences of the general public. The use of sentencing circles or programs of restitution will not be equally congenial in all provinces.

We will monitor the choices that are made for Ontario as well as case law that develops on the implementation of the *YCJA*. As new information becomes available, it will be posted on the Web site (www.youthinconflict2e.nelson.com) along with whatever commentary is needed to make it relevant to students and instructors alike.

Exercise 1

TRUE OR FALSE

1. T   F   The authors consider that there may be criticism of the *YCJA* because the age of 12 years is maintained as the lower limit.

2. T   F   There is widespread agreement that 11-year-olds should be covered by the *YCJA*.

3. T   F   The *YCJA* has a strong presumption in favour of custodial sentences.

4. T   F   In comparison with most countries in the world, Canada incarcerates fewer of its citizens.

5. T   F   Because of the *YCJA*, there are fewer decisions to be made by the police about how to deal with young persons.

MULTIPLE CHOICE

1. The Canadian experience has been that legislation dealing with young people in conflict with the law

    a) changes about every five years
    b) passes quite quickly and with little debate
    c) is received equally in all province
    d) none of the above

2. The *YCJA* favours responses to youthful offending that are

    a) prompt
    b) severe
    c) oriented toward treatment
    d) two of the above

3. According to the text, which of the following may consider warnings to be inadequate?

    a) parents of young people
    b) victims
    c) judges
    d) two of the above

4. Under the *YCJA*, custodial sentences

    a) are encouraged with repect to first time offenders in order to "nip crime in the bud"
    b) are reserved for persons who have had three or more noncustodial sentences
    c) are reserved for the most severe occurrence
    d) two of the above

5. Under the *YCJA*, the police will need to take ___ informal actions than previously.

    a) more
    b) fewer
    c) about the same number of
    d) exactly twice a many

SHORT ESSAYS

1. Why might some people object to the minimum age of 12 years in the *YCJA*?

    _____

    _____

    _____

    _____

    _____

_____

_____

_____

_____

_____

_____

_____

_____

2. Indicate two possible advantages of having a presumption in favour of "less intrusive interventions."

1) _____

_____

_____

_____

_____

_____

2) _____

_____

_____

_____

_____

3. What do we mean when we say that the *YCJA* has a "presumption against custody"?

_____

_____

_____

_____

_____

_____

_____

_____

_____

_____

_____

_____

_____

4. Identify two advantages of having a "presumption against custody."

1) _____

_____

_____

_____

2) _____

_____

_____

_____

5. Indicate two ways in which the *YCJA* has an impact on how police officers do their work.

1) _____

_____

_____

_____

2) _____

_____

_____

_____

Glossary

Absolute discharge: A disposition under which the court releases a young person with no obligations or restrictions on his/her freedom.

Alternative measures: Under the *Young Offenders Act,* ways of dealing with young persons who are in conflict with the law in a manner that reduces continued formal processing in the criminal justice system. Nonjudicial alternatives to dealing with young offenders.

Bail: The conditions, usually financial, under which a person will be released with a promise to appear in court.

Bail hearing: A judicial process where it is decided whether and under what circumstances a person charged with an offence will be released.

Cautions: Notices to young persons and their parents about the offence that has been alleged.

Child endangerment: A generic term to identify child maltreatment and neglect as well as emotional and physical abuse, including sexual molestation.

Community service orders (CSOs): Part of a disposition involving service work within the community, often with a voluntary organization. A judge may require the young person to perform up to 240 hours of community service.

Compensation: This usually involves a monetary payment when the offender cannot make restitution or it is inappropriate in the circumstances. It can also involve "compensation in kind" by way of personal service.

Conditional discharge: A disposition that allows for the young person "to be discharged on any conditions as the court considers appropriate." A typical condition imposed by the court would be that the offender remain at work, or return to school and be supervised. Once the young person fulfills the conditions imposed, the sentence has the consequences of an absolute discharge.

Conditional supervision: A disposition that allows young persons to serve part of their sentence in the community with a set of restrictions or "conditions" which they must comply with.

Crimes cleared: A crime is most often cleared when an arrest takes place or the crime is otherwise "solved."

Crimes known to police: A count of all crimes which the police are aware of, whether solved (cleared) or not.

Criminal Code of Canada: A compilation of Canadian criminal statutes. The first *Criminal Code of Canada* was compiled in 1891 drawing together a diversity of common laws and existing statutes.

Crown prosecutor cautions: The *YCJA* makes provision for provinces to establish a program that authorizes prosecutors to administer cautions to young persons, rather than starting or continuing judicial proceedings. The *YCJA* does not explicitly give a name to such cautions, but it is implicit that they are Crown prosecutor cautions.

Culpability: The notion of blameworthiness and accountability for one's actions; culpability requires that a person acted purposefully and knowingly in the commission of a criminal act.

Custody and supervision: A period of incarceration plus a period of supervision. The supervision period is to be one half as long as the custody. The notion is that the supervision part of the sentence will assist in the rehabilitation and re-integration into society of the young person.

Day release: A type of leave usually allowing the young offender to be absent from the institution during the day to perform some duty and then return at night.

Disclosure: The sharing of information among counsel concerning the facts of a case. The basic rules of disclosure that apply to adult cases also apply to those of young persons. In general, the Crown must disclose its case—including evidence and the names of potential witnesses—to the young person's counsel before the trial.

Extrajudicial measures: Ways of dealing with young persons who are in conflict with the law in a manner that reduces continued formal processing in the criminal justice system.

Extrajudicial sanctions: Formal interventions administered to a young person who has been accused of an offence, but where the process is a noncourt (extrajudicial) one.

Fine: A financial penalty. The young person can be fined an amount no larger than would be required of an adult for a similar offence. The maximum fine under the *YCJA* is $1,000.

Higher degree of restraint: One of two levels of custody referred to in the *YCJA*. One level is the "least degree of restraint," the other level is referred to variously as "more than a minimal degree of restraint," "a higher degree of restraint," and "increase the degree of restraint." Ontario has decided to use the more well-known term "secure custody."

Houses of refuge: An institutional response to the problem of juvenile crime that grew out of the juvenile sections of the English workhouses of the 16th and 17th centuries. Their principal features were that they kept youths separate from adults and focused on hard work and discipline.

Hybrid offences: Offences, such as some types of assault, that can be treated as either summary or indictable offences at the discretion of the Crown.

Indictable offences: Offences where the potential penalty is greater than either six months in jail or a fine of more than $2,000. More often, indictable offences carry sentences of two or more years imprisonment (including life).

Industrial school: A late 19th century institution designed to fit between the ordinary public schools, which were coming into existence, and the reformatories. Wayward and neglected youths were targeted for the industrial schools as much as young offenders were. Industrial schools were meant to teach job-related skills for the new industrial economy.

Intensive rehabilitative custody and supervision: An exceptional order under subsection 42(7) of the *YCJA*. Such orders may only be made when the following conditions are met: the young person has been found guilty of a presumptive offence; the young person is suffering from a mental illness or psychological disorder; a plan of treatment and intensive supervision has been developed; and the program has been determined to be available and appropriate for the young person.

Intensive support and supervision program: To be used if the provincial director has determined that a program to enforce the order is available. Such programs are to address the needs of the young person and contribute to rehabilitation and re-integration without placing society at risk.

Juvenile court: A special court having jurisdiction over children and young people. The first formal juvenile court was opened in Chicago in 1899.

Least degree of restraint: One of two levels of custody referred to in the *YCJA*. This involves a minimal degree of restraint in contrast to other levels referred to variously as "more than a minimal degree of restraint," "a higher degree of restraint," and "increase the degree of restraint." Ontario has decided to use the more familiar term "open custody."

Legal infant: English common law defined a person between the ages of seven and 14 years as a legal infant; that is, a person with limited ability to form criminal intent.

Mens rea: A guilty mind; a legal concept used to denote criminal intent.

Neglected minors: According to the New York Family Court Act of 1963, any minor "under 18 years of age…whose environment is injurious to his welfare or whose behaviour is injurious to his welfare or that of others."

Notification to the parent: When a police officer arrests and keeps a young person in custody, section 26 of the YCJA obliges the officer notify the parent of the young person as soon as possible. The parent must be contacted and told, either orally or in writing, where the young person is detained and the reason for the arrest.

Official statistics: Information on crime collected by official agencies, such as the police, the courts, and the corrections system.

Onus: Burden of responsibility or proof.

Open custody: The removal of a young person from his or her home and placement in a group home for a fixed length of time.

Parens patriae: A Latin term meaning "parent of the country" used to denote the role of the state as guardians of underage and disabled persons. Under this doctrine, the jurisdiction of the Chancery Court could be invoked to intercede on behalf of children when their parents or guardians were neglecting or mistreating them.

Person in authority: Under the YCJA, an adult who is directly involved in the administration of justice or prosecution of offences. This would normally include probation officers and anyone who is a peace officer.

Persons in need of supervision (P.I.N.S.): The New York Family Court Act of 1963 created a separate category of youths appearing in front of the family court known as persons in need of supervision or P.I.N.S. This classification was an attempt to deal with "obnoxious" or "undesirable" youthful behaviour not strictly of a criminal nature.

Phase I offenders: In Ontario, these are young persons who are between the ages of 12 and 15 years when they commit an offence. They become the responsibility of the Ministry of Community, Family, and Children's Services.

Phase II offenders: In Ontario, these are young persons who are between the ages of 16 and 17 years when they commit an offence. These young people become the responsibility of the Ministry of the Solicitor General and the Ministry of Public Safety and Security.

Plea bargain: A trade-off in which both attorneys weigh the likelihood of conviction against the cost of conviction to the accused and the cost of prosecution to the community.

Pre-sentence assessments: Occasionally, a young person may be suffering from disturbances that are severe enough that the court should consider them when making a disposition. Section 34 of the YCJA indicates the conditions under which the court can order an assessment of the medical, psychological, or psychiatric condition of the young person. Those assessments should be based on a clinical evaluation of the emotional, cognitive, and social functioning of the young person along with the needs of that person, the individual and social risk posed, and the need for intervention.

Pre-sentence report: A report, usually prepared and written by a probation officer or "youth worker," to assist the youth court judge in the sentencing process. Pre-sentence reports contain information gathered from the young person, the young person's family, victims, and others who might have relevant information.

Presumptive offence: An offence under subsection 2(1) that is committed by a person who has attained at least the age of 14 years and which falls into one of the following categories: first-degree murder or second-degree murder; attempt to commit murder; manslaughter; aggravated sexual assault; or a serious violent offence for which an adult is liable to imprisonment for more that two years, after having had at least two judicial determinations, at different proceedings that the young person has committed a serious violent offence.

Prison hulks: English ships used to house inmates in the early 19th century. Mostly decommissioned military vessels, these ships generally had their masts removed and were moored in the Thames river. The practice was abandoned after about 1840.

Probation order: An order that the young person must "keep the peace and be of good behaviour" and must "appear before the youth justice court when required to do so."

Prohibition: The forbidding by youth justice court of a young person from owning something that they could otherwise legally possess if they had not been involved in the commission of the offence.

Proportion: The number of cases in a subgroup divided by the total number of cases in the whole group.

Provincial director: A term found often in the *YCJA*, it applies to a fairly broad category of people. Generally, it refers to a person, a group or class of persons or a body appointed by a province to perform a function under the *YCJA*. Those in charge of probation services as well as persons in charge of provincial correctional facilities, for example, are provincial directors.

Publication: The public release of information relating to the offence, hearing, adjudication, disposition, or appeal of a young person. There are strict limitations on what information can be released to the public.

Publication ban: The prohibition in the *YCJA* [ss. 110(1)] is clear: "No person shall publish the name of a young person, or any other information related to a young person, if it would identify the young person as a young person dealt with under this *Act*."

Rate: A type of ratio with a large number—usually 1,000 or 100,000—as its fixed base. It is used to compare events that actually occurred with the potential number of events that could have occurred.

Ratio: The comparison of one portion of a population count with another, as in the number of women in a community in comparison with the number of men.

Recognizance: A promise to do something, typically appear in court, that may be with or without the posting of surety. Where no bond is required, it is called personal recognizance.

Referral to a program: Referral to a program or agency means to a service in the community that may assist the young person not to commit offences in the future. Such referrals are considered to be a more serious intervention than a caution, but stop short of starting judicial proceedings.

Reformatory: A penal institution for young offenders where the emphasis is on reformation as opposed to punishment. Reformatories started to appear in the late 1850s.

Reintegrative leave: At the discretion of the provincial director, a young person may be allowed to be absent from custody with or without an escort. It is used for medical, compassionate, or humanitarian reasons, or for the purpose of rehabilitation or re-integration into the community.

Reprimand: A statement by the youth justice court judge that indicates to the young person that some law has been violated. The statement may indicate the severity with which the offence could be dealt with and the reasons why, on this occasion and in these circumstances, the judge considers that the young person should have learned the appropriate lesson.

Responsible person: An adult who is willing and able to take care of, and exercise control over, the young person and under whose care the young person is willing to be placed.

Restitution: The returning of any property that may have been taken to its rightful owner.

Reverse onus: This refers to the onus or burden being shifted from the Crown to the young person to show cause as to why release is justified.

Secondary caution: When an interview takes place, the police officer must advise the young person of his or her legal rights. It is also essential to give the young person what is known as a "secondary caution." This is to help ensure that the young person has not been pressured or coerced into giving a statement.

Secondary victimization: This usually happens after the police or social service agents leave the scene of an offence or complaint. The offender retaliates because the victim either called or was responsible for calling the police.

Secure custody: The placement of a young person in a more restrictive (higher level of restraint), jail-type facility with bars and electronic surveillance.

Self-report survey: A survey asking people how much crime they have committed.

Sentencing hearing: This hearing takes place after the issue of guilt has been decided. At this point, the court decides on the merits of an application of a youth sentence or of an adult sentence.

Status offence: An act that is considered to be an offence or crime that would not be an offence if committed by a person who was an adult.

Summary offences: Offences where the potential penalty is a fine of not more than $2,000 or imprisonment for six months, or both.

Surety: The posting of money or other collateral to ensure the accused person's appearance in court.

Temporary detention: Normally refers to the period when the young person is in a detention centre before sentencing. Typically, this would occur if the young person has committed a very serious offence or has a history of nonappearance and had been denied bail as a consequence.

Temporary restraint: This occurs when the young person is in the custody of a police officer before a youth court justice can remand the young person to a detention centre.

Unfounded crime: An offence reported to the police that either did not take place or a behaviour that, upon investigation, does not constitute an illegal act.

Victimization survey: A survey asking people if they have been the victim of a crime.

Warnings: Informal notices or admonitions issued to a young person by a police officer.

Workload data: Information that provide a general idea of how much crime the community thinks is important enough to report and the amount of activity engaged in by the local police.

Young person: Under the *YCJA*, someone "who is or, in the absence of evidence to the contrary, appears to be 12 years of age or more, but under 18 years of age."

Youth justice court: Under the *YCJA*, any court that deals with a young person.

References

Abramovitch, R., K.L. Higgins-Biss, and S.R. Biss. 1993. Young persons' comprehension of waivers in criminal proceedings. *Canadian Journal of Criminology* 35: 309–22.

Abramovitch, R., M.P. Badali, and M. Rohan. 1995. Young people's understanding and assertion of their rights to silence and legal counsel. *Canadian Journal of Criminology* 37: 1–18.

Allen, F. A. 1964. *The Borderland of Criminal Justice: Essays in Law and Criminology.* Chicago, IL: University of Chicago Press.

Avison, W.R., and P.C. Whitehead. 1997. *Evaluation of London Family Court Clinic's (YOA) Section 13 Assessments.* London, ON: London Family Court Clinic.

Avison, W.R. and P.C. Whitehead. 1998. *Evaluation of the London Family court Clinic's Clinical Support Program.* London, ON: Ontario Ministry of Community and Social Services.

Bala, N. 1997. *Young Offenders Law.* Concord, ON: Irwin.

Barnes, H. E. 1972. *The Story of Punishment.* Montclair, NJ: Patterson Smith.

Brown, J.A., P.C. Unsinger, and H.W. More. 1990. *Law Enforcement and Social Welfare: The Emergency Response.* Springfield, IL: C.C. Thomas.

Canadian Centre for Justice Statistics. 1998. *Youth Court Statistics, 1996-97.* Ottawa, ON: Statistics Canada, Cat. #85-522-XMB.

Canadian Centre for Justice Statistics. 1999a. *The Juristat Reader.* Toronto, ON: Thompson Educational Publishing.

Canadian Centre for Justice Statistics. 1999b. *Youth Court Statistics, 1997-98.* Ottawa, ON: Statistics Canada, Cat. #85-522-XMB.

Carrigan, D.O. 1998. *Juvenile Delinquency in Canada: a History.* Concord, ON: Irwin.

Carson, B.A., and B.K. Macmurray. 1996. Child abuse and neglect. In Hendricks, J.E., and B.Byers, (Eds.). *Crisis Intervention in Criminal Justice/Social Service (2nd ed.).* Springfield, IL: C.C. Thomas.

Cavan, S., and T.N. Ferdinand. 1975. *Juvenile Delinquency (3d. ed).* Philadelphia, PA: Lippincott.

Creechan, J.H., and J. Grekul. 1998. *Encouraging Directions: A Preliminary Review of Promising Non-Custodial Youth Justice Programs.* Edmonton, AB: Population Research Laboratory, University of Alberta.

Edmison, A. 1977. Some aspects of nineteenth-century Canadian prisons. In McGrath, W.T. (Ed.), *Crime and Its Treatment in Canada.* Toronto, ON: Macmillan.

Government of Canada, Dept. of Justice. 1965. *Juvenile Delinquency in Canada.* Ottawa, ON: Government of Canada.

Hagan, J., and J. Leon. 1977. Rediscovering delinquency: social history, political ideology and the sociology of law. *American Sociological Review* 42: 587–98.

Hobbs, T. 1996 (1651) *Leviathan.* Cambridge, UK: Cambridge University Press.

Hurley, A. 1905. Necessity for the lawyer in the juvenile court. *Proceedings of the National Conference of Charities and Correction* 32: 172.

Kenney, J.P., D.G. Pursuit, D.E. Fuller, et al.1989. *Police Work with Juveniles and the Administration of Juvenile Justice.* Springfield, IL: C.C. Thomas.

Kieran, S. 1986. *The Family Matters: Two Centuries of Family Law and Life in Ontario.* Toronto, ON: Key Porter.

Kohlberg, L. 1981. *The Meaning and Measurement of Moral Development.* Worcester, MA: Clark University Press.

Kuczynski, J. 1967. *The Rise of the Working Class.* Toronto, ON: McGraw-Hill.

MacGill, H.G. 1925. *The Juvenile Court in Canada: Origins, Underlying Principles, Governing Legislation and Practice.* Ottawa, ON: Canadian Council on Child Welfare.

Maxim, P.S. and P.C. Whitehead. 1997. *Explaining Crime.* Boston, MA: Butterworths.

Mennel, R.M. 1973. *Thorns and Thistles.* Hanover, NH: University Press of New England.

Mewett, A.W. and M. Manning. 1978. *Criminal Law.* Toronto, ON: Butterworths.

Piaget, J. 1951. *The Child's Conception of the World.* London, UK: Routledge & Kegan Paul.

Platt, A. 1969. *The Child Savers.* Chicago, IL: University of Chicago Press.

Platt, P. 1991. *Police Guide to the Young Offenders Act.* Markham, ON: Butterworths.

President's Commission on Law Enforcement and Administration of Justice. 1967. *Task Force Report: Juvenile Delinquency and Youth Crime.* Washington, DC: U.S.G.P.O.

Rendleman, D. K. 1971. *Parens patriae:* from chancery to the juvenile court. In F.L. Faust, and P.J. Brantingham (Eds.). *Juvenile Justice Philosophy.* St. Paul, MN: West.

Sacco, V.F. and L.W. Kennedy, *The Criminal Event.* Scarborough, ON: ITP Nelson.

Salhany, R.E. 1997. *The Police Manual of Arrest, Seizure and Interrogation.* Scarborough, ON: Carswell.

Sanders, W.B. 1974. Some early beginnings of the children's court movement in England. In F.L. Faust, and P.J. Brantingham (Eds.). *Juvenile Justice Philosophy.* St. Paul, MN: West.

Scott, W.L. 1952. *The Juvenile Court in Law (4th ed.).* Ottawa, ON: Canadian Welfare Council.

Sellin, T. 1930. The house of correction for boys in the Hospice of St. Michael in Rome. *Journal of Criminal Law, Criminology and Police Science* 20: 533–53.

———. 1944. *Pioneers in Penology: the Amsterdam Houses of Correction in the Sixteenth and Seventeenth Centuries.* Philadelphia, PA: University of Pennsylvania Press.

Stewart, V.L. 1974. *The Development of Juvenile Justice in Canada.* Philadelphia, PA: Center for Studies in Criminology & Criminal Law, University of Pennsylvania.

Sutherland, E.H., and D.R. Cressey. 1974. *Criminology (6th ed.).* Philadelphia, PA: Lippincott.

Treger, H. 1981. Police-social work cooperation. *Journal of Contemporary Social Work* 62: 426–33.

Waite, E.E. 1921. How far can court procedure be socialized without impairing individual rights? *Journal of Criminal Law, Criminology and Police Science* 12: 339.

Whitehead, P.C., and W.R. Avison. 1998. *An Evaluation of the Impact of Changes in Funding on Section 13 Assessments under the Young Offenders Act.* London, ON: Ontario Ministry of Community and Social Services.

Wolfgang, M.E., T.P. Thornberry, and M.F. Robert. 1987. *From Boy to Man, from Delinquency to Crime.* Chicago, IL: University of Chicago Press.

Index